# BIG GOVERNMENT IN HARD TIMES

# CONTRIBUTORS

HOWARD GLENNERSTER is Reader in Social Administration, London School of Economics. He is author of *Social Service Budgets and Social Policy* (1975) and of numerous articles and chapters on social service planning and budgeting.

ROYSTON GREENWOOD is Senior Lecturer in Politics, Institute of Local Government Studies, University of Birmingham. He is author (with J. D. Stewart) of *Corporate Planning in English Local Government* (and with K. Walsh, C. R. Hinings and S. Ranson) of *Patterns of Management in Local Government* (1980), as well as numerous articles, chapters and research papers on local government organization and finance.

KEITH HARTLEY is Reader in Economics, University of York. He is author of *A Market for Aircraft* (1974), *Problems of Economic Policy* (1977) and many articles on applied economics and UK defence policy.

CHRISTOPHER HOOD is Lecturer in Politics, University of Glasgow. He is author of *The Limits of Administration* (1976) and of articles on central non-departmental organizations in Britain.

MAURICE KOGAN is Professor of Government, Brunel University. He is a former civil servant in DES and author

of several books on education policy, including (with E. Boyle and R. Crosland) *The Politics of Education* (1971), *The Government of Education* (1971), *Education Policies in Perspective* (1979) and (with T. Becher) *Process and Structure in Higher Education* (1980).

MICHAEL LEE is Professor of Politics, University of Bristol. He is a former civil servant and author of books and articles on administration in many contexts, including *Social Leaders and Public Persons* (1963), *Colonial Development and Good Government* (1967), *African Armies and Civil Order* (1969), *The Scope of Local Initiative* (1974) and *The Churchill Coalition 1940-45* (1980).

ARTHUR MIDWINTER is Lecturer in Administration and EDWARD PAGE is Lecturer in Politics at the University of Strathclyde. Jointly and separately, they have produced many articles and research papers on Scottish local government, including *Remote Bureaucracy or Administrative Efficiency? Scotland's New Local Government System* (1980).

MAURICE WRIGHT is Reader in Government, University of Manchester. He is author of many articles and several books on central government and public spending control in Britain, including *Treasury Control of the Civil Service* (1969) and *Public Spending Decisions* (1980).

# BIG GOVERNMENT IN HARD TIMES

*edited by*

CHRISTOPHER HOOD
MAURICE WRIGHT

Martin Robertson · Oxford

© Martin Robertson and Co., 1981

First published in 1981 by Martin Robertson & Company Ltd.,
108 Cowley Road, Oxford OX4 1JF.

British Library Cataloguing in Publication Data

Big government in hard times.
1.  Great Britain — Economic policy — 1945—
I.  Hood, Christopher
II.  Wright, Maurice
338.941        HC256.6

ISBN 0-85520-416-8
ISBN 0-85520-417-6 Pbk

Typeset by Pioneer Associates Ltd, Flimwell
Printed and bound in Great Britain by Book Plan, Worcester

# Contents

*List of Tables and Figure*                                                vi
*Preface*                                                                  vii

PART I   INTRODUCTION
1 Big Government in Hard Times: The Restraint of            3
Public Expenditure *by Maurice Wright*

PART II   GOVERNMENT ORGANIZATION AND
STRUCTURE IN 'HARD TIMES'
2 Whitehall and Retrenchment *by Michael Lee*              35
3 Cutting Local Spending — the Scottish Experience,        56
1976-80 *by Arthur Midwinter and Edward Page*
4 Fiscal Pressure and Local Government in England          77
and Wales *by Royston Greenwood*
5 Axeperson, Spare That Quango . . . *by Christopher*      100
*Hood*

PART III   AREAS OF POLICY AND 'CUTS'
6 Defence: A Case Study of Spending Cuts *by Keith*        125
*Hartley*
7 Education in 'Hard Times' *by Maurice Kogan*             152
8 Social Service Spending in a Hostile Environment         174
*by Howard Glennerster*

PART IV   CONCLUSION
9 From Decrementalism to Quantum Cuts? *by*                199
*Christopher Hood and Maurice Wright*

*Index*                                                                    227

# List of Tables and Figure

*Tables*
1.1 Public expenditure as a percentage of GDP (at market prices)  4
3.1 Three mechanisms for central government influence over Scottish local authority spending  59
3.2 The relative importance of factors influencing grant changes to Scottish local authorities  60
3.3 The extent of over- and under-spending by Scottish local authorities  64
3.4 Correlation coefficients for percentage growth in Scottish local authority budgets as between one year and another  66
3.5 Percentage variation between Scottish local authority budgets and RSG target figures for eight services  70
3.6 Percentage change in Scottish local authority spending by service  73
4.1 Potential expenditure reductions caused by fiscal pressure, 1974-80  80
4.2 Changes in aggregate local authority current expenditure in England and Wales (1974-80) compared to government guidelines and changes in aggregate Exchequer grant  83
4.3 Extent of local authority compliance with government guidelines; 1974-80 (England and Wales)  86
4.4 Association between levels of current local authority expenditure and fiscal pressure, 1974-80  87
4.5 Association between fiscal pressure and gross expenditure (annual changes), 1974-80  88
6.1 UK defence expenditure, 1948-79  128
6.2 Savings from the 1975 Defence Review  138
6.3 Functional costing, expenditure and UK force structures  141
6.4 Defence manpower cuts  142
6.A Defence substitutes and votes  150
8.1 General government expenditure, 1951-78 (UK basis)  175
8.2 Social service spending in 1975/76, 1979/80, 1983/84 (GB bases, 1979 survey prices)  177
*Figure*
Public expenditure 1973/74 to 1983/84 (1979 prices)  4

# Preface

'Government growth' is a cliché of social science. Government has grown 'big', in terms of organization and activities, in most developed countries since the 1930s. Modern ideas about government behaviour are largely based on the experience and presumption of government growth. But, increasingly, 'big government' seems to be facing a crisis. The resources that it needs for maintenance and expansion of its activities are becoming harder to obtain as economic growth declines. Rising unemployment and an ageing population make further heavy demands on government's purse, making government's activities more expensive just at the time when its income is coming under pressure. As a result, there is talk everywhere of retrenchment and disengagement, of 'cuts' dramatically announced and noisily protested. 'Blaming the cuts' has quickly emerged as a convenient catch-all way of excusing every administrative failing on the part of government officials. If 'big government' is facing 'hard times', do we need to revise accepted accounts of government behaviour and to look for different kinds of problems?

This book, based on observation of recent government cutbacks in Britain from the standpoint of a variety of academic disciplines and subject specialisms, explores how government agencies respond to 'hard times'. 'Hard times' in this context means a background of economic standstill, financial stringency and pressures for disengagement. This is explained more fully in Chapter 1, which sketches out the background to the present-day financial problems of government in Britain and outlines some of the main political and administrative issues that may face government in hard times. The four chapters that follow look at particular parts of the structure of government against this background: the central machinery of government in Whitehall, relatively protected from the impact of cutbacks in the recent past; local authorities, subject to strong pressures from central government to cut their spending, but able to offset the effect of reduced grant-aid from central government by large increases in the property tax rate; and the so-called 'quangocracy', facing attempts to cut back the growth of *ad hoc,* semi-independent public bodies that have grown up outside the ambit of central government departments in Britain in recent decades.

The focus of the book then moves from particular institutions of government to exploring the impact of hard times on three areas of policy that are crucial for 'big government'. A chapter is devoted to looking at the response of government agencies in defence to a long period of pressure for spending cuts in Britain at a time when other activities of government were growing. The next two chapters discuss the more recent impact of retrenchment on two 'welfare state' areas of government that expanded in Britain up until the 1970s and were linked with the expansion of local authority activities at that time — specifically, education and the social services. Cutbacks in all of these areas may involve grappling with hazy and intangible concepts of 'need' developed by administrative and professional stakeholders. Sir Robert Peel once remarked that: 'If you adopt the opinion of military men, we are never safe'; and that remark could well be adapted to other fields of policy. Such questions form part of the theme of the final 'overview' chapter, which highlights the common factors and contrasts in accounts of government behaviour offered in earlier chapters, and also briefly explores the wider socio-political problems of 'reducing expectations' that a move from standstill through 'decrementalism' to 'quantum cuts' would raise.

The issues explored in this book are detailed more precisely by Maurice Wright in the first chapter. They include the gap between appearance and reality in cuts, since spending 'cuts' are a far more slippery thing to define and identify than might at first appear; the response of public agencies to pressure for cuts; and the related issue of the impact of cutbacks on the efficiency and effectiveness of government. Such themes are of both academic and practical importance, directly relevant to anyone who is caught up in the financial crisis of modern government.

This book is not a polemic for or against government spending cuts. Its aim is to begin to develop a conceptual understanding of institutional problems and responses in the context of spending and manpower pressures, rather than merely to report events or to present *engagé* arguments for or against public spending cuts. Given the relative novelty of the phenomenon under study, this is a 'first generation' book in a field where ideas and language are still developing and where 'cuts' remain more of an illusion than a reality in most countries. Of course, we are not alone on the planet in either an intellectual or a geographical sense. The management of cutback and decline and the response of public organizations to fiscal pressure has begun to develop a growing literature in several countries, attracting the interest of organizational analysts, business management specialists and political scientists. But Britain was a particularly good 'laboratory site' for taking some early observations of government behaviour in hard times, especially in the period 1979-80. This was a time when to the general economic pressures that had been developing over a period to threaten the continuance of government growth were added the activities of a newly elected government ideologically committed to (if not uniformly successful in) cutting back the public sector. The British experience may thus be of particular — and perhaps ghoulish — interest to overseas readers in those countries where the prospect of 'hard times' for government has scarcely begun to appear over the horizon.

Most of the chapters in this book began as a set of papers presented to the British Political Studies Association conference at Exeter University in the spring of 1980, but Michael Lee subsequently produced an entirely rewritten contribution and three other chapters were added to the book from other sources. An earlier version of Chapter 5 had already appeared when this book was conceived, but it was included in modified form because of the importance of the quasi-non-governmental area in the rhetoric of public sector cutbacks in 1979-80. Only reasons of space prevented us from including a chapter on the state-owned industries (for which falling revenue coupled with government-imposed limits on borrowing also spell decidedly hard times); even so, a wide span of policy areas and institutions is considered here.

Preliminary versions of Chapters 5 and 8 appeared in *Policy and Politics* in August and December 1980, and we thank the editors of that journal for permission to reproduce the substance of those articles in a modified and updated form. We are also indebted to the Controller of HM Stationery Office for permission to use materials in publication. Further, our thanks are due to Avril Johnston of Glasgow University for her cheerful help in producing endless re-drafts of our chapters; to Gillian Hood for preparing the index; and to numerous colleagues (notably David Heald of Glasgow University) for insights obtained in informal discussion.

Christopher Hood
Maurice Wright
December, 1980

# PART I

# INTRODUCTION

CHAPTER ONE

# Big Government in Hard Times: The Restraint of Public Expenditure

by MAURICE WRIGHT

Cuts in public expenditure are not new in Britain. Economy and retrenchment, the watchwords of mid-Victorian finance, found modern echoes in Geddes' axe of 1922, and the budgets of Gaitskell and Thorneycroft in the 1950s. More recently, following the dictates of Keynesian economics, concern with the stabilization of the economy has led governments to use public expenditure to help depress (and stimulate) the level of aggregate demand in the economy. In practice, cuts in public expenditure made at such times were often of a 'paper' kind, relating to the future rather than to the present. Before the time came to implement cuts, as often as not the winds blowing through the economy veered in a new direction (Wright, 1977).

In the last decade the winds have become more persistently chilling; hard times are no longer 'just around the corner'. The 'treble affluence' of the 1950s and 1960s — rising GDP, public expenditure and take-home pay — began to crumble. The smooth upward progression of public spending during those decades was interrupted in the 1970s and for a time reversed as cuts occurred more frequently, began to bite more deeply, and proved enduring. Since the apogee of the growth era in the middle 1970s, when the ratio of public expenditure to GDP reached 46.5 per cent and public expenditure rose in real terms by 8.5 per cent in a single year, the general trend has been downwards, or where growth has resumed it has done so at more modest levels.

TABLE 1.1
PUBLIC EXPENDITURE AS A PERCENTAGE OF GDP
(AT MARKET PRICES)

| | |
|---|---|
| 1972/73 | 39 |
| 1973/74 | 41.5 |
| 1974/75 | 46.5 |
| 1975/76 | 46.5 |
| 1976/77 | 45 |
| 1977/78 | 41 |
| 1978/79 | 42.5 |
| 1979/80 | 42 (estimate) |

Source: *The Government's Expenditure Plans 1980/81 to 1983/84* (1980)

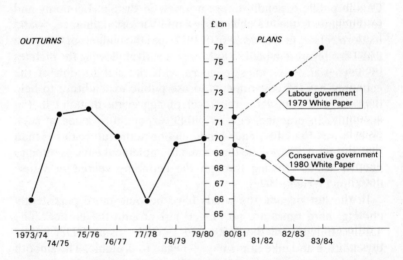

Figure 1.1 *Public Expenditure 1973/74 to 1983/84* (1979 prices)

Source: *The Government's Expenditure Plans, 1980/81 to 1983/84,*
        Cmnd 7866, HMSO, 1980.

One of the major assumptions of this book is that 'the party is over', however reluctant some of the guests may appear to be to take their leave and to adjust to a more austere environment. Since the middle 1970s governments have cut and cut again, while the 1980s began with a declaration of intent from the Conservative government to reduce the absolute level, rather than the rate of growth, of public spending for the next four years. This may not succeed, but no previous government has systematically *planned* to cut back expenditure over such a long period of time.

Our argument is that an era of growth has been displaced by one of restraint and decline. The evidence for this abounds. Take for example what has happened to capital expenditure. A prime target for governments looking for 'soft cuts' in the 1970s, it was so savaged that by 1980/81 it was in total some 40 per cent less than its 1974/75 level; almost all of the burden fell upon local authorities. In real terms, current and capital spending on industrial programmes was down by 40 per cent in 1980/81 compared with 1974/75, and that on housing, agriculture and roads and transport by between a third and a quarter. On the principle that 'some sacred cows should be allowed to safely graze', there were winners as well as losers. For example, social security increased its share of total public spending from 20 to 27 per cent, and health and personal social services programmes continued to expand by modest amounts throughout the period.

In an era of restraint some programmes have to be cut (in easier times they might have grown more slowly than others) simply to accommodate inescapable commitments and 'inertia growth' elsewhere in the public sector. Thus we shall argue in later chapters that the perception and experience of hard times will vary with people, organizations and levels of government, and will help to determine what cuts are made and where.

If we are right in our assumption of hard times, what kinds of problems does an era of restraint pose for government? Are they of a different kind, or merely the obverse of those experienced at a time of growth? How do public bodies respond to restraint? Is there a gap between appearance and reality? Do governments have to learn a new science of 'cutback management' and spending authorities to devise and employ strategies and tactics different from those used in the management of growth? What effect does restraint have on bureaucratic behaviour and the process of decision-making? Can the incrementalism of the growth era be effortlessly converted into 'decrementalism' in an era of decline? Can cutback be managed within organizations adapted for growth?

Do attempts to prune government spending result in 'leaner', more efficient government services, or do they produce perverse, counter-productive outcomes because of the political and bureaucratic priorities that shape the process of retrenchment? Can expectations about growth and the continuance of growth be scaled down?

Some of these questions are addressed directly in the chapters in Parts II and III; others, which raise larger issues of the implications of hard times for the structure and operation of government, the relationship between government and citizens, and the stability of the politico-economic system, are discussed in the concluding chapter. The remainder of this chapter is in two parts. The first part looks at the relationship between economic growth and public expenditure, while the second part introduces the concept of cutback management and discusses in broad terms some of the issues that arise when governments attempt to practise it.

## ECONOMIC GROWTH AND
## PUBLIC EXPENDITURE

In this section I shall examine the conjunction of economic growth and public expenditure. The aim is not to enter economists' debates about the dependency of that relationship, but rather to show that the assumption of economic growth was an important condition of the growth of public expenditure. The 'take-off' for public expenditure in the 1950s was predicated on the assumption that a continuous improvement in the standard of living (real disposable income and public goods and services) was possible through growth. Growth became the major economic objective of all British governments for the next twenty years. The abandonment of that objective in the middle 1970s posed an awkward problem of transition from a growing to a stationary economy — the problem of 'the landing'.

### The phenomenon of growth

The rise and fall of the growth of GDP as a major economic objective of UK governments spans no more than a generation. References to economic growth as a policy objective of the UK (or any other) government were rare before the 1950s (Arndt, 1978). As the short-term economic problems of the immediate post-World

War II period began to disappear, economists and then governments began to discuss the feasibility of raising the real standard of living by the active pursuit of faster economic growth. In 1954 the Chancellor of the Exchequer, R. A. Butler, committed the Conservative government to doubling the standard of living in the next twenty years. Raising the standard of living by deliberate policy commitment and action had arrived on the political agenda, soon endorsed by the theoretician of the social democrats, who argued that 'A rapid rate of growth and efficiency . . . at least for the next decade, so far from being inconsistent with socialist ideals, is a pre-condition of their attainment' — and, it was emphasized, a pre-condition for attaining office (Crosland, 1956, p. 378). From 1960 onwards economic growth occupied 'an exalted position in the hierarchy of goals of government policy' (Arndt, 1978, p. 55). In the UK, Macmillan's 'dash for growth' in 1962, the setting up of NEDC, the establishment of medium-term growth targets, even the 1965 National Plan, were evidence of a continuing preoccupation with raising the performance of the UK economy to the levels achieved in other industrial countries.

While the British economy grew, it did so at much lower rates than governments wished or planned for, though they nevertheless proved eternally optimistic about the prospects for future growth. It was assumed, for all but the short periods when the economy had to be deflated, that the economy would go on growing and at rates higher than achieved in the immediate past. This had an important consequence for the growth of public expenditure.

A sharp rise in the trend of public expenditure is observable from about 1957 onwards. Until that time the trend in the 1950s was for public expenditure as a proportion of GNP to fall; thereafter it rises quite sharply, with a sudden lurch upwards between 1973 and 1975 (Else and Marshall, 1979). By that time public expenditure was nearly 60 per cent of GNP[1] and excited considerable public debate (Wright, 1977). What is important in the comparison of GNP and public expenditure for the present argument is not whether the public sector was pre-empting an 'undue share' of total resources at the expense of private sector claims. It is that where GNP growth fell below that forecasted, or hoped for, the commitment of resources to the public sector was not restrained *pari passu.* In volume terms public expenditure more than doubled between the 1950s and 1975; GNP grew at a much slower rate. More importantly, when GNP levelled out and then declined in the middle 1970s, public expenditure grew in volume terms at a faster rate still.

With the commitment of resources through PESC (Public Expenditure Survey Committee — see Wright, 1977) up to four years ahead, it would have been difficult to rein back public expenditure when the expected growth failed to materialize where those commitments were firm and the room for manoeuvre limited in the short term. But in any case, there was little political incentive to do so and almost no political will. Public expenditure was encouraged to grow (apart from the years immediately following the 1967 devaluation) on the assumption that the economy could and would do better in the future than in the past. The high point of this ill-conceived optimism occurred in the 1975/76 Expenditure White Paper, before the IMF crisis of late 1976. The assumptions in the Medium Term Assessment (MTA — an economic forecast) that underpinned the public expenditure plans for the years 1975/76 to 1979/80 were of such heroic proportions that they required 'almost an economic miracle' in the performance of the economy. To achieve the government's objective of full employment and equilibrium in the trade account, manufacturing output was assumed to grow faster than at any time since World War II; private fixed investment to increase at a rate faster than achieved for any three-year period since 1955; and exports to increase at an unprecedented annual rate. Taxed with the unrealism of these assumptions by the Select Committee on Expenditure (1976, Q.213), Joel Barnett, Chief Secretary to the Treasury, admitted that the assumptions were highly optimistic but that if you based your views on what had been achieved in the past 'you are giving up all hope'.

## Changed attitudes towards growth and public spending

Until the mid-1970s, government's response to the poor performance of the British economy was to proceed as though rates of economic growth could be improved mainly by macro-economic management of the aggregates of demand (in the metaphor of the times: the belief that while the ship was frequently 'blown off course', touches on the tiller would bring it round again). By the middle of the decade, government had begun to accept what had become increasingly obvious: that the economy could no longer be managed to provide simultaneously for growth, stable prices and full employment. The changed response to 'hard times' was partly intellectual — an admission that a new bag of economic tools was needed to replace those that Chancellors had toted since the acceptance and implementation of Keynesian techniques. It was also partly a change or re-ordering of priorities in economic policy-making; and partly a change in attitudes towards the role of public spending and the size of the public sector.

It is impossible to date precisely the end of the Keynesian era, in the sense of the dominance of Keynes' ideas in the economic philosophy of British government; but the change in 'ideas-in-good-currency' and in the 'appreciative judgement' of Cabinet ministers and Treasury and Bank of England officials occurred some time in the early 1970s.[2] Conventional Keynesian responses to problems of unemployment, rising prices and sluggish growth were manifestly less efficacious than a decade earlier; the 'Barber boom' of 1973 was the last attempt to expand demand in order to reduce unemployment. The trade-off between unemployment and inflation no longer seemed to work within the tolerances apparent in the 1950s and 1960s; indeed it seemed as though there were no limits to the concurrence of rising unemployment, rising inflation and diminishing growth.

The introduction of the new orthodoxy — concern with the supply and circulation of money, interest rates, the Public Sector Borrowing Requirement (PSBR), the restraint of public expenditure — did not occur overnight, nor was it the prerogative of one political party. Even today parts of the Treasury and Bank of England, let alone front-benchers in both of the main political parties, remain wholly or partly unconvinced by the efficacy of the new tools of economic and financial management; pockets of reconstructed and unreconstructed Keynesians survive. Nevertheless, the monitoring of the money supply (the setting of targets for M3 and for PSBR) began in the middle of the decade, in April 1976; this was also the date of the introduction of cash limits on central and local government expenditure, and tighter control of borrowing by nationalized industries. Rolling targets have continued since, and led to the introduction in 1980 of a medium-term *financial* plan. Any doubts that a real revolution of ideas and practice had taken place were finally dispelled by the arrival of the Conservative government in 1979. Keynesian economics had not merely been abandoned; it had been stood on its head, with the explicit rejection of 'fine-tuning' and demand management approaches to economic management and with the doctrine that higher public spending could no longer be allowed to precede growth in the private sector.[3]

The intellectual revolution was also partly a response to a change in the major economic objectives. The pursuit of faster economic growth was no longer the overriding objective, as it had been since the 1950s. From at least 1975 (though arguably since the beginning of Edward Heath's counter-inflationary policies in 1973) the main objective of Labour and Conservative governments' economic and financial policies has been to reduce the rate of inflation. The abandonment of growth was accompanied by the abandonment of the goal of full employment. The aims of the famous 1944 Employment White Paper, to which all post-World War II British governments had subscribed, were no longer attainable. This was tacitly admitted and condoned by the trade unions in the negotiation of the 'Social Contract' with the Labour government in 1974/75, and assumed by all governments since. The abandonment was reflected in the annual Expenditure White Paper where the conventional calculation of the MTA on the assumption of achieving full employment by restoring the economy to equilibrium by the end of the plan-period was dropped in 1977.

The abandonment of macro-economic management to stimulate aggregate demand was accompanied by fresh attempts to stimulate the supply side of the economy. This had been emphasized after the collapse of the National Plan in 1966, most controversially through the activities of the Industrial Reorganization Corporation and the powers inherent in the 1968 Industrial Expansion Act. But it was Edward Heath's 'U-turn' away from 'disengagement' in 1972 that provided the means for the Labour government's subsequent increasing intervention at the level of the individual industry and firm through the 1972 Industry Act, the Price Commission and the Manpower Services Commission.

A change in attitudes towards public expenditure within the Treasury, among ministers and in Parliament was an important part of the overall change in ideas, goals and instruments. After the crisis of public expenditure control in 1974/75, bringing public spending 'under control' became a new objective of government policy. For some this meant reducing the absolute level of the public sector; others thought public sector growth should be restrained and related more closely to the new lower levels of GDP growth. In a technical sense it meant ensuring a closer correspondence between what was planned to be spent and outturn expenditure. The introduction of cash limits to supersede volume control of public spending in 1976 was partly the Treasury's response to that technical problem, but more importantly cash limits were seen as a means of more closely controlling government borrowing as part of an increasing emphasis on limiting the growth of the money supply. In practice, the effect was to heighten the significance of the financing of public expenditure programmes. Resource planning through five-year public expenditure plans gave way to short-term financial control through cash limits. Increasingly, governments began to treat the aggregate total of public spending as a 'residual' determined by stipulated target levels for government borrowing, which in turn reflected broader monetary strategies. Implicit in this approach was the abandonment of the use of public spending as an instrument of demand management.

## RESTRAINING PUBLIC EXPENDITURE: MANAGING CUTBACK

*What are 'cuts'?*

The concept of 'cuts' in public expenditure planning and control is a confused and confusing one. It can be and is used to mean several different things, and governments have frequently exploited the ambiguity of the concept to present their public expenditure plans and outturns in the most favourable light. There are at least six important distinctions that have to be borne in mind when assessing 'cuts'. At the simplest level, a cut in public sector spending does not necessarily mean that all or even most of the constituent programmes and sub-programmes are being reduced. Some may continue to grow, others may decline or stabilize at previous levels. Second, cutting public expenditure may mean a decision either to reduce the future *rate of growth* of a programme or to reduce the future level of resources below that allocated the previous year. Third, it may mean a reduction either in the volume of a programme (e.g. staff, vehicles, building) or in the monetary costs of financing that volume. If pay and prices in the public sector rise faster than planned or allowed for, or than occurred in the previous year, a reduced volume of expenditure may cost as much or more to finance than a higher volume the previous year.

Fourth, cuts may be made in the plans for public spending, but the actual expenditure may be higher or lower than the plans. A comparison of plans with projected or actual outturn can cause confusion. Different rates of growth or decline can be shown by comparing, for two successive years, plans with plans, plans with outturn, outturn with plans, and outturn with outturn. Fifth, cuts may result from an intended and announced course of action, as in a White Paper or Chancellor's 'package', or from unplanned and unintended action where programme managers fail to spend their planned and cash limited volumes. In some years unintended and unplanned cuts — shortfall in spending — have been greater than those planned and intended. Finally, decisions to cut spending in any of these ways do not ensure that expenditure will be so cut. Even assuming the political will to do so, an exact correspondence between planned and outturn expenditure is almost impossible to achieve. Expenditure by some spending authorities is impossible to monitor and control within fine limits — e.g. local authorities' current spending, or borrowing by local authorities and nationalized industries.

In addition to these distinctions, it is useful in discussing cuts and cutback to distinguish between *decremental* cuts (which are typically general and small) and *quantum* cuts (which are typically selective and substantial) (Glassberger, 1978). Of course, there is no *a priori* method of distinguishing one from the other quantitatively (although the conventional wisdom in the British Civil Service Department (CSD) prior to 1979 was that 3 per cent cuts in manpower could be achieved by improved efficiency; beyond that level cuts entailed 'loss of functions'). The crucial characteristic of decremental cuts is that they are or may be temporary and likely to be restored — or that ministers and administrators regard them as such. Thus the 'paper cuts' referred to earlier that were made to public expenditure plans in the 1960s and the first half of the 1970s could be described as decremental in this sense. If programme managers expect such cuts to be restored in the future, they are likely to favour strategies for defending the budgetary 'base' of a programme. Thus future capital expenditure that is restorable may be offered for sacrifice ('fairy gold'), 'organizational slack' taken up, housekeeping economies made, revenue balances drawn upon, and so on. If, however, the expectation of restoration appears remote or disappears in a period of more permanent restraint, the strategies of 'defending the base' may become less attractive and more selective quantum cuts made. In an era of sustained quantum cuts, strategies developed for dealing with incremental changes (whether of increase or decrease) may become inappropriate.

## How much and where?

Government has to decide: by how much to cut present and future levels of public spending; the division between capital and current expenditure; which category of spending authority shall bear what proportion of the cuts; and, within those categories, which programmes shall be cut and by how much. The starting-point may be, as in 1979, a figure plucked out of the air at the time of a general election; but, whatever its antecedents, the size of the package of cuts (and perhaps its broad distribution between central and local government and the nationalized industries, and the broad disposition among services) is decided in Britain by the Cabinet after recommendations made by the Prime Minister and Chancellor and submissions by government departments. In the present context, that judgement is very much the result of consideration of a broad economic and financial strategy, in which taxation, the costs and methods of financing levels of public expenditure and meeting stipulated targets for government borrowing are likely to predominate. For example, in late 1980 the Chancellor of the Exchequer and the Prime Minister proposed a target figure of an extra £2 bn. cuts in planned expenditure for 1981/82 to offset increases in public spending in 1980/81 and the resulting rise in PSBR above target.

Once the broad parameters of cuts have been established, the second-order decision-making is not dissimilar to the familiar horse-trading in Cabinet over marginal increases in expenditure at the time of the Public Expenditure Survey in the summer and early autumn, where the case for more, moderated by the Treasury view, comes up from the departments to be met at sub-Cabinet or Cabinet level by the Chancellor's judgement of what extra can (or ought to) be afforded. But until 1980 the annual review of public expenditure plans through PESC had not been used for planning a reduction in real terms; previous cuts had taken place outside that process.

Another difference was that the Conservative government elected in 1979 was committed electorally through its manifesto to reducing the size of the public sector (there is a precedent, but not an encouraging one, in the commitment of the 1970-74 Heath government to roll back the public sector).

The subscription of all Conservative ministers to such an electoral undertaking gives rise to a novel variant of the potential conflict of interests that ministers experience in their roles as departmental heads and members of the Cabinet. In times of growth (or assumed growth) the interests of the Cabinet collectively and of ministers individually tended more or less to coincide, although the occasion of (temporary) cuts produced clashes and occasionally resignations. Wearing their departmental (spending) hats, ministers were expected to 'fight their corners'. Despite the commitment to reduce the size of the public sector, Conservative ministers continued to behave in the traditional manner in each of the five rounds of cuts in 1979-80 — most obviously so in the autumn of 1980 when ministers like Francis Pym at Defence, Michael Heseltine at Environment and Mark Carlisle at Education were so successful that after prolonged and bitter argument the Treasury was able to make only half of the £2 bn. cuts it required, and was obliged to raise National Insurance contributions (social security taxes) to finance the additional cost of government spending in 1981/82.

Where the burden of cuts is to fall and how they are to be made entail judgements and choice about the distribution among and within programmes. As with the allocation of increments, the allocation of cuts raises issues of equity and efficiency and the trade-offs between them. Where there is growth, or the expectation of future growth, additional increments can be allocated according to rough notions of equity: programmes can continue to grow at similar rates, whether they be greater or smaller than those of past years. Reallocation does occur (and may be marked over time, as the chapters on defence, education and Scottish local spending show); and some programmes do get squeezed relative to others, or absolutely. Nevertheless, allocations made on the basis of agreed norms, established standards and historic costs are easier than those that entail an examination of needs, priorities and effectiveness and lead to a revision of norms and established standards of service.

The strategies and tactics adopted by individual spending authorities will depend partly upon how different groups and interests perceive and experience the effects of cuts. What a 'strategic coordinator' in the Treasury or a local authority treasurer's department perceives as a 'rational' strategy in a time of restraint may be different from the 'rational' response of politicians and bureaucrats in spending departments, or from that of professional workers and unionized employees at the 'sharp end', or of consumers. Such differences emerge clearly in a comparison of defence and social services spending discussed in Chapters 6 and 8.

Cutting expenditure equitably — 'sharing the pain' or 'equal misery' — is an attractive strategy for politicians and administrators (a point that is developed in Chapter 9), and has been the basis of many cutback exercises in the last two decades. It avoids difficult questions of identifying relative priorities and of re-opening negotiated agreements on established programmes; it is less painful than winding down specific organizations and programmes. But at some stage of sustained restraint, 'sharing the pain' may begin to erode and weaken the integrity of particular programmes. Adding piecemeal to programmes is very much easier than taking them apart bit by bit. The interdependencies of many programmes, with myriad linked 'decision centres', make unscrambling a complex process. Charles Levine (1979) has called this 'the paradox of irreducible wholes', arguing that the 'lumpiness' of public organizations stems from the growth process in which critical masses of expertise, political support, facilities, equipment and resources are assembled. Hence, Levine argues, 'Taking a living thing like an organization apart is no easy matter; a cut may reverberate throughout a whole organization in a way no one could predict by just analyzing its growth and pattern of development' (p. 180).

Where programmes have been protected from cuts in the past, or have suffered only mildly, it may be possible initially to make decremental cuts, or to offer up 'fairy gold' and token savings. Such a response may become more difficult or impracticable in a period of prolonged restraint where a spending authority has suffered a succession of cutback shocks over several years, as has happened for example, in housing, roads, defence and education. In such circumstances a strategy of decremental cutting may prove inappropriate or inadequate. With each successive wave of cuts the need to be more selective becomes more urgent. Decremental strategies give way to quantum ones. Spending authorities are obliged to 'think the unthinkable', to contemplate the abandonment of established programmes and to make more than marginal and temporary cuts in others. They need to devise strategies other than those calculated to defend the base and protect the core; to scrutinize and cut into base-spending in some programmes in order to sustain current levels of spending in other programmes and to leave room for inescapable commitments, as well as some margin for the development of existing programmes and the initiation of new ones. In some programmes, spending authorities have proved adept at protecting the core. For example, in the 1970s, the non-core elements of education — school meals, adult education and nursery schools — bore the brunt of spending cuts. The core — the teaching of 5—16 year olds and the provision of courses in working skills for 16—18 year olds — suffered only marginally. By 1980 politicians and bureaucrats were unsure how much longer they could continue to protect the core.

## Organizational decline and death?

The most obvious symptom of organizational decline in the labour-intensive public sector is the reduction in staff levels by leaving vacancies unfilled, freezing new appointments, and redundancy. Freezing recruitment and leaving vacancies unfilled is relatively easy to introduce and sustain over a short period, but may store up difficulties for the future by creating shortages of special skills and promotion bottlenecks. In the 1970s this was something that all public sector organizations learned to cope with. Like a pay freeze, it buys government time and preserves options, but in itself solves nothing and is neither an equitable nor an efficient way of achieving economies.

Until 1974/75 local authority manpower had been growing annually by more than 5 per cent for more than twenty years (Stewart, 1980). Since then, the size of the local authority labour force has been the subject of continual critical attack from central government. Despite that, and considerable reductions in the level of central government grants, the number of local authority employees continued to rise, by nearly 2 per cent between 1974 and 1980, with a greater increase still in the number of those employed full-time. There were years of reduction, notably 1976/77 and 1979/80, but these were more than offset by the years of increase (*Joint Manpower Watch,* June 1980).

Until the election of the Conservative government in 1979, the civil service had been more insulated from cutback than local authority manpower, although the introduction of cash limits in 1976 provided governments with a mechanism for squeezing numbers and pay indirectly and less publicly than by a frontal assault. On entering office, the Conservatives gave a high priority to reducing the size of the civil service, eliminating waste and promoting greater efficiency. As Michael Lee explains in Chapter 2, the Prime Minister herself took a close personal interest in these matters. In mid-1979 the government introduced a three-month freeze on new appointments, and announced a target reduction of 60,000 civil service jobs by 1983. Like their Labour predecessors, Conservative ministers considered the implications for their departments of cuts of 10, 15 or 20 per cent. Some refused to contemplate cuts in the higher ranges; others used 'bleeding stump' arguments to show how damaging cuts of 20 per cent would be to their programmes; the Ministry of Defence refused to consider any of the options, and drew up its own separate proposals.

The result of this first cutting exercise, announced at the end of 1979, was a planned reduction of 39,000 jobs, averaging 8 per cent over three years at an estimated saving of £212 m. Many of these cuts, however, were not quite what they seemed. Far less money would be saved than appeared on paper. For example, the largest cuts, at the Ministry of Defence (£41 m.) and the Property Services Agency (£29 m.), were to be achieved very largely by shifting the responsibility for maintenance, cleaning and catering work from civil servants to private contractors. The net saving of such an exercise depends on the contract terms that government can negotiate, and is therefore conveniently blurred. Very similar 'cuts' were effected by the Heath government in 1970/71.

The target was revised in April 1980 when the Prime Minister announced a further reduction in the size of the civil service, from 732,000 (May 1979) to 630,000 by April 1984. This decision was criticized by the Select Committee on the Treasury and Civil Service as 'based on intention rather than calculation' (1979/80b). This remark was prompted by the government's inability to state which services were to be affected by the proposed cuts in evidence to the committee; government was also unable to estimate how the cuts would fall as between the industrial and non-industrial parts of the civil service, between headquarters and the regions, and on particular grades. As a result of this, the committee began to take a close interest in the government's control of manpower. On the basis of quarterly progress reports from the CSD, it started to monitor the new savings arising from any cuts, the extent of the transfer of the tasks involved to the private sector, the effects of cuts on the geographical and grade distribution of civil servants, the extent to which cuts entail a loss or curtailment of existing services, and the total financial saving to the Exchequer.

Because governments have multiple and often conflicting policies and objectives, cuts and increases can occur simultaneously. While the Conservative government was announcing further cuts in the civil service it was also taking on additional staff to deal with the administrative consequences of rising unemployment. Once unemployment went beyond 1.8 million in mid-1980, each subsequent 100,000 unemployed required an extra 2,000 civil servants to administer unemployment, social and welfare benefits (Select Committee on the Treasury and Civil Service, 1979/80b). Similarly, the allocation of an additional £250 m. to the Manpower Services Commission in late 1980 to help the jobless required 1,000 more employees in a 'quango' that had been singled out as a ripe target for cutback. While some civil service posts were frozen, others remained unfilled because of a shortage of suitable candidates.

Attempts to eliminate waste and to improve efficiency in the civil service by the reduction and redeployment of staff and by special 'waste-finding' inquiries (as described by Michael Lee in the next chapter) may prove counter-productive. There are signs of a sharp deterioration in civil service morale similar to that occurring in the early 1970s when there was unrest over pay and conditions. It was partly the result of the way that the government handled manpower reductions, and partly a reaction to continual public and ministerial attack on bureaucratic behaviour. In 1980 the Official Head of the Civil Service (Sir Ian Bancroft) twice spoke in public against the unjustified 'public vilification' of the civil service (CIPFA, 1980; RIPA, 1980). In an era of growth, Sir Ian said, civil servants were required by governments to administer a rising level of public expenditure and to expand public services quickly. But in a period of cutback they were accused of wasting resources and of inflating the size of the bureaucracy.

Still more resentment at government policies towards its own employees arose from the decision, taken without consultation, to suspend the Pay Research Unit, which established the rates of pay for work elsewhere in the economy that could be compared to civil service work and traditionally formed the basis of pay negotiations. Instead, anxiety to hold down wages in the public sector and to avoid the embarrassment of large 'staged' pay increases such as occurred in 1979/80, led the government to try to impose a general 6 per cent pay limit for 1980.

In other parts of the public sector, the prospect of redundancies arose as a result of tight cash limits on spending (or on borrowing, in the case of nationalized industries, among which the industries whose revenues were falling in recession were particularly hard hit). Grant-aided bodies like the BBC were forced to economize on labour, in that case through a reduction in the grant for overseas broadcasting and government refusal to increase the TV licence fee.

At the level of the individual spending authority, however, there have been few deaths up to now. The two government departments to disappear in 1979 were both merged with other departments rather than wound up completely. The disappearance of the Overseas Development Ministry into the Foreign Office was part of an old see-saw game played by successive Labour and Conservative governments since the setting up of the Department of Technical Co-operation in the early 1960s. The other department to disappear in 1979 was the Department of Prices and Consumer Protection: its rationale had been weakened by the ending of price controls and the winding up of the Price Commission. Its residual functions disappeared into the Department of Trade. Neither of these departmental 'deaths' was solely attributable to the restraint of expenditure. The closure of educational institutions is the most obvious and numerically significant example of 'organizational death', but this partly reflects changes in demographic demand working through the system as well as changes in prevailing norms and standards of service derived more directly from an era of restraint. The nature and impact of this response is discussed in Chapter 7.

The quasi-non-governmental sector looks prime 'killing ground', but appearance of death and decline, fostered sedulously by the Conservative government in 1980, was deceptive; the reality is quite different, as Christopher Hood explains in Chapter 5. A more promising bet for a government bent on reducing the size and cost of the public sector is 'privatization'. Plans for the disposal of public assets in aerospace, airways, oil, docks, buses, freight, rail subsidiaries and the investment portfolio of the National Enterprise Board (NEB) would, if carried through to a successful conclusion, mark a substantial shift in the balance between public and private. In this case, Conservative ideology was strengthened by the desire to reduce government borrowing in the short term. In practice, any immediate financial benefits to government might be balanced or outweighed by benefits forgone in the longer term. Selling assets is a once-for-all gain, and reduces the level of government borrowing only once — unless the assets involved are loss-making and dependent on government financing, in which case it is likely to be difficult to sell them to private buyers. Second, some assets may be difficult to capitalize quickly without risk of loss (such as the British National Oil Corporation, the state oil company) and the destruction of their potential to contribute a more substantial and sustained reduction in government borrowing in years to come by enhanced profit-earning capacity. Third, 'privatization' poses difficult questions about control and accountability in mixed government-private enterprises — questions raised on a smaller scale by the involvement of the NEB and its sister organizations in industrial investment.

## CHANGES IN STRUCTURE AND DECISION-MAKING PROCESSES

As cutting exercises became more frequent in the 1970s and 1980 — the Conservative government had five expenditure reviews in its first eighteen months, the Labour government thirteen budgets and mini-budgets in five years — and the period of restraint lasted longer, especially at the local level, the response of some spending authorities was to look more closely at the efficiency and effectiveness of their use of existing resources. This resulted in some changes in structure and process at both the local and central levels. However, the evidence needs to be interpreted with caution. Changes in structure and process do not necessarily lead to changes in organizational behaviour. For example, despite the existence of long-term plans and some elements of programme budgeting in the Department of Health and Social Security (DHSS) in the 1970s, there is evidence (some of it discussed by Howard Glennerster in Chapter 8) that the department continued to respond to restraint through the incrementalist mode. In 1980 it was fiercely criticized by the Select Committee on the Social Services (1979/80) for the lack of a coherent strategy, and its ministers were criticized for not knowing the implications of spending cuts on their own policies. 'Policy is made by taking decisions about specific items and then having a retrospective look to see what their combined effect turned out to be' (p. xviii, para. 15).

At the local level, some local authorities responded to the restraint of public expenditure after 1974 by 'retreating' from corporate management: typically these were authorities where corporate practices had been precariously established in the wake of the Bains Report and reorganization. Others responded by trying to make corporate management work better, either by centralizing policy planning or by adopting a decentralized and participatory form of management (Hinings *et al.,* 1980). It is more difficult to establish any such connection at the central level of government in Britain. However, there is some evidence that there was a change in the structures of central departments contingent upon the changing assumptions of ministers and civil servants about the role of the state in the economy (Lee, 1980). This occurred most obviously in the structures of the Treasury and the economic and industrial departments as the role of the state in the economy has become more openly and determinedly interventionist and discriminatory since the early 1970s.

It is hardly surprising that more far-reaching changes have occurred in the processes of decision-making, especially in budgetary processes. If the latter have developed over the past twenty-five years on the assumption of continuing growth, it is likely that the removal of that assumption, other than temporarily, will affect those processes. Here there is a very striking contrast between what is happening at the local and central levels. If we accept that the budgetary processes of both have in the past been characterized by incrementalism (indeed, it can be argued that the growth of resources is intrinsic to that concept), there is some evidence that suggests that local authority budgetary processes have become less incremental and more economically rational as a response to the restraint of public expenditure. For example, Greenwood *et al.* (1980) have shown that in some local authorities there was a widening of the parameters of budgetary review to include the hitherto sacrosanct base-spending in order to make room for 'inescapable commitments' and some further innovation. At the same time, changes were made in the mode of analysis employed to include the introduction and use of the techniques and procedures of 'strategic and issue analysis' associated with the principles of corporate planning. More recent research confirms these findings. Those local authorities that suffered a reduction of Rate Support Grant (RSG) from central government tended to adopt more rational analysis in their budgetary process than those whose RSG was increased. Where resources were squeezed or declining, zero-based budgeting, or some variant of it, became more attractive to programme managers.

The comparison between the experience of local authorities and that of central government can be made at two levels. First, the comparison with the central allocative system in Britain, PESC. Whether PESC in the late 1960s and early 1970s provided the means to make a more economically rational allocation than had been the case with the pre-PESC system, can be put to one side (see Wright, 1980, pp. 89-91, 114-17); what is certain is that the system has been changed considerably by the need of the Treasury and other departments to respond to the changed conditions in an era of restraint. Here the turning point is 1976 and the introduction of cash limits on government spending. Before that date, PESC had become geared to the distribution over several years ahead of additional increments, and sizeable increments at that. In the first five years of the 1970s public expenditure grew in real terms by an average of 5 per cent per annum.

The budgetary process was until the mid-1970s about negotiating and bargaining for additional increments; the characteristics are familiar and do not need elaboration here (Heclo and Wildavsky, 1974; Diamond, 1975). Equally familiar is the shock to the system sustained in the 'crisis of control' that occurred in 1974—75 (Wright, 1977). Cash limits followed, and early-warning devices to monitor resource use and cash flow were hastily installed throughout Whitehall. The immediate effect, and the one most desired by Treasury officials, was to bring public expenditure under control, in the sense that what was consumed in real terms and paid for in money did not exceed what was planned. So successful was this exercise that there was a considerable shortfall of expenditure for the first three years of the operation of cash limits.

As yet, the assumption was one of restraining growth rather than cutting spending absolutely, although the incidence of shortfall had a greater than intended effect on reducing growth. Nevertheless, PESC began to change: the current financing of public expenditure — the monetary costs of programmes — became more important than planning future levels of real resources. PESC plans continued, but cash limits had primacy. The credibility of PESC as a planning system was steadily eroded as the time-horizon became attenuated, the Medium Term Assessment forecast abandoned, and swingeing cuts made in future capital commitments. By the end of the 1970s it had been transformed from a mainly planning system to one in which short-term cash control predominated.[4]

A still tighter squeeze on public expenditure has contributed further to these developments. After May 1979 there was an even more explicit emphasis on the financing of public spending, and there is now greater scepticism in the Treasury about medium-term planning in aggregate for *all* programmes, an acceptance that while looking ahead for four years is necessary for some programmes, for others such plans are subject to such large margins of error that the figures produced are often spurious and misleading (HM Treasury, 1980).

This argument was used by the Chancellor of the Exchequer in defence of his 1980 Expenditure White Paper (*The Government's Expenditure Plans 1980/81 to 1983/84*) when criticized for failing to provide detailed allocations of spending for other than the first year of the plan, a break with the practice of the previous ten years. Nor was there any indication how cuts totalling some £6 bn. were to be allocated in subsequent years, or how the burden was to be divided between capital and current expenditure. Without such information, it was 'impossible to assess the impact of the plans on the economy or on different sections of the community' (Select Committee on the Treasury and Civil Service, 1979/80a, p. 13).

So great was the delay in agreeing the planned cuts that the government, making a virtue out of necessity, published the Expenditure White Paper simultaneously with the Financial Statement and Budget Report in 1980. Hence, by an accident of timing, expenditure plans and revenue projections were brought together for the first time. The government seized the opportunity to present the two as part of a coherent economic strategy. The

medium-term financial plan, as it was called, was a logical conclusion
to the shift in emphasis from resource to financial planning begun in
1976. For the first time a government announced target figures for
four years ahead for the aggregates of government borrowing and
the money supply, as well as for expenditure, together with
projections of revenue and GDP growth assumptions for the same
period. Paradoxically, while the government was emboldened to
commit itself on the finance and revenue side further into the future
than previous governments had been willing to do, expenditure
planning through the White Paper appeared to be moving still
further away from the 1961 Plowden 'forward look' principles. This
trend was confirmed by the decision announced shortly afterwards
that in future expenditure plans the time-horizon would be reduced
from four to three years.

Cutback on the scale envisaged in the 1980 Expenditure White
Paper was wholly without precedent. While the PESC process had
been used in the past to cut the rate of growth of expenditure over a
four-year period, it had never been used to plan and allocate cuts in
the absolute levels of expenditure. Such cuts were in fact made in
the 1970s, most notably in 1976, but they took place outside the
PESC planning cycle in a period of acute economic or financial
crisis. They were brief, and often bitter, exercises in crisis
management. To embark at much greater leisure, without any
immediate external threat, upon an exercise to achieve reductions
in public spending determined by financial targets set for the growth
of the money supply and the PSBR was positively to invite ministers,
politicians and bureaucrats to close ranks in the protection of
threatened programmes. Had the Treasury attempted to negotiate
with spending departments the precise nature and distribution of
the cuts, as it did when bargaining over increments of growth, it
would have failed as surely as the more modest exercise in cutback
for just one year ahead came to grief on the rocks of ministerial and
bureaucratic intransigence in late 1980. Wisely perhaps, this task
was not attempted; the details of the cuts planned for future years
were to be filled in 'later'.

Cash limits have had consequences other than controlling the
monetary costs of programmes. Used by both Labour and
Conservative governments as an instrument of controlling public
sector pay, they have produced a squeeze on the volume of
expenditure still greater than that planned and announced at the

time of the prescription of cash limits each April. Because target or policy forecasts of the movement of public sector pay and prices have been incorporated into the limits, the provision of goods and services has been squeezed through the 'back door' as hard or harder than through the front door of publicly announced cuts. What this means was well described by a participant: 'We have a great argument about the volume of spending next year. When the Treasury is defeated by the forces of the anti-Christ, they regroup and try again through the back door of cash limits' (*Guardian,* 15 November 1980). In each of the three years 1976/77 to 1979/80, the shortfall of expenditure averaged 3 or 4 per cent of total public spending — a more significant amount than the government's announced expenditure cuts.

The use of cash limits to secure 'back door' cuts is a theme that recurs in several chapters of this book and is considered further in Chapter 9. It is attractive as a strategy for government because it avoids having to make public choices about what to cut and how; that vexed and potentially divisive question is left in the hands of the programme managers, who in turn may pass it on 'down the line' to professionals, 'street bureaucrats' and those who deliver services.

Changes in the budgetary process have been taking place within central government departments as well. Unlike those made to PESC, these changes have more in common with the practices described by Greenwood *et al.* at the local level after 1974; but we should be cautious in ascribing the changes to similar stimuli. The proximate causes are less the displacement of growth by restraint, standstill and decline — which in any case were experienced much less severely at the centre than the periphery in the period 1974–78 — than a felt need to enhance departmental negotiative capacity in PESC bargaining with the Treasury by formulating and clarifying priorities more clearly. Throughout the decade, the centralization or integration of resource allocation, policy planning, research and intelligence, and personnel and management functions took place in many central departments and led some of them into new ways of thinking about the analysis of policy and the monitoring of its implementation. One product of that is a proliferation of planning systems as mechanisms for obtaining centrally allocated resources. Most of these were designed specifically for the purpose of allocating and reallocating resources in particular policy areas according to criteria other than the customary ones associated with historic costs. This has provided an additional stimulus to local authorities and other regional and local bodies that participate in the preparation and implementation of those and other plans (such as regional strategies or local authority corporate plans) to pay closer attention to the relative priority of the activities that they help to finance. It is also an encouragement to adopt corporate planning and to use corporate management techniques.

The planning system that has attracted most attention is that of the DHSS where, following reorganization, a new and comprehensive system was introduced. It was claimed that a rational decision-making system had been substituted for an older planning system that had focussed on the increment rather than the total resources available. In the new system, by contrast, plans were to 'reflect reconsiderations of priorities and possibilities of advantageously redeploying existing resources from year to year' (DHSS 1976, para. 1.3.2). One objective of National Health Service (NHS) reorganization in the mid-1970s was to increase the influence of the centre in decisions about priorities, and the new DHSS planning system provides for the strategic and operational plans prepared by regions, areas and districts to be checked for consistency with national priorities set at the centre. Another objective was to inject more rationality into the distribution of resources by substituting formulae based on criteria of 'need' for those of historic costs. The new ('RAWP') formulae were used as the basis for allocations to NHS regions for the first time in 1977/78.

These 'changes in the system of financial allocation and control were designed to move the NHS from a system of incremental budgeting to a rational system in which resources were balanced against and determined by need' (Hayward *et al.,* 1979, p. 45). It is too early to judge the extent to which the allocation of resources within and between regions has really become more 'rational'; but the Institute for Health Studies has carried out some limited research in one region to see if health authorities are looking more at the totality of resources and not merely at the increment. Is there more scrutiny of base-spending? The Institute's conclusions, while pointing to more rational outcomes, suggest that these are not necessarily the consequence of a more rational decision-making process.

The new management structure, based on notions of rational

decision-making, through which the messages about central priorities and so on flow, does not seem to have been a major factor in determining outcomes . . . the decision-making process within these health authorities on these issues was essentially political, with interests deploying information to their own advantage. [Hayward *et al.,* 1979, p. 50]

In other words, the outcomes might be justified more in terms of their political than their economic rationality, a point that is taken up and developed in greater detail by Howard Glennerster in Chapter 8 in a discussion of the significance of different kinds of rationality as determinants of spending decisions.

One of the principal objectives of the DHSS three-year plans for the social services (which replaced the ten-year plans abandoned in 1975 with the onset of spending cuts) was to provide a more rational basis for the allocation of resources. The main stimulus was the need for central government to take a firmer hand in the control of local expenditure, following the crisis of 1974—75. In his evaluation of the achievement of the plans, Booth (1979) is critical of the approach adopted, which he sees as reinforcing incrementalism through the progressive improvement in existing levels and standards of provision. Booth may well be right in asserting that the failure to address questions of outputs and the impact of services is inconsistent with a rational planning system; but it is nevertheless clear that the planning exercise does give greater emphasis to resource planning and allocation. As resources become scarcer in the 1980s, it is possible that the planning exercise might be used as the basis for the development of more rational analysis, for example by scrutiny of base-spending.

The need to link resource planning and allocation more clearly to the PESC process stimulated an integration of programme budgeting and PESC forecasts in DHSS at the time of the 1975 spending cuts. By the following year the programme budget had become established as 'a tool for linking policies to resources, considering priorities within the DHSS . . . [and] of use to the Department in the review of public expenditure' (Banks, 1979, p. 167). Programme budgeting helped in the reallocation of some existing allocations at the national level.

A similar concern with planning and the determination of priorities is apparent in some other central departments. The

Department of Transport has planning and resource allocation systems for Inter-Urban Highways and for Transport Policies and Programmes (TPPs). More recently, the Department of the Environment (DOE) has introduced comprehensive Housing Investment Programmes (HIPs) to 'provide a framework within which both central and local government can deploy resources more effectively in response to housing needs' (Expenditure Committee, 1978, p. 3).

Bidding for more resources through separate policy initiatives in fields such as housing, transport, water and health has led to the setting up of different planning systems, each with their own different time-scales, criteria and procedures. Within the same central department there is often difficulty in relating one planning system to another, even where the activities overlap or interact, as in the DOE where the Inner City Partnership Programme, HIPs and local authority Structure Plans coexist. Second, the proliferation of planning systems within departments gives rise to problems of coordination and allocating resources to several different programmes within the overall budgetary structure. Third, where the policies and resource allocation procedures of different planning systems interact and overlap (e.g. HIPs, TPPs, health, social service and employment planning), there is the problem of achieving a coordination or integration of resource allocation within the larger framework of PESC. Most planning systems are new, and with greater experience departments may achieve a greater degree of integration between them. There are two possible developments that have implications for the central and local budgetary process. First, if the potential for linking together a variety of functional plans is exploited, corporate planning at the central government level may follow. This has already happened in the Scottish Financial Plans. Second, while the emphasis at present tends to be on securing resources for short-term developments, there is some evidence that the emergence of planning/programming systems is in fact marginally encouraging the development of longer-term resource planning, as in the case of Community Land and Housing Programmes. If this continues, there may develop a tension between these systems and PESC, with its shorter time-scales and emphasis on financial planning and control.

One general consequence of hard times has been an increase in parliamentary and public pressure upon the Treasury and spending departments to explain and justify how and why resources are allocated and used. The Public Accounts Committee, the Expenditure Committee, and the fourteen select committees that succeeded the Expenditure Committee in 1979 have been particularly energetic in this respect in recent years. Whether such pressures will encourage the wider adoption and use of procedures and techniques of rational analysis similar to those described above, and if so, whether they can contribute to more efficient and effective policy outcomes, are questions on which opinions may differ. Two contrasting views are presented in the chapters on defence and social services. What the role of the 'centre of government' should be in all of this — for example, whether the control of resource allocation should be centralized in the Treasury or divided between two departments — is discussed, together with other 'machinery of government' issues, in the next chapter.

## NOTES

1. Public expenditure was defined more narrowly soon afterwards and the ratio was reduced 'at-a-stroke'.
2. *The End of the Keynesian Era* (Skidelsky, 1977) was based upon essays that appeared in the *Spectator* between May 1976 and January 1977.
3. Economists still dispute whether 'fine-tuning' the economy through demand management was stabilizing. Some argue that, if it did work, the stabilization was temporary (a decade or so) and that higher inflation and unemployment appeared next time round. On this argument, boosting public expenditure provided only a temporary improvement in employment and, if it contributed to inflation, then next time round unemployment would have to be very much higher to deal with higher inflation; and so on. See Dow (1965) and Blackaby (1978).
4. The changes in PESC in the 1970s are discussed in greater detail in Wright (1980) Chapter 6.

## REFERENCES

Arndt, H. W. (1978) *The Rise and Fall of Economic Growth* London, Longman

Banks, G. T. (1979) 'DHSS programme budgets' in T. A. Booth (ed.)

Blackaby, F. T., (ed.) (1978) *British Economic Policy 1960-74* London, Cambridge University Press

Booth, T. A., (ed.) (1979) *Planning for Welfare* Oxford, Blackwell & Martin Robertson

CIPFA (1980) Speech by Sir Ian Bancroft to Annual Conference of Chartered Institute of Public Finance and Accountancy, Brighton, June

Crosland, C. A. R. (1956) *The Future of Socialism* London, Cape

DHSS (1976) *The National Health Service Planning System* London, HMSO

Diamond, Lord (1975) *Public Expenditure in Practice* London, Allen and Unwin

Dow, J. C. R. (1965) *The Management of the British Economy 1945-60* London, Cambridge University Press

Else, P. K. and Marshall, G. P. (1979) *The Management of Public Expenditure* Policy Studies Institute, Vol. XLV, No. 580, March

Expenditure Committee (1975/76) *4th Report 1975/76,* HC 299 1975/76, London, HMSO

Expenditure Committee (1978) *8th Report 1977/78,* London, HMSO

Glassberger, A. (1978) 'Organizational responses to municipal decreases' *Public Administration Review* Vol. 38, pp. 325-32

Greenwood, R., *et al.* (1980) 'Incremental budgeting and the assumption of growth' in Wright (ed.)

Hayward, S. C., *et al.* (1979) 'The outcome of NHS reorganization' *Public Administration Bulletin* No. 31, December

Heclo, H. and Wildavsky, A. (1974) *The Private Government of Public Money* London, Macmillan

Hinings, C. R., *et al.* (1980) 'The organizational consequences of financial restraint in local government' in M. Wright (ed.)

H.M. Treasury (1980) Paper by senior Treasury official to RIPA seminar, February

Lee, J. M. (1980) 'The context of central administration' in M. Wright (ed.)

Levine, C. H. (1979) 'More on cutback management: hard questions for hard times' *Public Administration Review* Vol. 39, pp. 179-83

RIPA (1980) Speech by Sir Ian Bancroft to AGM of Royal Institute of Public Administration, December

Select Committee on the Treasury and Civil Service (1979/80a) *The Budget and the Government's Expenditure Plans 1980/81 to 1983/84* HC 584 London, HMSO

Select Committee on the Treasury and Civil Service Department (1979/80b) 4th Report, *Civil Service Manpower Reductions* HC 712-I/II London, HMSO

Select Committee on the Social Services (1979/80) 3rd Report *The Government's White Papers on Public Expenditure* HC 702 London, HMSO

Skidelsky, R., (ed.) (1977) *The End of the Keynesian Era* London, Macmillan

Stewart, J. D. (1980) 'From growth to standstill' in Wright (ed.)

Wright, M. (1977) 'Public expenditure in Britain: the crisis of control' *Public Administration* Vol. 55, Summer

Wright, M., (ed.) (1980) *Public Spending Decisions* London, Allen and Unwin.

PART II

# GOVERNMENT ORGANIZATION AND STRUCTURE IN 'HARD TIMES'

# CHAPTER TWO

# Whitehall and Retrenchment

by MICHAEL LEE

A Cabinet committee set up in 1942 by the World War II coalition government and chaired by Sir John Anderson produced the classic definition of the fields to be covered by official consideration of the machinery of central government in Britain. The fields were: Cabinet organization; the distribution of functions among ministers; non-departmental organizations; and any questions raised in the conduct of the executive's relationship with Parliament, such as the scope of questioning by select committees or the extent to which MPs should be disqualified from holding specific public offices (Lee, 1977).

This definition established a style of management. The Head of the Civil Service advised the Prime Minister on machinery-of-government changes after conducting inquiries through the machinery-of-government division in the Treasury. That unit, established in 1945, symbolized a doctrine that regular reviews of the subjects listed by the Anderson Committee would lead to a central 'fund of experience' on which officials could regularly draw. Official advice on such matters was seen to have a technical basis, because the Treasury as the central department had been equipped to undertake appropriate research and to store the results. For at least twenty years after World War II, this approach provided a language and an orthodoxy for the discussion of machinery-of-government questions, which were handled in a 'top-down' style of management after collective official and ministerial consideration.

But in recent years, and in the context of hard times for government, two further approaches have been developed that are at variance with the framework established by the Anderson Committee. First, the internal arrangements of government organizations have become increasingly subject to scrutiny, on a case-by-case basis, by management review teams drawn from the departments involved as well as from the Civil Service Department (the central organization responsible for promoting efficiency in government, including the machinery-of-government division originally established in the Treasury in 1945). The transfer of the machinery-of-government division from the Treasury to a separate Civil Service Department (established in 1968) has had the effect of linking questions about the allocation of functions among ministers to questions about the relationships between permanent secretaries, finance officers and establishments officers. This change of emphasis acquires its significance from a wider debate about the accountability of public servants, but it has been given a special force by retrenchment in public expenditure. Second, civil servants themselves have been claiming that they ought to be consulted about the consequences of changes of policy for the administrative activities that they carry out — an issue that is clearly likely to be sensitive at a time of financial cutbacks. A number of different strands are involved in this development. Some technical staff criticize the paternalist attitudes of generalist policy advisers who often have an important influence over the management of resources, but lack an appreciation of the work 'on the ground'. Moreover, officials have come to see the machinery of government as much in terms of the jobs to be provided and the basis of recruitment to be maintained as in terms of ministerial responsibility or accountability to Parliament.

Hence, particularly in hard times, ministers may become more conscious of the difficulties in the way of implementing their wishes. The public sector has become more politicized since Sir John Anderson's day, and more subject to disputes among major trade unions. Managers in many different kinds of public service (in local authorities and other agencies as well as civil service departments) are quick to point out the effects of organizational changes on the morale of their staff. There is an increasing reluctance to leave the determination of the machinery of administration to a discussion of constitutional principle alone. This reluctance takes its origins from a gradual transformation of popular respect for public service jobs, but it is of course magnified whenever governments announce their intention to reduce the public sector.

To what extent may retrenchment in public spending be expected to bring a return to the top-down style of management associated with the Anderson Committee? Or does retrenchment instead emphasize that the approaches developed in recent years represent a permanent adaptation of Whitehall to both technical and social change? These questions are difficult to answer because of the problem of isolating the effects of retrenchment from other political developments. Moreover, there has been little public discussion of recent developments in approaches to machinery-of-government questions — the examination of internal organization, department by department, and the recognition of syndicalist and consultative elements in public sector management.

The first development, the increasing emphasis on reviewing internal organization of government agencies, touches on the roles and self-images of ministers and senior civil servants. Any modification in what a minister does as the 'manager' of his own department, or in what his officials regard as the functions for which they are directly accountable, cannot be undertaken without questioning many long-accepted central conventions and involving the expectations and aspirations of ambitious people. Particularly in the context of retrenchment, policy and government organization become very closely intertwined — raising important issues about the spheres of influence of ministers and officials that do not fit easily into the Andersonian conception of how machinery-of-government consideration related to policy. Questions are raised about the appropriate balance between what needs to be handled centrally — through central departments such as the Treasury, the Civil Service Department and the Cabinet Office — and what is best left to the individual agency concerned. The Anderson Committee's vision of a central research capacity has been superseded by a more complex set of considerations.

The second development, the claim that administrators should have a greater participation in the design of the government machine, has a particular interest in a context of retrenchment. Civil servants have organized themselves to oppose public spending cuts through bodies such as the National Steering Committee Against the Cuts (an umbrella organization including twelve public sector unions in its membership). Indeed, even in times of growth, one of the lessons learned by applying the 'human relations' style of management to the public sector is that civil servants set great store by the actual content of their jobs, meaning that the claim to participation may go beyond 'conditions of work' in some neutral sense to questions more closely related to the design of policy and organization. It looks as if the worsening conditions in public service industrial relations are partly a product of policy changes that impose administrative tasks of such doubtful feasibility that the staff concerned can only protest; and specific policies of reducing the size of the public sector may aggravate these tendencies. The Anderson Committee's conviction that personnel management was a field of investigation separable from other aspects of the machinery-of-government problem has been abandoned.

This chapter describes what happened to these two post-Anderson approaches to machinery-of-government questions during the period of retrenchment immediately following the election of Mrs Thatcher's Conservative government in 1979. This is a particularly interesting test-bed for observing the behaviour of government in 'hard times', because it combined strong pressures for cutting public spending (pressures that had to some extent also been exerted by the previous Labour government) with a specifically Conservative desire to 'roll back the frontiers of the public sector'. The chapter begins by considering the internal organization of government departments and then looks at the recognition of claims for consultation; it also briefly comments upon the part played by departments at the centre of Whitehall at a time of retrenchment.

## THE INTERNAL ORGANIZATION
## OF DEPARTMENTS

In attempting to cut public spending, the methods and approach of Mrs Thatcher's government bring to light deeply embedded traditional conceptions of the respective roles of ministers and civil servants in government departments. They also reveal very clearly that those relationships and other basic features of departmental organization often flow directly from parliamentary appropriation and audit procedures, or from the tacit approval that ministers have collectively given over the years to a common code of practice for civil servants. Some of these relationships rest on statute, such as Comptroller and Auditor-General's right to see departmental files; but others, such as the position of finance and establishment officers, depend upon the gradual acceptance by ministers in successive governments of collective arrangements that override their otherwise exclusive authority to manage their own departments. Any examination of the internal organization of departments shows how loose a confederation central government can be, but also how much the practices of coordination in Whitehall depend upon the conventions of what ministers and civil servants expect from each other.

This point is important because 'ministerial management' lay at the heart of Mrs Thatcher's conception of how public spending might be reduced. Ministers were required — individually more than collectively — to take the lead in planning to 'roll back' the public sector. The whole strategy of the government was to use the drive inherent in ministerial office. After all, the formalities of law and organization place responsibility for government's activities in the hands of ministers. Relatedly, any effective application to the details of dismantling public services has to begin with a review of departmental powers, and with the identification of those changes that require legislation if they are to be introduced. The Cabinet and the central departments may stimulate innovation and make arrangements to systematize what ministers wish to do, but they cannot themselves undertake the detailed investigations that may be needed.

But to question the costs of government through individual ministerial initiative highlights the extent to which the expansionary era had altered the conventions of business in Whitehall. The government's desire to 'disengage' threw a fresh light on the elaborate administrative networks that hold government together. For example, inside each government department the permanent secretary is supported by a principal establishments officer concerned with staffing questions, and each of these officials has contacts with his opposite number elsewhere. They are locked into common procedures and bound by regular meetings. The permanent heads of department themselves see each other weekly with the minimum degree of formality, as well as at a number of official committees; departmental finance officers have regular contact with the Treasury Officer of Accounts; and establishment officers attend monthly meetings at the Civil Service Department. Many of these procedures originated with extensions of Treasury control after World War I.

Apart from common conventions and inter-departmental links, a different kind of constraint on a managerial approach to slimming down government is the desire of both ministers and permanent secretaries to be adequately briefed on all matters that impinge on their responsibilities, no matter how far removed from their immediate concerns. For example, proposals to 'hive off' functions formerly carried out by government departments to non-departmental or other bodies outside Whitehall tend to provoke requests from departments for staff to be retained at the centre in order to liaise with hived-off bodies. The desire to 'hive in' is very strong, and hiving off policies may be seen as a threat to official careers. Ambitious civil servants prefer to remain within easy range of the permanent secretary's eye, because good performance within the Whitehall networks of association is essential for promotion.

Pressures such as these present difficulties for a government aiming to reduce the numbers of senior posts in Whitehall. Indeed, part of the Conservative government's suspicion of the high ranks of the civil service may have stemmed from the apparent expansion of the 'top hamper' of senior staff in Whitehall as a result of changes in the structure of central departments in the early 1970s. In 1972 a unified system of pay and grading was introduced for all posts of under-secretary and above. This was known as the 'open structure', and all civil servants who had enjoyed the status of comparable work, but had previously not been counted in these general grades, were at last included. The effect on total numbers in the grades of permanent secretary, deputy secretary and under-secretary was an increase from 417 in 1971 to 718 in 1972. Subsequently, the numbers in these posts rose further, partly due to a reclassification of posts and partly due to an expansion of posts (it is difficult to assess the relative importance of these two factors from published statistics). The result was that by 1980 there were over 800 in the 'open structure'. There were 28 permanent secretaries and 79 deputy secretaries in 1971 (CSD, 1971), and 39 permanent secretaries and 156 deputy secretaries in 1980. Any government seeking to roll back such an increase faces questions of extreme sensitivity in the management of individual careers.

Unlike the previous Conservative government of 1970—74, Mrs Thatcher's scheme for retrenchment in the public sector was not set in the context of some overall scheme for administrative reform. Implicitly, working relationships and operations seem to have been taken to be more significant than formal structures and procedures. Given such a philosophy, there were many advantages in continuing the newly developed habits of management review rather than returning to something more like the Andersonian style. Indeed, the Prime Minister's chief personal initiative on civil service management was a variant on the management review philosophy: she selected Sir Derek Rayner of Marks and Spencers stores to be her personal adviser on the promotion of efficiency and the elimination of waste. Significantly, Leslie Chapman, the author of *Your Disobedient Servant* (1978), whose well-publicized personal campaign against civil service waste had impressed the Conservatives in opposition, was *not* chosen — perhaps because the approach he favoured was to recruit a 'private army' that would root out the malefactors (Kellner and Crowther-Hunt, 1980, 287-8).

By contrast, the essence of Rayner's approach was 'an inside job', which would get each minister to go beneath the civil service 'top hamper' and secure advice from the assistant secretary or principal level. Moreover, Rayner's presence in the Cabinet Office was not conceived as an Anderson-style 'central capability' like the Central Policy Review Staff, which undertook research or briefed ministers collectively. Rather, his function was to advise upon and process the action of individual departments on a case-by-case basis. The approach recommended by Rayner involved a set of inquiries, conducted normally by one or two officials (there were twenty-nine such projects in 1979 and thirty-seven scrutinies in 1980), which brought departmental ministers into direct contact with their 'shop floor', at which civil servants are themselves eager to recommend improvements. The intention was to oblige ministers to look more closely at the 'inside' of their departments, by themselves supervising the Rayner studies. The Cabinet's decision to have a scrutiny programme of this type and the Prime Minister's personal backing for Sir Derek gave the programme a powerful momentum; but, as with all such initiatives, much depends on the impact of the first series of reports. There is, as Rayner recognized, a danger that this might lapse into a 'staff suggestions scheme', in which a low proportion of proposals arising from junior staff are actually applied. (For details of the scrutiny programme, see Select Committee on the Treasury and Civil Service, 1979/80.)

Apart from individual case studies, the provision of 'management information' for ministers on a regular basis was thought to be a useful way of helping ministers to eliminate waste and non-essential functions. Superficially, this arrangement looks something like the application of the Anderson Committee principle of central research, but applied at the level of each individual department not of the civil service as a whole. Basically, the notion involved each directorate within a department providing its minister with periodic statements of the tasks performed and the resources committed to those tasks — enabling the minister to assess the deployment of resources in his department in relation to his political priorities and providing civil servants themselves with a sense of what their activities cost. Sir Derek Rayner considered that a 'management information' system of this kind was the best method of ensuring cost-consciousness and 'good stewardship' in departments.

But the re-emergence of Andersonian principles is perhaps more apparent than real. There is not much evidence that ministers are likely to re-examine their managerial functions in the context of a collective strategy. Governments are not normally equipped to take a systematic approach to ministerial skills. In spite of the Prime Minister's personal backing to those involved in the Rayner exercises, not many ministers naturally warm to the managerial role. Their parliamentary experience does not accustom them to running large organizations. They naturally prefer to approach retrenchment by activities that create political capital without involving them in complex managerial tasks. That is why the elimination of quangos in 1980 — shedding a few non-departmental organizations, as described in Chapter 5 — was both elementary and satisfying.

The concept of ministers-as-managers is therefore unlikely to be uniformly applied or to lead to major changes in departmental organization. But in some cases it was linked to attempts to reduce the size of departments. The most notable case is that of the Department of the Environment, whose political head, Michael Heseltine, was one of the few government ministers to have publicly stated the doctrine that ministers should be managers, in a much-reported speech to the British Institute of Management in 1979 (Heseltine, 1980). Heseltine's formulae were familiar if not trite; for example, his emphasis on setting clear objectives and designing a strategy to meet them, plus a monitoring system based on regular reports, involved nothing that a good permanent head of department should not already be doing. But several DOE divisions disappeared as a result of Michael Heseltine's MINIS control exercise, or at least in connection with it.

As will be described in more detail in Chapter 5, Heseltine also played a leading part in another major initiative to reduce costs in the public sector — the elimination of non-departmental organizations that failed to provide convincing evidence of their need to continue. More than the 'managerial information' initiative, this exercise had some distinct echoes of the Andersonian style, in that it combined with the post-Andersonian style of individual departmental reviews a top-down, government-wide approach that involved a degree of central research and 'funded experience'.

As in the case of the Rayner waste-finding exercise, the Prime Minister showed a preference for an 'inside job'. She chose a permanent secretary on the point of retirement, Sir Leo Pliatzky, to undertake an inquiry into non-departmental organizations throughout government. In the style of the 1940s, Pliatzky was housed in the Civil Service Department while he conducted his inquiry. He had the full support of the CSD management services group and his report (*Report on Non-Departmental Bodies*), which appeared early in 1980, was full of material acquired from the CSD's machinery-of-government division. Moreover, the report became in large measure a vehicle for the projection of ideas that had already been developed at official level, embodying the CSD's experience since the Fulton Report on the civil service of 1968, and indicating what appeared to be the most appropriate 'regimes' for various types of non-departmental bodies. It packed a good deal of accumulated experience into asking 'how to find the right balance between disengagement from detail and reserved powers of supervision or intervention' in the creation of non-departmental bodies. The degree to which the Pliatzky Report heralded 'real retrenchment' in non-departmental bodies is considered in Chapter 5; but the Pliatzky exercise demonstrated that, at least on some issues, moves towards retrenchment may involve an element of the Andersonian approach to handling machinery-of-government questions.

However, the main institutional legatee of the Andersonian approach, the Civil Service Department, moved somewhat closer to the case-by-case management review approach in its internal composition during this period. In order to bring CSD's organization into line with government thinking on retrenchment and other matters, the management services group was split into two under-secretary divisions. One half was renamed 'Functions and Programmes' and given responsibility for staff inspection (staff inspection entails regular visits by CSD inspectors to departments to determine the levels of grading for established civil service posts). This broke new ground in bringing staff inspection closer to considerations of waste and inefficiency. The other half of the management services group was renamed 'Management and Organization', retaining a link between machinery-of-government questions, audit and operational research.

## CONSULTATION AND MORALE

Turning to the second of the post-Andersonian developments, a drive to cut public spending and to reduce the size of the public sector has interesting implications for the claims to rights of consultation by public servants. The waves of unrest and discontent over pay within the public sector during the 1970s encouraged greater trade union membership and activity, and transformed what had once been conceived in staff association terms into something more akin to the conventions of industrial relations in the private sector. It became unrealistic centrally to design different regimes for staff in departments and in fringe bodies solely by appealing to the principles of good management and effective performance. The disposition of public offices and their supporting staff was in some sense an exercise in industrial management. Calculations about the prospects of introducing new technology into administration and about the likelihood of redundancies had a direct bearing on decisions about the machinery of government.

In the face of these developments, the election of a Conservative government in 1979, committed to cutting public spending as a desirable end in itself (not merely a regrettable necessity, as its Labour predecessor saw spending cuts), might perhaps have been expected to herald an abrupt change back towards central and uniform direction of the public service. Conservatives at this time were attracted by Bacon and Eltis's view (1976) that the British economy had 'too few producers' and too many employees providing non-marketed public services (that is, services provided by government that were given away rather than bought and sold). This had implications for the central core of the civil service, since

'Crown bodies' are by and large 'not in the market'.

Moreover, some Conservatives were both suspicious of the privileges acquired by civil servants within the definitions of 'the Crown' (particularly their index-linked pensions in a period of high inflation) and apprehensive about the degree to which expansion of the public services in the past had been a boost to supporters of the Labour party. It was rumoured that one of the first suggestions made to the policy unit attached to No 10 Downing Street after the Conservatives' election victory was that it should investigate how civil servants might best be 'deprivileged' (see Stephenson, 1980, especially pp. 28-43). There was also a desire to find out whether there were any discernable links between political affiliation and public sector employment, or between forms of public sector unionization and patterns of labour unrest. The Conservatives had taken an interest in opposition in formulating a strategy to resist strikes by public sector unions in connection with their plans for denationalization, identifying areas (particularly in key nationalized industries) in which it was wise to avoid confrontation with trade unions. (This was done by a study group under Nicholas Ridley in 1977-78: see *The Economist,* 27 May 1978).

In fact, senior managers in the civil service had long been accustomed to view the machinery of government in terms of the extent to which different blocks of work vary in terms of staff turnover, absenteeism and trade union militancy. Indeed, the dissatisfaction of public sector workers with the pay restraint policies attempted by Labour governments in the 1970s has inculcated in the senior management of the civil service a strong interest in public sector trade unions, and an awareness of the impact on the civil service itself of ramifications in the much larger world of public sector employment. The traditional system of departmental 'Whitley' Councils, consultative machinery composed of a management and a staff side, has been shaken by the regular threats of industrial action by civil servants since 1973.

Apart from problems of managing the central civil service, there is a tendency for those who are not senior managers at 'the centre' and who work in provincial out-stations to interpret proposals for change in terms of a struggle for power between interested parties; and retrenchment is likely to intensify this tendency. The machinery of government is considered in a much more tendentious manner than the Anderson Committee would have ever conceived. The balance between central control and agency autonomy is being fixed in a process of continuous negotiation, not by accepted conventions that settle the appropriate staff regime according to centrally agreed and stable criteria.

Outside the civil service altogether, comparisons of pay and conditions of employment have led those outside the boundaries of the 'Crown' service to question the authority of those within it. From the periphery, the central agencies of Whitehall appear much less bound by the criteria of performance that they seek to impose on others. As Royston Greenwood reports in Chapter 4, local government officers often seem to resent the lack of discipline that they think they perceive at the centre, and they sometimes imagine that central civil servants take advantage of the weakness of local authorities to pursue a rather special set of departmental interests. The staff of nationalized industries also often express dislike of what they regard as the intolerable interference of sponsoring departments. At all levels in the public sector, workers have been taught by experience to question the doctrines that provide a rationale of accountability and control.

The Conservative government's attempt to 'break out' from the handicaps that it associated with a large public sector brought these discontents, and existing anxieties about the structure and functions of government, into a sharper focus. The government was in fact itself divided over the extent to which public spending should be cut, public services 'reprivatized' and the market economy restored. Some senior members of the government believed that reducing the public sector had to be approached carefully, because public servants had clients and customers whom it might be politically damaging to neglect (many thought that the Conservatives had been voted into office to some extent because of popular distaste for the hardships imposed on the recipients of public services during the public sector industrial disputes of the winter of 1978/79). A speech by Sir Ian Gilmour in early 1980 (reported in *The Times,* 12 February 1980) on the need for the Conservative government to take a 'caring' approach to 'people who are in trouble' and the Cabinet's watering-down of a Treasury proposal for £2 bn. of spending cuts in November 1980, are examples of this line of thinking.

Commitment to retrenchment was therefore not always matched by actual performance (a theme that is echoed elsewhere in this book); and even when politicians hang together it is likely to be difficult to bring about retrenchment through a process of genuine staff consultation and without further politicization of the public sector. Reverting to the simple doctrine that an individual minister is responsible for all the actions of his department, and therefore has the right to impose views on policy that run counter to those developed by civil servants, runs sharply up against the claim of departmental employees that they have a right to satisfying and responsible roles. Indeed, the Conservative government's policies posed not only a threat to the continuance of existing jobs (in fact, the vast majority of job losses were effected by natural wastage — that is, a hiring freeze) but also a challenge to established professionalism, whether it were 'generalist' or specialist administration. The formalities of law and the practices of individual ministers did not fit in easily with the activities of officials whose skills lay in building institutions that combined the principles of accountability with the requirements of measured performance and good morale. Instead, as we have seen earlier, the whole enterprise of reducing the scope of government seemed to depend on the style of interpretation adopted in each department. Thus local authorities and other semi-autonomous agencies such as Health Authorities were threatened with, and in some cases subjected to, administrative action and discriminatory cuts in grant; non-departmental bodies due for abolition were suspended until the appropriate legislation could be passed; local authority services that had been mandatory (that is, were required by law to be provided in specific circumstances) were cut back while they were being transformed into permissive arrangements (that is, services that might be provided or not, at the discretion of each individual authority). Indeed, the distinction between the mandatory and the permissive services of local authorities was said by some to have been nullified, because local authorities had no funds available for discretionary activities.

Examples such as these indicate how the government's policies of cutbacks could be seen as 'riding roughshod' over the skills and practices of professional administrators, and as ignoring what those administrators considered to be important symbols of legitimacy. Ministers making cutbacks without extensive consultation with advisers could be viewed by officials as indulging in ideological postures rather than caring for the institutions in their charge.

Policies of retrenchment may therefore have a sharp impact on the morale of public servants. Morale had been recognized as a problem in management of the civil service before Mrs Thatcher's government added its particular ideological twist to pressures for retrenchment. For example, the Civil Service Department had implemented the suggestions of one permanent secretary who wanted a campaign to improve the image of the civil service, and it went as far as to produce a magazine, known as *The Quarry*, for internal circulation in the civil service (see *The Times*, 19 September 1978). It had also responded to the emergence of an industrial relations problem by setting up an industrial relations division and encouraging a new Whitehall network of industrial relations experts. Even so, morale in the higher civil service was fairly low in 1979/80, because senior civil servants were under attack from all sides and had to translate the proposition that ministers should be managers into concrete policies that were far from uniformly welcome to the staff concerned.

Will continuing pressures for cutbacks further accentuate the importance attached to central consideration of projects for maintaining civil service morale or for containing industrial unrest? Perhaps; but the style of handling these matters is unlikely to return to the Anderson Committee's conception. Immediately after the Anderson Committee had reported, permanent secretaries of major government departments, in their capacity as managers, used to meet in official Cabinet committees to discuss specific problems of the civil service or of organization, and to make recommendations. That mode of conducting business seems nowadays much less important: the present style is informal and *ad hoc*. In recent years the Head of the Civil Service has held weekly informal meetings with the official heads of department to exchange information and to anticipate difficulties, but without the formal papers and minutes of an official committee. By means such as these, Whitehall is equipped to respond quickly in a crisis. Indeed, it has become perhaps too fond of contingency planning based on the model of a 'war game', the drill for responding to attack by atomic weapons that involves the minimum investment to ensure the survival of a few without spreading the gloom and despondency of a visible civil defence corps for the many. As a model for handling retrenchment, this has a certain logic about it; but it runs the risk of exacerbating problems such as trade union militancy.

## PRIVATIZATION, RETRENCHMENT, AND INSTITUTIONAL RELATIONS

In terms of the machinery of government, the policies that made the greatest impact on the discussion and professional opportunities and morale in the public service in the early period of Mrs Thatcher's government were those dealing with the return to the private sector of a number of major public corporations. Plans for 'disengagement' were made and pursued in the sponsoring departments with the characteristic zeal of a newly elected government. But an ideological unity in Cabinet — at least in its public appearance — will not guarantee a uniformity of ministerial practice, and styles of 'disengagement' varied from department to department.

Indeed, there was nothing to prevent ministers from choosing individually to 'disengage' in ways that disrupted the processes of government as a whole. A dramatic example was the behaviour of the Department of Industry in early 1980, facing the first nationwide steel strike since 1926. Instead of actively involving his department in the pursuit of an early settlement of this dispute, as might have been the style of a different kind of minister, Sir Keith Joseph (the Secretary of State for Industry) stuck closely to the doctrine that a minister shall not interfere in the day-to-day management of a nationalized industry.

Apart from the short-term disruption and long-term effect on industrial relations of 'disengagement' in this style, disengagement and privatization contain potential ambiguities. In practice, disengagement may mean exchanging one form of government engagement for another, rather than a total withdrawal from all administrative activities. There may even be potential conflict between spending cuts and privatization. For example, a process of privatization will not necessarily reduce the propensity of central government departments to intervene in the work of organizations under their sponsorship, or the opportunities available to ministers to make their personal attitudes felt. Indeed, governments that 'roll back the public sector' may well in certain fields require more professional advice, not less; and arrangements made ostensibly to delegate management functions outside Whitehall to other agencies may in practice bring about new forms of centralization.

Thus during 1979-80, Department of Environment officials were being asked to reduce contacts with local authorities, in the sense of abandoning specific controls and over-use of central circulars, but at the same time to design instruments that measured local authority financial performance. Similarly, Department of Industry officials devised legislation to return nationalized assets to the private sector, but also continued to consider how they should give special assistance to particular companies through the provisions of the Industry Act. Returning activities to the private sector in terms of ownership is not necessarily the same as returning them to market forces outside the sphere of government intervention. For example, the selling of government shares in British Aerospace is unlikely to entail any withdrawal of ministerial concern about the design and sale of British aero-engines and airframes.

Anticipating the theme of the next two chapters, the retrenchment policies of Mrs Thatcher's government also made an impact on central-local relationships and on working concepts of central government control over local authorities. The Conservative government's extension of its predecessor's use of 'cash limits' on public spending as techniques of retrenchment (discussed in Chapters 3 and 4) made central departments appear highly 'interventionist' in the affairs of local authorities and other public bodies. The Local Authority Associations found that the reduction in the number of detailed central controls that the Conservatives had promised (*Central Government Controls over Local Authorities,* 1979) tended to consist of obsolete or little-invoked powers, and that they were accompanied by a much tighter set of regulations in areas that mattered. Indeed, many Conservative local authorities strongly objected to the new conceptions of central government control over local authority spending embodied in the new 'block grant' system of finance (discussed in Chapter 4; see also Roweth, 1980, pp. 173-86). Similarly, in 1979-80 the chairmen of nationalized industries made it clear that they saw a serious conflict between the required rates of return on capital (set for each industry following the Labour government's White Paper on nationalized industry control of 1978) and the cash limits on the sums that nationalized industries were allowed to borrow if their expenditure exceeded their income. In practice, cash limits overrode financial targets; and in the context of recession, which reduced the income of nationalized industries, limits on the industries' ability to borrow meant very steep price increases. Hence nationalized industry chairmen wanted a new code of practice and perhaps a global cash limit for all nationalized industries (so that industries with buoyant income in recession, such as gas, could in effect subsidize those with falling revenues). They thought that nationalized industries were being forced into sharp price increases as a result of the government's financial stringency, and that they would have the difficult task of explaining to their consumers that such price increases were the result of Whitehall decisions rather than of board policy (see *The Economist,* 8 December 1979 and *The Times,* 26 January 1980).

Indeed, the screwing down of public expenditure generally by the use of cash limits had the effect of encouraging professional administrators at all levels to make privately expressed protest against the awkward '*sauve qui peut*' situations that they faced. It required some degree of courage for officials at all levels to persuade their superordinate authorities to avoid taking decisions based on expediency, and to consider which fundamental values needed to be preserved. It was not simply wage claims in the public sector that were at stake, but the defence of skills in professions that allowed scope for initiative and creativity (a point developed by Maurice Kogan in Chapter 7). Local government officers, local councillors, voluntary grant-aided bodies, teachers, actors, consultants and contractors all had to reassess their position in the public sector.

Interestingly, anxiety about the drive to reprivatize and to cut public spending resulting in more government intervention and more Whitehall control over the administrative periphery did not emanate so much from academic lawyers at this time as from professionals in administration outside the centre. The effect of reprivatization may be to increase the administrative instruments available to government for intervention in the affairs of reprivatized agencies and attempts to cut local authority spending have resulted in legislation increasing the powers of ministers (for example, the 1980 Local Government Planning and Land Act, which introduced the block grant regime for local authority finance, also provided for the minister to penalize local authorities that he considers to be 'inefficient', and to deprive them of their power to maintain 'direct labour' organizations for building works if those organizations fail to meet a prescribed rate of return on capital). In the next section, I revert to developments at the 'centre' itself, and their relation to public spending cuts.

## THE CENTRE

The agency directly responsible for civil service staffing, pay settlements and efficiency — the Civil Service Department — has long been criticized for its ailing condition. Like the Ottoman Empire in the eyes of nineteenth-century statesmen, it lumbered along in the 1970s without causing major upheavals but without arousing loyalties and passion. In the light of anxiety about control of public spending and civil service staffing levels, a case has often been argued in favour of joining together the Treasury's responsibilities for public expenditure control and the CSD's powers over the staffing and grading of posts (Select Committee on the Treasury and Civil Service, 1979/80). As was mentioned earlier, this combination existed in the Treasury until 1968, when its management side was removed to form the nucleus of the new Civil Service Department. Such a conjunction could emulate the Office of Management and Budget in the United States (cf. Select Committee on Expenditure, 1976/77, 746-759). But its main virtue would be to simplify the process of controlling the number of public servants; it would not reconcile some of the incompatibilities between doctrine and practice that may be disguised by the immediate reactions to public spending cuts.

Indeed, the location of the machinery-of-government division as between the Treasury and the CSD is not a crucial factor in the evolution of thinking about central government. The secretariat of the Anderson Committee was in the Cabinet Office because of that committee's official Cabinet status, and a number of the committees of permanent secretaries that succeeded it kept the Treasury division in regular contact with the Cabinet secretariat. The location of the unit collating official advice on government machinery will change from time to time according to what is perceived as the most appropriate point in the centre for the Prime Minister's senior advisers; but any reshuffling of the units that make up the centre of government would be unlikely by itself to change official perceptions of what needs to be done.

It is doubtful whether retrenchment alone is the major force that has led the centre to move away from thinking in Andersonian terms of research capacity and funded experience for handling machinery-of-government questions. Although it can be argued that the rise in oil prices and the rapid increase in rates of inflation during the early 1970s compelled the Treasury to move from thinking largely about real resources to tackling the problems of financing, it is difficult to construct a parallel argument that the CSD was shifted by the same circumstances from a preoccupation with grouping government functions into manageable units to considering the wider social significance of government employment. If there *is* a connection between Britain's economic decline and its arrangements for considering the most appropriate divisions of labour in central government, the link has not been directly identified and publicly discussed.

What might be more plausibly argued is that cuts in public spending have made it easier to recognize what has been happening to the conceptions that were originally outlined by the Anderson Committee and that were modified over the next thirty years or so by the growth of central government's activities. First, retrenchment has simplified the acceptance by Cabinet and officials that there will always be a distinct element of bureaucratic politics in any proposals to change the government machine. The habit of looking at the operation of government departments one by one and from the inside (as in the case of the periodic management reviews that are conducted jointly by the CSD and the agency concerned) is an admission that there cannot be an adequate central fund of experience from which principles are derived. Each adjustment is different and demands an element of negotiation. Moreover, it seems to be a widely held assumption among senior civil servants that there can never be a single or unchanging mechanism for promoting efficiency or deploying manpower. The combination of forces of inertia and of the capacity of the system to adapt to new initiatives means that any particular style of central management is likely to face diminishing returns over time — particularly when the stakes are high, as in a period of retrenchment. Nothing can survive for long without becoming sluggish. It is better to have an occasional foray than to wage a long war.

Second, retrenchment has compelled ministers to accept that the privileges of civil service employment no longer carry the same weight in popular imagination or guarantee the same discipline that previous generations used to expect. Public authorities are vulnerable to the embarrassments caused by the disclosure of information by their employees, and this may be heightened during a period of public spending cuts. 'Leaks' of documents to the media can often be traced to a disgruntled official or to a partisan insider. Moreover, thinking about institutions in terms that recognize that the staff are legitimate participants represents an assent to the doctrine that decisions on the government machine should always be related to decisions on personnel management. There seems to be a place for consultations with junior staff, as well as negotiations with senior officials, whenever a new disposition of government offices is contemplated, although retrenchment has compelled a more realistic appraisal of the work involved.

The longer-term changes in thinking, to which public expenditure cuts have drawn attention, centre on those activities of government that fall somewhere between the processes by which policy is made and the mechanics by which administrative decisions are implemented on the 'shop floor'. Retrenchment has focussed attention on the middle ground in central government between what is clearly 'policy' and what is clearly 'implementation', highlighting a fresh approach to the major points of 'transmission' from the engine of policy to the wheels of administration. For example, one of the reasons why the Rayner waste-finding programme aroused such interest was its determination to get beneath 'the top hamper' of Whitehall to the actual heads of line divisions. One of the suggestions considered within the Rayner programme was that a whole level of the official hierarchy could be removed by abolishing the office of under-secretary. This implied that one of the greatest obstacles to improved efficiency was the influence exercised by middle management at this level in Whitehall.

It was precisely the growth of official coordination at middle management level that marked the transition of Whitehall from conditions that the Anderson Committee knew and understood to those that the Civil Service Department came to manage in the years after 1968. It is not surprising that the Anderson Committee's approach has been abandoned, even if the structure of central government it designed has remained. Is it perhaps time to abandon this term 'machinery of government' altogether? It now carries connotations that Lord Haldane would not have recognized and Sir John Anderson would have dismissed from his agenda.

As was indicated earlier, many of the important effects of retrenchment on the public sector in the period covered here have come outside the centre of Whitehall rather than within it. Accordingly, the next two chapters look at the response of local authorities to central government pressures to restrain spending in the years up to 1980, and the final chapter in this section looks in more detail at the attempt to cull non-departmental bodies.

## REFERENCES

Bacon, R, and Eltis, W. A. (1976) *Britain's Economic Problem: Too Few Producers* London, Macmillan

*Central Government Controls over Local Authorities* (1979) Cmnd. 7634, London, HMSO

Chapman, L. (1978) *Your Disobedient Servant* London, Chatto and Windus

CSD (1971) *Staff in Post* Civil Service Department

Heseltine, M. (1980) Speech to British Institute of Management *Management Services in Government* May, pp. 61-8

Kellner, P. and Crowther-Hunt, Lord (1980) *The Civil Servants* London, MacDonald General Books

Lee, J. M. (1977) *Reviewing the Machinery of Government 1942-52: An Essay on the Anderson Committee and Its Successors* London, Birkbeck College

Roweth, B. (1980) 'Statistics for policy — Needs assessment in the rate support grant' *Public Administration* Vol. 59, Summer

Stephenson, H. (1980) *Mrs Thatcher's First Year* London, J. Norman

*Report on Non-Departmental Bodies* (1980) Cmnd. 7797, London, HMSO (Pliatzky report)

Select Committee on Expenditure (1976/77) 11th Report Session 1976/77, *The Civil Service,* HC 535-II

Select Committee on the Treasury and Civil Service (1979/80) HC 333-iv and HC 333-X, XI, Minutes of Evidence, London, HMSO.

CHAPTER THREE

# Cutting Local Spending –
# The Scottish Experience, 1976-80

by ARTHUR MIDWINTER and EDWARD PAGE

The impact of hard times and of pressures for spending restraint is not confined to the centre of the government machine, as Michael Lee stresses in the last chapter. Local government spending inevitably also comes under pressure from central government, whatever the party complexion of the government. This is because local spending in Britain accounts for about a quarter of public expenditure and local government employs over 11 per cent of the working population (roughly double the 1952 figure: see Stewart, 1980), meaning that the annual wage settlements for local government workers now have major implications for central government's spending targets.

Local authority spending and employment grew steadily over twenty years from the 1950s to the mid-1970s. Thereafter the situation changed, with stronger pressures for retrenchment and spending restraint. This involved some contradictions for governments caught between manifesto commitments to 'local democracy' (in the name of which local government was reorganized into larger units in the mid-1970s, ostensibly to create units more capable of resisting pressure from central government) and commitments to cut public spending – a large part of which is in the hands, not of Whitehall, but of local authorities. The strategic relations between local and central government are thus a key factor in the behaviour of government in hard times.

This chapter explores some of the weapons used by central

government to reduce spending by Scottish local authorities in the period 1976—80, and the reactions to them. The English and Welsh experience, as discussed by Royston Greenwood in the next chapter, is in many ways similar. On the face of it, this is odd, because the Scottish local government system is distinct from that of England and Wales in both institutional and political terms. With only sixty-five local authorities, it is relatively small *vis-à-vis* England and Wales; it is controlled by a multi-functional 'provincial' government department in Edinburgh, which makes the concept of 'central' government somewhat ambiguous; and the country is heavily dominated by the Labour party, even at a time when the Conservatives are in power at Westminster. All of these features might at first sight be supposed to make an 'abrasive' programme of cutting local spending more difficult for central government to develop and carry out in Scotland.

This chapter is divided into two main parts. The first part looks at the attempt by the Scottish Office to influence the aggregate spending of local authorities in Scotland. What strategies were used? What effect did these strategies have on the local government system as a whole, and what was the response of *individual* local authorities? In the second part, we turn from aggregate spending to individual services. Did aggregate expenditure reflect priorities for the development of individual services as laid down in Rate Support Grant settlements negotiated between central and local government; and what was the scope for variations to meet the needs of individual localities?

## THE SCOTTISH OFFICE'S STRATEGIES FOR INFLUENCING AGGREGATE SPENDING

The first dimension of central influence over local spending concerns the aggregate total of that spending. By and large, the aggregate figure in which central government is interested is that part financed by local property tax (rates) and central government grants. Local authorities may, of course, to some extent compensate for reductions in rates and/or grants by increasing charges for services, so that the actual amount of services provided does not necessarily rise and fall proportionately with rate and grant income. Most of the discussion in this section refers to local expenditure net of service charges, though we shall briefly discuss gross expenditure at the end.

Central government can affect local spending directly — notably, by reducing the money it gives to local authorities as grants. Alternatively, it may use indirect weapons. Of the latter, a particularly important device is the issuing of 'indicative guidelines', which attempt to put pressure on local authorities to conform to central government spending plans by suggesting broad levels of net spending for each individual local authority (for a discussion of the control implications of this device, see Dunsire, 1980).

The Scottish Office can alter the level of financial assistance to local authorities in three main ways. First, it may change the proportion of approved local spending to be covered by central government grant. This is known as the 'percentage support' and, as Table 3.1(a) shows, it was used to effect cuts in 1977 and 1978.

Second, the Scottish Office may alter the base figure upon which the percentage support is calculated, by specifying a different *level* of approved local spending upon which central government is prepared to pay Rate Support Grant. This is a 'volume' control, in that it is set in constant-price terms. It is known as the 'expenditure allowance', and Table 3.1(b) shows the change in expenditure allowance since 1976 (the percentage change, as can be seen, differs according to whether this year's expenditure allowance is compared with last year's expenditure allowance or with last year's actual spending, because expenditure allowance is set in constant-price terms at the beginning of the financial year).

Expenditure allowance is set in constant-price or 'volume' terms; but government pays Rate Support Grant (RSG) to local authorities as a fixed cash sum. Hence the third instrument available to the Scottish Office for altering the level of financial assistance to local authorities is to vary the extent to which it allows for likely cost increases in arriving at a cash figure for Rate Support Grant. Since the advent of the 'cash limits' regime for controlling the bulk of public spending in 1976, government has been able to set the cash limit at levels lower than the actual cost increases incurred by local authorities, instead of automatically adjusting the cash amount of grant to maintain a given volume of services, as in the pre-1976 system. In this way local authorities lose out, less dramatically than by the first two methods discussed above, by the conversion of 'funny money' to 'real money' (Wright, 1977). Since cash limits were first applied, the allowance for cost increases in the cash limits has become progressively lower than actual increases in costs, as can be seen by inspecting Table 3.1(c).

TABLE 3.1
THREE MECHANISMS FOR CENTRAL GOVERNMENT
INFLUENCE OVER SCOTTISH LOCAL AUTHORITY SPENDING

(a) *'Percentage support'* (proportion of spending to be financed by government grants)

| | |
|---|---|
| 1976 | 75 |
| 1977 | 72.5 |
| 1978 | 68.5 |
| 1979 | 68.5 |
| 1980 | 68.5 |
| 1981 | 68.5 |

(b) *Percentage growth in 'expenditure allowance'*

| | Over previous year's expenditure allowance | Over previous year's actual spending |
|---|---|---|
| 1977 | 6.4 | 1.0 |
| 1978 | 0.5 | 0.5 |
| 1979 | 0.9 | 3.9 |
| 1980 | 3.2 | 2.7 |
| 1981 | −2.3 | NA |

(c) *Percentage increase for rising costs allowed for in cash limits and in local authority budgets*

| | Cash limit | Local expenditure |
|---|---|---|
| 1977 | 5.9 | 8.8 |
| 1978 | 6.4 | 9.2 |
| 1979 | 9.3 | 12.5 |
| 1980 | 9.8 | 16.9 |
| 1981 | 13.0 | 20.0* |

* estimated

The collective effect of these three strategies has been slightly to reduce the amount of grant paid to Scottish local authorities in real terms from 1976 to 1980 — the real level of grant fell by 4 per cent in 1978 and is likely to fall by 2 per cent in 1981. Moreover, this standstill in the real level of central grants has been achieved largely by the setting of cash limits below the level of likely cost increases.

This point is demonstrated by Table 3.2, which shows the relative impact of four factors on the overall level of central grant received by Scottish local authorities in the period 1977—81. Column (a) shows the difference between the level of grant that *would* have been received if the grant had been calculated with the same 'percentage support' as in the previous year and the actual level of grant received (that is, the percentage of spending to be financed before taking into account the erosion of grant levels by the cash limit mechanism described above). Column (b) shows the impact of the 'expenditure allowance' in terms of the percentage change in the approved volume of spending compared to the previous year allowed by this mechanism (in this case, before the effects of the cash limit and percentage support mechanisms start to operate). Column (c) shows the adjustment in the real level of grant effected by the setting of grants in cash-limited terms that do not fully cover cost increases.

TABLE 3.2
THE RELATIVE IMPORTANCE OF FACTORS INFLUENCING
GRANT CHANGES TO SCOTTISH LOCAL AUTHORITIES

| Year | Percentage support | Expenditure allowance | Gap between actual cost rises and cash limit | Automatic increment | Total per cent change in grant |
|------|------|------|------|------|------|
| | (a) | (b) | (c) | (d) | (e) |
| 1977 | −3.5 | +6.4 | −2.7 | 0 | +0.1 |
| 1978 | −5.7 | +0.3 | −2.5 | +2.7 | −4.8 |
| 1979 | 0 | +0.9 | −2.9 | +2.6 | +0.6 |
| 1980 | 0 | +3.2 | −6.4 | +2.9 | −0.2 |
| 1981 | 0 | −2.3 | −6.1 | +6.4 | −2.0* |

* Assumes 20 per cent cost increases and no raising of cash limit

Column (d) shows an effect of cash limits that works in the opposite direction in its impact on grant levels — an automatic increment that is made on the basis of the effect of cost increases in the previous financial year. Space does not permit us to explain this device in detail; briefly, it is a mechanism that has the effect of compensating local authorities for actual cost increases that ran ahead of cash limits in the previous financial year. Column (e) shows the combined effect — the 'bottom line', in terms of the percentage change in total grant over the previous year.

Table 3.2 demonstrates the increasing reliance on the cash limit mechanism as a strategy for reducing the level of central government grant to local authorities over this period. The other two mechanisms have been used as well — the percentage support weapon being used in 1977 and 1978 and the expenditure allowance being cut in 1981 at a time when cash limits were held closer to the likely level of cost increases. Perhaps central government's preference for the cash limit mechanism for cutting grants arises from the fact that, in the complex of factors that go to make up the level of central government grants, cash limits are least visible in the sense of provoking less public discussion than changes in percentage support and expenditure allowance. The political attractiveness of cash limits as a device for cutting public spending is a theme that appears elsewhere in this book, and is discussed further in Chapters 8 and 9.

### Indirect tactics: the use of circulars and guidelines

A less direct tactic available to central government in attempting to cut local spending is that of exhortation and target-setting. In 1977, the Scottish Office began to issue expenditure guidelines for each local authority — that is, an indication of a level of spending consistent with the provisions of the Rate Support Grant settlement, so that local authorities can 'plan their own spending'. Before 1977, guidelines were cast in aggregate terms that did not lay down levels of spending for the individual local authorities (district and regional authorities) in the nine Scottish regions. Since then, they have become much more specific. The use of guidelines — a familiar device of 'indicative planning' — to influence local spending in Scotland does not necessarily imply that financial control by the Scottish Office is stronger than DOE control over English and Welsh local spending (Layfield, 1976, p. 85). In fact, there is some evidence that the guidelines were requested by Scottish local authorities themselves rather than imposed unilaterally by the Scottish Office (Convention of Scottish Local Authorities (COSLA), 1976, pp. 120-1 and 1977, p. 37).

In the first three years of the guideline regime (1977—79), the guidelines attempted to bring the higher spenders among district (lower-level) authorities into line with other authorities by giving them lower guideline spending targets per head of population than the lower-spending authorities. But in 1980 the tactics changed completely, and in this case it was the higher spenders that were given higher per capita spending guidelines — in effect, reinforcing the *status quo* of past spending patterns rather than trying to punish the big spenders and reward the parsimonious. Broadly, the same picture applied to the regions, with some *ad hoc* adjustments.

In the first two years of the Conservative government elected in 1979, the use of guidelines by the Scottish Office has been reinforced by circulars issued to local authorities *after* the budgets for the year have been fixed, pointing out the extent to which aggregate local authority budgets exceed the amount of spending allowed for in the RSG settlement, and calling for cuts. But, like the pre-1977 guidelines, such circulars are not discriminatory — they refer to aggregate spending by all Scottish local authorities and are issued to all local authorities, irrespective of whether their budgets are within the guidelines or not.

### The response of the local authority system to Scottish Office influence

In aggregate terms, local government spending outturns in Scotland over the period 1976—79 corresponded fairly closely to the level of spending envisaged by the Scottish Office in the spending guidelines and the RSG spending allowance; and the pattern seems likely to be repeated in 1980. In 1976, the aggregate outturn was some 5 per cent above the Scottish Office target, but thereafter spending has remained within the target and was substantially below it in one year, 1978. This hardly conforms to the picture of local authorities 'defying' central government spending targets that is so often painted in the press and in political rhetoric.

However, as Maurice Wright points out in the first chapter, we have to be careful in determining whether cuts are 'cosmetic' or 'real'. As was mentioned earlier, the figures that have been quoted refer to expenditure net of charges for services and miscellaneous income, such as school meal charges and licence fees. We have already remarked that it is one of the peculiarities of local government finance in the UK that bargaining between central government and local authorities typically ignores service charges and miscellaneous income, and the conventional statistics on local authority spending refer to net rather than to gross spending. Is it possible that local authorities have responded to Scottish Office pressures for cuts in net spending by increasing charges and other income?

It seems unlikely that this has occurred to any great extent. Only about 7 per cent of Scottish local authority spending is financed by fees and charges, which would hardly seem to give local authorities a great deal of scope for cushioning themselves from cuts in net spending (the figures are for 1975, the latest year for which data are available, and refer to spending on rate-funded services other than housing). Moreover, there is no evidence that the relationship between the number of workers employed by Scottish local authorities and their net spending has greatly altered, as one might expect if wage costs were increasingly being loaded onto service charges and other income. Of course, manpower is by no means the only item of local government spending, but it is a very important one and it is probably the area most resistant to cuts. Indeed, over the whole period 1976—80 wage costs have tended to take a slightly increasing share of net spending by Scottish local authorities — implying, as one might predict, that local authorities have responded to pressure for spending cuts to some extent by reducing non-wage costs rather than by sacking people. There is not much evidence of local authorities raising fees and charges to keep real spending constant.

## Individual local authority responses

Aggregate local government spending may have met aggregate Scottish Office targets, as was explained above. But this does not mean that all authorities responded to the targets uniformly. A target can be met even if some authorities overspend substantially, so long as this is offset by underspending on the part of other authorities.

This is in fact what has happened in Scotland in the period 1977—80. There are noticeable differences between upper- and lower-tier authorities as groups, and also among individual local authorities at both levels. As far as the first point is concerned, there has been a consistent tendency for the districts (lower-level authorities) to set their budgets substantially above the targets set by the Scottish Office guidelines. In 1980, for example, the total budget of the districts exceeded the guideline figure by over 19 per cent. On the other hand, the regions (higher-level authorities) have tended to budget as a group fairly close to their guideline figures. Since the high over-budgeting by the districts only involves relatively small amounts of money, the overall level of over-budgeting is comparatively small.

Similarly, when these groups are disaggregated, somewhat varying responses among individual authorities can be discerned. A statistical measure of 'spread' in percentage growth of Scottish local authority budgets, 1977-80, (the 'coefficient of variation', or the standard deviation divided by the mean in order to standardize for size) shows no marked increase in the homogeneity of local authority responses to Scottish Office requests for financial stringency: the index rises and falls, but there is no evidence of a trend one way or the other, among districts or regions.

Table 3.3 presents an indication of the diversity of the pattern

TABLE 3.3
THE EXTENT OF OVER- AND UNDER-SPENDING BY
SCOTTISH LOCAL AUTHORITIES

| | 1977 | | 1978 | | 1979 | | 1980 | |
|---|---|---|---|---|---|---|---|---|
| | D | R | D | R | D | R | D | R |
| Number of authorities: | | | | | | | | |
| Under-spending | 13 | 0 | 23 | 3 | 21 | 0 | 4 | 0 |
| On target | 8 | 3 | 6 | 3 | 2 | 3 | 0 | 2 |
| Over-spending | 6 | 5 | 11 | 3 | 9 | 6 | 9 | 5 |
| Substantially over-spending | 26 | 1 | 13 | 0 | 21 | 0 | 40 | 2 |

D = district authorities (lower tier)
R = regional authorities (upper tier)

from a slightly different angle, showing the number of Scottish local authorities underspending their guidelines, those that were on target (defined as plus or minus 2 per cent), those overspending (by between 2 and 10 per cent), and those substantially overspending (by over 10 per cent). Again, it can be seen that the response of local authorities to the guidelines was far from uniform. But this does not necessarily mean that the guidelines had no effect because, as was explained earlier, before 1980 the guidelines attempted to rein back high spenders and to 'reward' or spur on low spenders. For example, in 1977 Glasgow district (a high spender) was given a guideline spending target 11 per cent below the 1976 level of spending, whereas Annandale and Eskdale (a low spender) was given a target of 43 per cent above the 1976 level. Obviously, an authority's ability to keep within its guidelines in the 1977—79 period was largely a function of the degree of stringency implied in those guidelines; an authority facing a target of 11 per cent cutbacks is far less likely to stay within its guidelines than one allowed to raise spending by 43 per cent. Indeed, there are strong correlations throughout this period between the degree of overspending and the degree of stringency implied in the guidelines (around $-0.85$ for regions and districts alike in each of the years shown in Table 3.3).

It is, of course, a familiar dilemma of target-setting that if too difficult a target is set, it will be missed and lose credibility. Hence it is interesting to see whether those authorities that overspent their financial targets (and these, as we have seen, were invariably those that had been set stringent guidelines) were nevertheless influenced by those guidelines, in the sense of containing spending growth below what it otherwise might have been. If, for the overspending authorities, one examines the relationship between the level of spending growth envisaged in the guidelines and the level of growth in the budgets drawn up by local authorities, there is a noticeable correlation between the two for 1977, the first year of the guidelines regime (0.71 for districts and 0.69 for regions), but thereafter the correlations tend to be weaker, though they vary from year to year. This may indeed indicate some loss of initial credibility and help to explain the change in the guideline system that took place in 1980.

Exploring the reasons for 'overspending' takes us on to difficult ground. There is a body of writing about local government that seeks to explain growth in local authority spending by reference to factors such as the political composition or socio-economic characteristics of local authorities, or their sources of finance. But such an approach makes the assumption that there are authorities that consistently have a higher propensity to increase spending than others; for the period covered here, no such assumption can be justified for Scottish local authorities. Table 3.4 shows the correlations between growth in any one year and that of the previous year for Scottish local authorities; as can be seen, these are generally weak or negative for both regions and districts, implying that higher growth in one year is not necessarily followed by higher growth in the next year. Thus, the Scottish local government world cannot be divided up into authorities with differing propensities to spending growth. There is, it would seem, no such thing as a general propensity to increase spending over time.

TABLE 3.4
CORRELATION COEFFICIENTS FOR PERCENTAGE GROWTH IN
SCOTTISH LOCAL AUTHORITY BUDGETS AS BETWEEN
ONE YEAR AND ANOTHER

|  | Regional authorities | District authorities |
|---|---|---|
| 1978 | −0.5 | 0.0 |
| 1979 | −0.5 | −0.3 |
| 1980 | 0.2 | 0.1 |

In view of this, it should hardly be surprising that growth in Scottish local authority budgets in the period 1976—80 can only to a very limited extent be explained by general hypotheses about the determinants of expenditure growth. A cumulative index of growth, derived by summation of standardized growth levels for the four years in question (that is, growth levels minus the mean and divided by the standard deviation) could be explained by three main variables — per capita expenditure in the 1975/76 period, domestic rateable value as a proportion of total rateable value and the complexion of the controlling party, with Labour control being associated with higher spending levels — but the overall $r^2$ level was only 0.30.[1]

The link between Labour control and higher spending growth is consistent with a number of other studies of the effect of political control on local spending levels, and is of particular interest at a time when Conservative governments are in power at Westminster — a point that will be discussed further in Chapters 8 and 9. Possibly linked with this is the influence of domestic rateable value, in the sense that local authorities that raise a high proportion of their local income through rates on residential property (rather than industrial or commercial property) are less likely to increase spending at a high rate.

Finally, the influence of the level of expenditure per head in the financial year 1975/76 may be interpreted as indicating a levelling effect among high and low spenders after 1975. Low spenders tended to increase spending at a faster rate than those with high spending per head in 1975/76. This is consistent with the Scottish Office's guidelines regime described earlier, but it is not in fact the guidelines alone that are responsible for this effect (a dummy variable for the guidelines substituted for per capita spending in 1975/76 actually reduces the explanatory power of the prediction equation).

The absence of any very clear determinants for overspending and the diversity of the response to Scottish Office calls for financial stringency suggest that the most powerful ways of explaining spending growth are likely to be *ad hoc* and time-specific. It would seem that central government grants set the overall limits of growth in the local government system as a whole but do not control the individual behaviour of local authorities: within the general parameters there is a degree of diversity that is not determined by the level of government grants.

An example of this is the behaviour of Lothian region for the financial year 1981. Amid great publicity, Lothian (a Labour-controlled authority) planned to raise spending by 2.4 per cent in real terms in spite of the Scottish Office target of a 2.3 per cent reduction in its spending level. Lothian was here 'stepping out of line' in the sense that a figure of 2.4 per cent growth is large in comparison with the spending plans of other Scottish local authorities at that time. To accommodate this expansion, Lothian raised rates by 41 per cent, in spite of the fact that the ratio of grants to rates in Lothian's income was already low. This is a dramatic example of central government's inability to control the spending of individual local authorities 'automatically' by setting grant levels. It is worth noting that this much-trumpeted 'rebellion' by Lothian involved an increase in real spending by no means out of the ordinary in comparison to the rates at which local authority spending was rising in the recent past; but even so, it prompted the Scottish Office to counter-measures. One weapon immediately available was the withdrawal of blanket Scottish Office consent for capital spending projects, meaning that Lothian region had to seek separate approvals from St Andrew's House for each individual item of capital spending. Moreover, at the time of writing the Scottish Office is proposing to meet the 'Lothian problem' by introducing legislation permitting the Scottish Secretary to reduce grants to local authorities retrospectively (i.e. after budgets and rates of local property tax have been fixed) if local expenditure is deemed to be excessive. This is similar in its essential strategic aspect to the new regime of central government grants to local authorities in prospect for England and Wales, as described in the next chapter. It means a move away from technocratic modes of fixing grants to a greater element of political choice, with interesting possibilities for 'brinkmanship' and dramatic conflict.

Similarly, a highly varied response greeted the Scottish Office's circular calling for cuts in local spending in the middle of the 1979/80 financial year. Only a minority of districts, but almost half of the regions, made any response to the circular. In a questionnaire survey of Scottish local authorities, almost one-third reported cuts in spending in response to the circular, but a majority did not. As with the guidelines, the tendency to cooperate was much greater among regions than among district authorities, but there were no distinctive features that marked out those authorities that made cuts from those that did not. Certainly, the response was not determined by the degree to which local authority budgets were running ahead of the Scottish Office's guidelines: most authorities were spending above their guideline targets but made no cuts, whereas Strathclyde region, which was very close to its guideline spending target, made further reductions. All of the regional authorities imposed spending cuts in the range of 0–3 per cent, whereas districts displayed a much more varied pattern, ranging from 3 per cent to 10 per cent increases in spending (but again, the comparatively small size of district budgets must be borne in mind when interpreting such figures).

Among the authorities that failed to make mid-year spending cuts in response to the Scottish Office's circular, various explanations were given by finance officers in interviews. For example, one finance officer explained that his authority was in fact in the process of considering cuts of the order of £1 m. at the time when the circular was issued, but that unforeseen pressures for expenditure increases ('outwith the Council's control') had offset the cuts that the authority had been able to make. Others claimed either that they had complied with the Scottish Office's guidelines and could do no more, or that their original budgets had been pruned to the limit. In view of Michael Lee's comments in Chapter 2 about the centre-periphery aspects of the retrenchment process, it is interesting to note the following attack made by one finance officer in an interview on the crudity and wastefulness of short-term spending cuts. He scathingly declared that:

> Experience of previous exercises of this kind has shown that a heavy-handed insensitivity to the management of the public sector results in damage to services provided . . . if public expenditure is to be reduced . . . then the exercise must be carried out in a planned and rational manner. Even a mixture of ingenuity and strict economy will not produce in the local authority sector the sums of money desired, in the timescale envisaged.

## SPENDING ON INDIVIDUAL SERVICES BY SCOTTISH LOCAL AUTHORITIES

A further dimension to spending cuts is the way that they are translated into spending on individual local authority services. At the time of retrenchment, did spending on individual local services reflect the Scottish Office's priorities as expressed in the RSG settlement? To illuminate this, we have chosen five regional services and three district services. Table 3.5 shows the aggregate variation between the spending envisaged for these services in the RSG settlement and the actual local authority estimates.

A few points about Table 3.5 deserve comment. It is interesting to note that, with the exception of leisure and recreation, the budget estimates were much closer to RSG targets in the years

TABLE 3.5
PERCENTAGE VARIATION BETWEEN SCOTTISH LOCAL
AUTHORITY BUDGETS AND RSG TARGET FIGURES FOR
EIGHT SERVICES

|  | 1976/77 | 1977/78 | 1978/79 | 1979/80 |
|---|---|---|---|---|
| *Regional services:* |  |  |  |  |
| Education | −0.8 | 0.8 | 2.2 | 2.1 |
| Roads and lighting | 0.1 | 5.4 | 1.1 | 7.3 |
| Fire | −0.5 | 4.4 | 7.1 | 5.0 |
| Social work | −1.5 | 2.1 | 1.3 | 5.0 |
| Sewers | 5.6 | 2.2 | 1.9 | 5.0 |
| *District services:* |  |  |  |  |
| Environmental health | NA | −10.2 | 11.2 | 4.5 |
| Leisure and recreation | 32.1 | 34.7 | 28.2 | 10.3 |
| Cleansing | −1.3 | 7.4 | 9.8 | 8.5 |

1976/77 and 1977/78, when the most stringent cuts in services were being sought. Second, as far as the regions are concerned, the high degree of divergence between actual budgets and RSG targets in 1979/80 reflects a big gap between the actual rate of inflation and that allowed for in the cash limit for that year. This was also a time when the formula for RSG was charged to favour the Strathclyde region (an industrial 'disaster area') and to favour the district councils *vis-à-vis* in the regions. Third, it is clear that within the regional services there is a tendency for RSG targets to be most closely approached in the case of education and social work. Both of these services are labour-intensive and make much more use of national standards than is the case with services such as sewerage or roads and lighting. Fourth, turning to district services, we see much greater divergence from RSG targets, as might be expected from the pattern of total spending described earlier (but, interestingly, this variation tends to be lowest in the case of cleansing — another service with a high labour component). Again, it must be stressed that this greater degree of divergence from RSG targets by district authorities involves much smaller totals of spending than is the case with the regions.

A fifth and final point to note from Table 3.5 is the extent to which local budgets have consistently been at variance with Scottish Office targets over spending on leisure and recreation. The difference appears to narrow towards the end of the period shown here, but this was not so much the result of local authorities 'coming into line' with Scottish Office targets as of the Scottish Office raising the spending targets by £10 m. in 1979/80. This represented a radical shift from the Scottish Office's argument up to this time that spending on leisure and recreation was the area with the most scope for spending cuts, and it is an intriguing political development. Does it represent the political popularity of local spending in this area — or is it more mundanely explained by central government underestimating the level of expenditure inherited by local authorities when they were reorganized into larger units in the mid-1970s?

For all of these services, then, there seems to be a tendency for Scottish local authorities to budget slightly in excess of the RSG settlement. Local authorities are, of course, subject to contradictory pressures from central government departments. On the one hand there are pressures for cuts in the totality of spending — and, as we have seen, local authorities tend not to spend the full amount laid down in their budget plans, thus in practice narrowing the gap between Scottish Office guidelines and expenditure outturn. On the other hand, officials and ministers in central departments responsible for particular services are naturally anxious to defend such services, and will tend to encourage local authorities to maintain or improve standards of service in the particular areas involved. Indeed, the central government guardians of particular functional services may even see the ability of local authorities to raise income through local taxes and other charges (as in the Lothian case discussed earlier) as a second line of defence against the Treasury axe. It is thus extremely misleading to suppose that all the pressures for retrenchment come from the Scottish Office, and that all the 'spend, spend, spend' pressures come from local authorities. The reality is far more complex.

*The degree of variation among local authorities in spending growth for individual services*

Having looked at the aggregate picture for spending on individual local authority services, we can explore the extent of variation among individual local authorities in the same way as we earlier analysed the total spending profiles of Scottish local authorities. Table 3.6 shows the degree of variation in growth in local spending on the five services discussed earlier, for regional and district authorities. The statistical measure of spread in the right-hand columns is the coefficient of variation described earlier (standard deviation divided by mean). The higher the coefficient of variation, the greater is the degree of 'spread' in spending patterns. The other columns show the percentage change sought by the Scottish Office in the RSG determination and the high and low points of the range in spending on that particular service.

Much as one would expect from the discussion in the last section, growth in spending on education and social work budgets by regional authorities shows the least variation. Spending on road budgets only exhibits a notable degree of variation in the year 1977/78, when there were strong Scottish Office pressures for retrenchment (cutting road maintenance has the advantage of being politically less immediate than measures such as sacking staff or closing schools). On the other hand, Table 3.6(a) shows a much higher degree of variation in spending growth in the case of fire services and sewerage.

A striking contrast to the picture for regional spending is presented in Table 3.6(b), showing the pattern of spending growth for district authorities. As might be expected from the picture painted by the last section, there is much greater variation in spending growth for district authorities. The one exception to this is the most labour-intensive service, cleansing. The range of variation in the high and low columns, although reflecting relatively small sums of money compared to the regions, is extremely wide in some cases. For example, growth in spending on leisure and recreation in 1979/80 varied from 400 per cent over the RSG target to 18 per cent below. Once again, patterns of growth in spending tend to show the greatest variation in years when the Scottish Office was calling for the biggest spending cuts — suggesting, perhaps, that local autonomy in spending is deployed to its fullest extent when pressures for retrenchment are strongest.

It would seem, then, that the scope for manoeuvre possessed by local authorities in responding to Scottish Office spending targets depends to a large extent on the type of authority and the type of service involved. RSG targets are by no means self-enforcing, but

TABLE 3.6
PERCENTAGE CHANGE IN SCOTTISH LOCAL AUTHORITY
SPENDING BY SERVICE

| Service | Year | RSG target | Highest | Lowest | Coefficient of variation |
|---|---|---|---|---|---|
| (a) *Regional authorities:* | | | | | |
| Education | 1977/78 | 8.0 | 12.9 | 6.4 | 0.21 |
| | 1978/79 | 11.9 | 17.6 | 9.8 | 0.19 |
| | 1979/80 | 14.0 | 17.4 | 11.4 | 0.20 |
| Roads | 1977/78 | −1.6 | 14.9 | −1.0 | 1.17 |
| | 1978/79 | 20.2 | 24.3 | 9.7 | 0.28 |
| | 1979/80 | 11.2 | 26.9 | 15.2 | 0.18 |
| Fire | 1977/78 | 4.5 | 20.0 | 5.6 | 0.45 |
| | 1978/79 | 14.8 | 17.8 | 7.5 | 0.29 |
| | 1979/80 | 28.8 | 37.0 | 15.1 | 0.36 |
| Social work | 1977/78 | 6.9 | 19.4 | 8.1 | 0.27 |
| | 1978/79 | 11.9 | 14.2 | 6.3 | 0.25 |
| | 1979/80 | 15.2 | 25.0 | 8.5 | 0.36 |
| Sewers | 1977/78 | 9.2 | 18.2 | 0.8 | 0.70 |
| | 1978/79 | 13.4 | 34.8 | 6.4 | 0.50 |
| | 1979/80 | 16.8 | 77.0 | 11.4 | 0.68 |
| (b) *District authorities:* | | | | | |
| Leisure and recreation | 1977/78 | −1.9 | 108.1 | −66.7 | 5.9 |
| | 1978/79 | +50.4 | 189.5 | −7.2 | 1.1 |
| | 1979/80 | +39.5 | 400.1 | −18.3 | 1.7 |
| Cleansing | 1977/78 | +7.7 | 39.6 | −12.5 | 1.9 |
| | 1978/79 | −0.4 | 56.0 | −2.1 | 0.1 |
| | 1979/80 | +17.9 | 48.0 | −10.0 | 0.6 |
| Environmental health | 1977/78 | NA* | 232.0 | −50.0 | 4.4 |
| | 1978/79 | −0.3 | 200.0 | −38.6 | 1.6 |
| | 1979/80 | +23.4 | 222.5 | −94.1 | 2.3 |

* 'Environmental health' comprises a group of services that were amalgamated for
RSG purposes from the year 1977/78 only.

nor are they invariably self-falsifying as sometimes happens with indicative planning targets. Much would seem to depend on the skills of departmental advocacy and the exercise of local political choice.

## CONCLUSIONS

In the period of retrenchment considered here, the role of the Scottish Office would seem to be more a matter of overall influence and constraint on aggregate spending than of effective control over spending on individual services or by particular local authorities. Aggregate local authority budget plans have generally exceeded the Scottish Office's spending guidelines, but expenditure outturns have been much closer. This has interesting implications for decision-making on retrenchment by central government. It is one thing for the Cabinet or the Scottish Office to decide that cuts should be allocated in a particular way, but quite another for those decisions to be reflected in the spending plans of the local authorities that actually deliver those services.

As was shown earlier, considerable variations in spending can be observed, particularly when services are not labour-intensive and where relatively small sums of money are involved, as in the case of some district services. More uniform spending decisions tend to be made in labour-intensive services, probably reflecting the difficulty of effecting large-scale redundancies; the same applies for the big spending programmes such as education, social work and police (the latter was not discussed earlier, since police services are funded by a specific grant outside the general RSG scheme, and are politically much harder to cut; see Page, 1980). Together, these 'big three' services account for some 70 per cent of regional authority budgets and are subject to national negotiations and standards. Not surprisingly, perhaps, 'local autonomy' in terms of variations in spending growth is greatest where relatively small amounts of money and manpower are involved.

The last point has to be borne in mind when assessing the degree of adherence to Scottish Office guideline spending targets. The existence of variations in spending does not necessarily mean that Scottish Office guidelines have no influence on local spending. Given the incremental nature of the budgeting process, decisions are taken by local authorities *around* the level of the guidelines. Authorities may go for a bit more or a bit less than the guidelines, but the guidelines do influence and constrain their choices. Indeed, the guidelines have assumed increasing importance in the public bargaining on finance between local authorities and the Scottish Office. Scottish Office ministers refer to the guidelines as if they had legal force, and as if the Scottish Office can objectively assess the correct level of spending for each local authority. On the other hand, the tactic of calling for spending cuts *after* local authority budgets have been drawn up throws the guideline system into some degree of confusion because, as we have seen, these requests for cuts are made to *all* councils and not only to those spending over the guideline levels. This, understandably, has led to attacks on the guideline system and even to demands that it should be scrapped altogether.

The 1976 Layfield Report on local government finance commented on the 'ambiguity and confusion' that characterize central—local relations in the finance of local services (Committee of Inquiry into Local Government Finance, 1976). Retrenchment, it would appear, tends to heighten this ambiguity and confusion. The status of the guidelines and Scottish Office calls for cuts in the middle of the financial year are two cases in point. A third is the tendency for central government to use the cash limit mechanism, which we described earlier, as a major tool for imposing cuts. This conveniently allows central government to claim that spending levels are being maintained in terms of such items as percentage support and expenditure allowance, whereas unrealistic cash limits are in fact enforcing cuts. This is a theme that is commented on further by Howard Glennerster in Chapter 8.

In the next chapter, Royston Greenwood takes up the story for England and Wales — a much larger, less close-knit institutional system in which one might expect central—local relations to have a different character (Page, 1978) and in which, at the time of writing, the issue of central control over local authority spending is far 'hotter politics' than is the case in Scotland. Do pressures for retrenchment produce a similar pattern in a different system?

NOTE

1. The resulting equation was:
   Cumulative growth index = 0.40 (Labour control) − 0.42
   (domestic rateable value)
   − 0.47 (per capita spending
   1975/76)
   $r^2 = 0.30$

REFERENCES

Committee of Inquiry into Local Government Finance (1976)
*Report* Cmnd. 6453, London, HMSO (Layfield Report)
COSLA (1976) *Minutes of the Convention of Scottish Local
Authorities,* Edinburgh, February
COSLA (1977) *Minutes of the Convention of Scottish Local
Authorities,* Edinburgh, February
Dunsire, A. (1980) 'Central-local relations in retrenchment: the UK
case', paper for EGOS Workshop on Organizational Analyses of
the Relationship between State and Local Government,
University of Bamberg, September
Page, E. C. (1978) 'Why should central-local relations in Scotland
be different to those in England?' *Public Administration Bulletin*
No. 28, pp. 51-73
Page, E. C. (1980) 'Grant consolidation and the development of
inter-governmental relations in the USA and the UK', paper for
5th PSA Workgroup on UK Politics, Cardiff, September
Stewart, J. D. (1980) 'From growth to standstill' in M. Wright (ed.)
*Public Spending Decisions* London, Allen and Unwin
Wright, M. (1977) 'Public expenditure in Britain: the crisis of control'
*Public Administration* Vol. 55, Summer.

CHAPTER FOUR

# Fiscal Pressure and Local Government in England and Wales

by ROYSTON GREENWOOD

The purpose of this chapter is twofold: to describe the economic context of local authorities in England and Wales from 1974/75 to early 1980, and to analyse local authority responses to that context. The years covered were characterized by financial discomfort, of restriction rather than of expansion, and it is important to appreciate how serious the discomfort was and the form it took. It will be shown in the following section that local authorities were faced with a serious and in some instances a widening gap between the increasing costs of service provision and the declining yield (in real terms) of resources from existing levels of local taxation. At the same time, local authorities faced pressure from central government to reduce the aggregate level of local government spending. In short, local authorities were faced with both *fiscal pressure,* i.e. increasing costs for *existing* levels of service provision coupled with a decline of available resources (Wolman, 1980, 1981; Alcaly and Mermelstein, 1977; Newton, 1980); and *pressure on expenditure* caused by the economic policies of the government.

The bulk of the chapter looks at how local authorities responded to these pressures. Did they increase taxes to cover the gap between income and the escalating costs of services? Did they follow central government's guidelines on the need to restrain and reduce total expenditure? And, given that answers to these and similar questions might be expected to vary from authority to authority, is it possible to trace the causes of compliance or non-compliance with national policies to the extent of financial distress?[1]

77

HOW HARD WERE THE HARD TIMES?

The history of local government in England and Wales from 1974/75 to 1980/81, at least from a financial point of view, is of mounting fiscal pressure. By fiscal pressure is meant:

> a situation in which local government faced with the necessity of achieving a balance between revenues and expenditure, must in time choose either to (1) increase taxes through changes in the tax rate structure in order to maintain existing real expenditure and service levels, (2) reduce real expenditures from the level of the previous year or (3) engage in some combination of these activities. [Wolman, 1981, p. 1]

In other words, fiscal pressure occurs where existing levels of expenditure can be maintained only by increasing the level of taxation. The causes of fiscal pressure may be several and two are of particular importance. First, there is the problem of rising costs that exceed the revenue yield obtainable from local taxes without raising tax rates. If the costs of providing the same level of services increase faster than the yield from taxation, fiscal pressure is the result. Secondly, the costs of providing services may remain unchanged but the tax yield may decline. Again, the result is fiscal pressure and the local authority is faced with the choice described by Wolman — between cutting expenditure to the level of tax income, or increasing tax rates to yield additional revenues.

Both sources of fiscal pressure confronted local authorities in England and Wales and it is necessary to assess their relative importance, beginning with the pressures that resulted from reduced tax yield. In Chapter 1, Maurice Wright described the government's economic strategy in the period covered here as one based upon tight control of public expenditure — a strategy that included moderation of, then reductions in, the scale of local government spending. Both capital and revenue spending were intended to fall over the period covered. To give substance to this policy, both Labour and Conservative governments produced annual guidelines on the appropriate volume of local government current and capital expenditure in England and Wales. Unlike the position in Scotland, described in the last chapter, these guidelines were an average for local government as a whole and were not specific to individual authorities.

But central government did not rely exclusively upon the willingness of local authorities to follow such guidelines. On the contrary, the government sought to persuade local authorities by reducing the level of grant,[2] thus making it difficult but not impossible for authorities to exceed the guidelines. In other words, government placed fiscal pressure upon local authorities as a means of securing conformity to expenditure guidelines.

The incidence of fiscal pressure was different for particular authorities. The government not only reduced the value of grant (by 1979/80 the Rate Support Grant[3] had fallen to 92 per cent of its 1974/75 level) but *redistributed* allocations among authorities. The result was that in some authorities grant receipts actually rose (in real terms) despite their fall for local government as a whole. By calculating the local rate of tax increases (or decreases) required to compensate for grant changes (the potential local tax effect), some indication may be obtained of the relative severity of grant-induced fiscal pressure. Examination of the 'potential local tax effect' upon the sample of twenty local authorities confirms the general impression that for the period as a whole the overwhelming majority of authorities suffered fiscal pressure resulting from loss of government grant.

The second cause of fiscal pressure on local authorities was the rapid upward movement of pay and prices. The vast bulk of local government income is derived from non-buoyant sources, i.e. the cash income remains static unless the rate of taxation or charging is altered. Increases in costs, therefore, immediately create fiscal pressure. *All* authorities suffered inflation-induced pressure and (if the sample of twenty authorities used here is indicative) the severity of that pressure was greater than the pressure from grant loss — often considerably greater. The major source of fiscal pressure operating upon local government over the five years was inflation, not loss of grant. For example, in 1975/76 the increase in local taxation necessary to finance existing services (i.e. to cover inflation only) was over 10 per cent for eighteen of the sample, and more than 20 per cent for fourteen of them. By 1979/80 these impacts were considerably reduced and were in single figures, but the impact of inflation still outran the effects of grant loss. Only in 1977/78 was this not the case.

Describing the incidence of fiscal pressure in terms of its *potential local tax effect* has the advantage of highlighting the importance attached to rate increases by local elected representatives when settling budget targets. An alternative way of assessing fiscal pressure, and which is worth noting briefly, is the effect of *not increasing tax levels* — in other words, the cuts in spending needed to maintain local taxes at a constant level. Had the twenty local authorities for which we have data pursued the latter option, the scale of expenditure cuts would have been severe. More importantly, they would have been much greater than the reductions called for by central government.

TABLE 4.1
POTENTIAL EXPENDITURE REDUCTIONS CAUSED BY
FISCAL PRESSURE, 1974—80

| Expenditure reduction % | Financial year | | | | |
|---|---|---|---|---|---|
| | 1975/76 | 1976/77 | 1977/78 | 1978/79 | 1979/80 |
| 0 | 0 | 1 | 1 | 0 | 0 |
| 1—5 | 0 | 2 | 2 | 4 | 0 |
| 6—10 | 1 | 5 | 4 | 11 | 13 |
| 11—15 | 3 | 8 | 8 | 5 | 0 |
| 16—20 | 5 | 4 | 4 | 0 | 0 |
| 21+ | 11 | 0 | 0 | 0 | 0 |
| No. of authorities | 20 | 20 | 20 | 20 | 13 |

As Table 4.1 shows, the potential expenditure reductions,[4] caused by the combination of grant loss and inflation, were for most authorities and in each year upwards of 5 per cent; indeed, until 1978/79 a majority of authorities faced cuts of over 10 per cent each year.[5] Although central government guidelines received considerable publicity, along with changes in the value of grant, the critical pressure upon local authorities was the rate of inflation. It is largely the impact of inflation that is reflected in Table 4.1.

For local government as a whole, then, five broad conclusions may be drawn. First, all local authorities faced fiscal pressure caused by increases in the costs of service provision and a static level of income from existing tax rates. Second, some local authorities (the majority) faced further pressure because of losses in grant received from the central government. Other authorities received additional grant that moderated the fiscal pressure caused by inflation. Third, the level of fiscal pressure caused by loss of grant was usually significantly *less* than that caused by inflation. Fourth, there was considerable variation between authorities in the incidence of fiscal pressure, especially at the beginning of the period. Fifth, and finally, for virtually all authorities the implication of *not* raising tax levels would have been cuts in expenditure deeper than those announced in the government's guidelines.

An interesting question is whether local authorities *did* raise local tax levels to meet the incidence of fiscal pressure, and, if so, by what amounts. One possibility is that local authorities might have preferred to follow government guidelines — that is, taking the guidelines as the initial determinant of aggregate expenditure and raising tax levels to meet the residual fiscal pressure (especially that caused by inflation). How far local authorities did adopt such a strategy is examined in the next section, which begins by presenting aggregate data for local government. To examine variations among authorities, we turn from aggregate data to data from our sample of twenty authorities.


## THE LOCAL AUTHORITY RESPONSE

### Local government

The noticeable and interesting feature of the debate on expenditure is that the focal point was (and remains) how far local authority spending goes beyond central government guidelines. Although the previous section showed that fiscal pressure from inflation was invariably more severe than that caused by loss of grant, discussions both in the national press and within local and central government have centred on whether the government's guidelines on expenditure should be accepted. For this reason, it is worth taking as a starting point the response of local authorities to the guidelines. Later the question of how local authorities treated fiscal pressure from grant loss and from inflation will be addressed more directly.

The importance of the guidelines in shaping local authority

spending decisions is reflected by the widespread practice throughout local government of beginning the financial year with a report from the Treasurer to elected members, setting out the prevailing economic circumstances, the government's guidelines on expenditure and the likely implications for the authority's pattern of expenditure. The Treasurer's report is intended to inform members and officers of the government's targets, to provide members with the opportunity to give an early indication of whether they intend to accept or deviate from those targets and to spell out the implications of the targets for the level of spending within the authority. Local authority departments then have a framework within which to draft estimates. (For a fuller description of local authority budgetary procedures see Howick, 1978, Greenwood, 1979, and Danziger, 1978.) Frequently, the Treasurer's report stresses that national guidelines are open to local interpretation and represent no more than an average or norm for local government. Local circumstances may be used to mediate between national guidelines and local implementation.

The response of councillors to the government's guidelines varied from authority to authority in the sample of twenty authorities. (Similar variation is reported by Blackburn, 1979.) For example, one (Labour-controlled) authority consistently denied their importance, stating that the authority rejected the government's guidelines as inconsistent with their electoral mandate. The same point was made in a Conservative-controlled authority. But the more usual response throughout the five-year period would be for a council to instruct its officers that the council intended to work within the government's guidelines and that service estimates should be drafted with those guidelines in mind.

Adoption of the government's guidelines as an initial yardstick did not mean that subsequent decisions would necessarily conform to them. Pressures more evident towards the end of the financial year (such as an adverse grant settlement, or political pressures to maintain services) could prompt an authority to underspend or overspend the guidelines, whatever the initial intention. Central government spokesmen have repeatedly declared that local authorities have taken the latter course and are overspending. The local authority associations and local leaders proclaim that the reverse is true (SOLACE, 1980; CIPFA, 1980).

The validity of these alternative positions is assessed in Table 4.2,

TABLE 4.2
CHANGES IN AGGREGATE LOCAL AUTHORITY CURRENT
EXPENDITURE IN ENGLAND AND WALES (1974–80) COMPARED
TO GOVERNMENT GUIDELINES AND CHANGES IN
AGGREGATE EXCHEQUER GRANT

| Year | Government guideline % change (a) | Exchequer grant % change (b) | Current expenditure % change (c) | Deviation (a–c) |
|---|---|---|---|---|
| 1974 | – | | | |
| 1975/76 | 4.8 | 11.2 | 5.1 | 0.3 |
| 1976/77 | 0 | −2.5 | 0.4 | −0.4 |
| 1977/78 | −1.0 | −6.0 | −1.7 | −0.7 |
| 1978/79 | +1.0 | 0.3 | 2.8 | 1.8 |
| 1979/80 | (−1.0) | (−3.4) | (1.4) | (2.4) |

which compares actual expenditure (column (c)) with the government targets (column (a)). The table shows the declining value of grants (column (b)). Interpretation of these figures involves important distinctions between *gross* and *relevant* expenditure, and between relevant and *current* expenditure. Gross expenditure is the total volume of expenditure irrespective of the source of funding (whether it be from grants, the local property tax, or fees, charges and sales). 'Relevant' expenditure (approximately 80 per cent of gross expenditure) is the volume of rate and grant-funded expenditure. In other words, relevant expenditure is gross expenditure *less* expenditure financed from fees, charges, sales, etc. Current expenditure is relevant expenditure *less* capital expenditure met from revenue, and loan charges. (Current expenditure is approximately 87 per cent of relevant expenditure.) The importance of these distinctions is that for purposes of economic management the government ignores gross expenditure and focusses instead upon either relevant or current expenditure. *In particular, the guidelines on expenditure refer to current expenditure.*

The importance of the distinction between gross and current expenditure will shortly become clearer but it is worth bearing in mind that a local authority could accept government guidelines to reduce current expenditure and at the same time maintain gross expenditure by increasing income from fees and charges. Such a practice of switching expenditure from one source of financing to another will be referred to as *resource substitution,* a concept to which I shall return in a moment.

Table 4.2 enables us to make comparisons between the government's expenditure targets and the outturn current spending patterns for local government (i.e. what was actually spent). Column (c) shows the percentage change in spending and column (a) gives the government's targets. The figures for 1979/80 are confused because of the changing targets introduced by the change of government in 1979 (see Greenwood, 1980, for a summary of the changing financial position). Ignoring that year, it seems that from 1975/76 to 1977/78 local authorities stuck firmly to the guidelines set and were as likely to underspend as to overspend. A larger overspend occurred in 1978/79 and even that was by less than two percentage points. The evidence is that local government spending was strongly influenced by the government's expenditure targets.

This points to the same conclusion as was noted in the previous chapter on Scotland: namely, the volume of current local government expenditure in England and Wales was largely consistent with the government's guidelines. However, the discussion in the preceding section concluded that the volume of cuts in expenditure would have to be much greater than those required by the guidelines unless the local authority was prepared to raise taxation levels to cover both cost increases *and* grant loss. Table 4.2 demonstrates that for local authorities collectively the financial response to the fiscal pressures described earlier was twofold. First, local authorities quite clearly followed government guidelines on the appropriate volume of expenditure. Second, they raised income (by increasing tax rates) to meet the higher costs of the new level of expenditure and to make up the deficiency caused by grant loss.

The latter aspect of the local authority response means that authorities practised both *cost compensation* (raising tax rates to produce income to meet the higher costs of existing spending) and *resource substitution* (switching the source of financing from central government grant to local taxation). (In view of this behaviour, it is interesting to speculate whether local authorities would have reduced expenditures even further if central government had provided no guidance whatever on the appropriate level of local expenditure. Without such guidelines, which effectively legitimate rate increases for purposes of cost compensation and resource substitution, local authorities might have opted to limit rate increases and cut expenditure.)

The idea of resource substitution may be explored further. It was noted earlier that central government guidelines referred to current and not gross expenditure. There was nothing to prevent an authority reducing current expenditure whilst maintaining its gross expenditure through increases in receipts from fees, charges and sales. (Indeed, in 1979 the Conservative government actively encouraged authorities to pursue this option by removing restrictions on various charges, of which the most significant related to school meals, as described by Maurice Kogan in Chapter 7.)

How far local government maintained gross expenditure may be assessed only up to 1977/78: records are not available for later years. Such figures as are available indicate that gross expenditure was maintained while current expenditure fell. For example, in 1975/76 current expenditure rose much faster than gross expenditure, reflecting the sharp increase in grant support for that year. In the next two years, however, the level of grant support fell and was accompanied by a fall in current expenditure. Gross expenditure, on the other hand, increased slightly in 1976/77, and fell in 1977/78 by only 0.5 per cent compared to a 1.7 per cent fall in current expenditure. In other words, local authorities were protecting expenditure by altering the source of finance. Additional resources were obtained from increased fees, charges and similar sources, and used to finance expenditure formerly funded from grants or the property tax.

In summary, then, the following picture emerges. Faced with fiscal pressure caused by grant loss and high inflation, local authorities used two principal strategies. First, they increased the volume of spending financed from fees and charges in order to maintain gross expenditure whilst allowing current expenditure to drift slowly downwards. This is one aspect of resource substitution, namely, the practice of removing items of expenditure from the category of expenditure to which government guidelines refer. This aspect involved switching funding from one *local* source of finance to another. Second, the remaining volume of current expenditure was financed by raising tax levels to cover increases in prices (cost compensation) and losses in grant (resource substitution). The twofold response by local government confirms Wolman's thesis (applied to local authorities in the USA) that 'local governments, *ceteris paribus,* will prefer revenue increasing to expenditure reducing strategies' (1980, p. 5).

*Variations between local authorities*

The conclusion that local government spending moved broadly in line with government targets ignores the fact that authorities varied in the closeness of their compliance. A simple analysis of whether local authorities planned to spend above or below the national guidelines, presented as Table 4.3, reveals that in each of the five years the current account estimates of a small proportion of authorities fell below the guidelines and those of a rather larger proportion went above them. Deviations from the guidelines were rarely dramatic (the largest occurred in 1978/79 when one authority exceeded the guideline by almost 5 per cent), but the interesting question is whether these variations between authorities were caused by the local incidence of fiscal pressure.

Earlier, attention was drawn to differences between authorities in the scale of fiscal pressure. The obvious question is whether these differences explain the differences in compliance with the government's guidelines. Are the authorities spending beyond the

TABLE 4.3
EXTENT OF LOCAL AUTHORITY COMPLIANCE WITH
GOVERNMENT GUIDELINES, 1974—80
(ENGLAND AND WALES)

| Compliance with guidelines | Financial year | | | | |
|---|---|---|---|---|---|
| | 1975/76 | 1976/77 | 1977/78 | 1978/79 | 1979/80 |
| Below the guideline | 8 | 3 | 3 | 5 | 3 |
| On the guideline ($\pm$ 0.5%) | 5 | 4 | 7 | 4 | 6 |
| Above the guideline | 6 | 13 | 10 | 11 | 10 |
| No. of authorities | 19 | 20 | 20 | 20 | 19 |

guidelines those that suffered the lower rates of inflation-induced fiscal pressure? Similarly, are the authorities spending above the guidelines those that gained additional grant? If answers to these questions are positive, then there is reasonable evidence that during times of financial stringency local authority financial behaviour is tightly constrained by resource availability and that the scope for local political discretion, and/or the willingness of local leaders to exercise local discretion, is much less than that observed under conditions of greater affluence. (The budgetary practices of local authorities under conditions of relative affluence are perceptively described by Danziger, 1978.)

The relevant data are given in Tables 4.4 and 4.5. Table 4.4 links fiscal pressure with changes in current expenditure, and Table 4.5 links fiscal pressure with gross expenditure. Both tables show the separate and combined effects of fiscal pressure arising from inflation and grant loss. In itself the impact of inflation does not appear to have been significant. Variations in spending between authorities were not affected by the local incidence of pay or price increases. The spending decisions reflected in Tables 4.4 and 4.5

TABLE 4.4
ASSOCIATION BETWEEN LEVELS OF CURRENT LOCAL
AUTHORITY EXPENDITURE AND FISCAL PRESSURE, 1974–80

| Fiscal pressure | Current expenditure changes | | | | |
|---|---|---|---|---|---|
| | 1975/76 | 1976/77 | 1977/78 | 1978/79 | 1979/80 |
| *Concurrent:* | | | | | |
| 1 Inflation | NS | NS | NS | NS | NS |
| 2 Grant | −.5931* | −5854* | NS | NS | NS |
| 3 Total | −.4890* | −.6268* | NS | NS | NS |
| *Lagged:* | | | | | |
| 4 1975/76 | — | −.8027* | NS | NS | NS |
| 5 1976/77 | — | — | NS | NS | NS |
| 6 1977/78 | — | — | — | NS | NS |
| 7 1978/79 | — | — | — | — | NS |
| *Cumulative:* | | | | | |
| 8 1974–80 | — | NS | NS | NS | NS |

Number of authorities: 20

TABLE 4.5
ASSOCIATION BETWEEN FISCAL PRESSURE AND
GROSS EXPENDITURE (ANNUAL CHANGES), 1974—80

| Fiscal pressure | Gross expenditure | | | | |
|---|---|---|---|---|---|
| | 1975/76 | 1976/77 | 1977/78 | 1978/79 | 1979/80 |
| *Concurrent:* | | | | | |
| 1 Inflation | NS | NS | NS | NS | NS |
| 2 Grant | −4965* | −4575* | NS | NS | NS |
| 3 Total | NS | NS | NS | NS | NS |
| *Lagged:* | | | | | |
| 4 1975/76 | — | NS | NS | NS | NS |
| 5 1976/77 | — | — | NS | NS | NS |
| 6 1977/78 | — | — | — | 5024* | NS |
| 7 1978/79 | — | — | — | — | NS |
| *Cumulative:* | | | | | |
| 8 1974—80 | — | −4427* | NS | NS | NS |

Number of authorities: 20

suggest that authorities maintained their levels of spending despite inflation. This is not the same as saying that inflation had no effect on spending. If the rate of inflation for each authority had been doubled then elected representatives might have been less willing to raise local tax rates in order to cover pay and price increases. In the event, however, local authorities preferred to raise taxes to compensate for inflation rather than reduce the volume of services.

In understanding this response, it is important to realize that central government was not exhorting authorities to reduce expenditure in cash terms (the percentage guidelines were in volume or constant-price terms). So it is perhaps not surprising that authorities apparently took last year's figures for outturn expenditure, *updated them for inflation,* and used the new cost figures as the base-line for applying guidelines on cutbacks. Indeed, the whole procedural framework of local authority budgeting has been based upon almost automatic updating in price terms (i.e. cost compensation of an existing volume of expenditure; Danziger, 1978). Whether this procedure will survive any of the severe reductions in expenditure anticipated for the 1980s is another matter.

Fiscal pressure resulting from inflation may, of course, have an effect acting in concert with losses of grant. The level of inflation on its own may be unimportant but could be extremely important if added to pressure resulting from loss of grant. Surprisingly, however, this was the case only for current expenditure (not gross) and only in 1975/76 and 1976/77. From 1977/78 onwards there was no apparent impact that could be traced to the combined pressure arising from loss of grant and local inflation. Why this should be the case will be considered later.

Similar results are found when the effects of changes in grant are examined. These effects may act or manifest themselves in three ways. First, there might be a *concurrent* effect between changes in grant and spending, i.e. spending plans could be affected by the level of grant support announced in the same year. When local authorities decide on planned expenditure for the forthcoming financial year they have a reasonable knowledge of likely grant receipts (although the problem of cash limits applied to grant has to be borne in mind as described in the last chapter). Hence, row 3 in Tables 4.4 and 4.5 shows the relationship between grant change and changes in planned expenditure for the same year. The principal conclusion is that loss of grant was important only in 1975/76 and 1976/77. In these two years spending decisions were tailored to the exigencies of grant receipts, but not thereafter. Partly, this may reflect the dampening of grant variations after 1976/77 (Crispin, 1980). Alternatively, it may provide some support for the view that from 1977/78 onwards local authorities were less willing to accede to government pressure on expenditure without reference to local factors. Authorities that lost grant after 1977 were willing to make up the shortfall in resources by raising the level of local taxation. From 1977/78 onwards, in short, there was a greater disposition to practise resource substitution.

A second possible grant effect is given in rows 4—7 inclusive. Spending plans could be affected by grant settlements of earlier years. For example, the level of spending in 1977/78 might be influenced by the changes in grant experienced in 1976/77. The lateness of grant announcements (at the end of the budgetary process) and the uncertainties of whether the provision for inflation built into central government grants will cover actual pay and price increases, may prompt an authority to set expenditure plans that are subsequently considered to be over-generous. A chastening grant experience might lead an authority to act more conservatively in *subsequent years*. That is, the effect of grant loss could be *lagged*. However, there is no consistent evidence in Tables 4.4 or 4.5 that fiscal pressure does have a delayed effect on expenditure.

The third possibility is that grant could have a *cumulative* effect upon expenditure. Losses of grant sustained over two or three years may be managed by resource substitution with comparatively little difficulty, but such a strategy could become decreasingly attractive if grant losses are sustained. Local leaders may baulk at the possibility of persistently and substantially raising local tax rates in order to avoid spending cuts. There may also be a belief prevalent during the earlier years of restraint that financial stringency is a temporary interruption to a longer process of growth and expansion. Stewart (1980), for example, has pointed out that the long tradition of government growth in the recent past engenders certain attitudes on the part of public officials, coupled with organizational procedures geared to the allocation of growing financial resources. The imposition of restraint, Stewart suggests, may at first be treated as an aberration and only later prompt a restructuring of attitudes and procedures. If this argument has any force, it would be reflected in grant losses having a cumulative effect upon spending levels. In fact, row 8 of Tables 4.4 and 4.5 gives little evidence that this had happened by 1979/80. There is *no* evidence, in other words, that cumulative grant loss affects changes in expenditure.

At the beginning of this section the question posed was whether the relative compliance of particular authorities to the government's guidelines was a function of fiscal pressure. The conclusion must be that in 1975/76 and 1976/77 such a relationship between grant-induced fiscal pressure and expenditure change did exist, but that thereafter other (unspecified) factors assumed greater importance. At the beginning of the period covered, the spending patterns of individual local authorities reveal the critical importance of grant-induced fiscal pressures as a determinant of expenditure change. The availability of resources proved a strong constraint upon local budgetary choice. But by the end of the period fiscal pressure appeared much less critical: authorities were more willing to practise resource substitution (raise additional *local* income) to replace losses in grant.

This suggests that the *onset* of hard times may provoke a response different from that characteristic of government decisions taken under conditions of *sustained* fiscal pressure. Certainly the behaviour of local authorities in England and Wales changed over the five years examined here. In other words, in seeking to understand how local authorities responded to the imposition of hard times it is important to trace changes in the assumptions of the actors involved and to anticipate that, as those assumptions change, so too will procedures and behaviour. For the social scientist, therefore, it is important to try to unravel why authorities should practise resource substitution coupled with cost compensation under conditions of sustained pressure.

There are three possible lines of argument. The rates of inflation were much higher in 1975/76 and 1976/77 than in later years, which meant that increases in local tax rates during the early years were dramatic. Faced with large tax increases necessary to cover the cost of inflation, local politicians may have been reluctant to countenance additional increases in local taxation to compensate for grant losses. A related point is that these early years were noticeable for widespread public concern over the apparent fragility of the national economy. At this time, there was a general acceptance that local authorities should follow central government's economic strategy. By 1977/78, however, these worries had abated and the rate of inflation had begun to fall. The slowdown in price increases meant that the increase in local tax rates necessary for cost compensation was much reduced, making it politically more acceptable to raise income to cover both inflation *and* grant losses. The scale of tax increases required to cover inflation was low enough to permit scope for additional increases to cover reductions in the value of grant. Resource substitution was less possible in 1975−77 because of the effects of cost compensation, whereas by 1977/78 and thereafter the more modest growth in prices (and the lower level of cost compensation consequently required) permitted at least some resource substitution.

The above explanation is essentially a financial one with political undertones. It rests upon the assumption that the most important determinant of resource substitution is the scale of local tax increase that political leaders find acceptable after the effects of inflation are removed. The second explanation, which draws upon the ideas of Peacock and Wiseman (1961), has a related theme but points to the changing conception of what an acceptable tax increase might look like. The substantial increases in local taxation of 1974/75, 1975/76 and 1976/77 were a departure from the much more modest increase throughout the 1960s and early 1970s. The public outcry was predictable. However, following three years of high tax increases, it is arguable that public expectations of likely increases in future years had altered. Instead of tax increases similar to those that occurred before 1974, larger increases were anticipated. Local politicians, intuitively aware of these changing public expectations, might have found it politically more acceptable to make further large tax rate increases than to cut expenditures.

These two arguments do not clearly explain why local politicians should wish to practise cost compensation plus resource substitution. The arguments merely state that it may have become easier to do so *if* the costs of inflation were not too severe and if public expectations of likely increases are consistent with increases that would enable resource substitution and cost compensation to take place. But why should local political leaders maintain expenditure irrespective of grant change? More accurately, why should some of those authorities that were losing grant practise resource substitution whereas some of the authorities gaining grant were prepared to cut expenditure?

There is little hard evidence bearing on these questions but a number of possible (if tentative) suggestions may be made. Interviews carried out in the sample of twenty local authorities gave the strong impression that relationships between central government and local authorities were less cooperative after 1976/77 than before. This was not a function of differences in party control. There was no evidence in any of the five years that the political complexion of the council *per se* affected an authority's response to fiscal pressure. This is not to deny that *some* Labour-controlled councils deliberately set out to avoid public expenditure cuts, especially after the election of the Conservative government in 1979. But the existence of *some* much-publicized rebel authorities under Labour control does not substantiate the case that Labour authorities in general oppose cuts in public expenditure. More particularly (especially in the present context) the existence of such rebels was not related to the level of fiscal pressure.

One reason for the worsening cooperation was a measure of frustration over central government's sometimes ill-informed approach to local expenditure. The government would accuse local authorities of overspending and threaten punitive action (for example, by reducing the resources built into the Rate Support

Grant to cover inflation) despite repeated claims by local authorities that the figures available to the government were misleading. In 1977, Peter Shore, the Secretary of State, admitted the error (DOE, 1977), but central government nevertheless continued the practice of judging local authority compliance with government targets on the basis of mid-year estimates. One consequence was that some authorities believed that the iterative cuts announced by the government penalized authorities that had remained close to the annual targets — a point made with feeling by at least one local authority chief executive.

Perhaps of greater importance was the feeling that national guidelines should be treated as norms whose interpretation depended upon local conditions. Authorities containing areas of high unemployment, urban stress or population movements throwing pressures upon existing service provision were able to present a convincing case for cutting less than the national average. The cases for maintaining expenditure would often be made by the service departments (such as education or social services) in much the way described by Wildavsky (1964), but the case was possible only because local politicians were sympathetic to the difficulties and hardship caused by cuts in public services. During the early years of financial stringency public officials met the call for restraint by squeezing inefficiencies from the organizational system, but such achievements must be an essentially short-term possibility; thereafter service provision is affected.

Local politicians are at the sharp end of cuts in service provision. It is they who have to make difficult decisions on which activities should be scaled down or held back. It is they who have to decide which items of expenditure should be jettisoned to make way for new services or to meet financial commitments. And, living in the locality, local politicians are often keenly aware of particular individuals suffering from those decisions. Whereas the role of those national politicians responsible for services provided by local authorities may allow them to focus exclusively upon the problems of supply and demand for services in the aggregate without the need to implement the strategy in its detailed form, local politicians frequently encounter individual cases of the hardship caused. In other words, one reason for the lack of association between fiscal stress and expenditure change may well be the relative and *growing* sharpness of political pressures within the local community. Local politicians see the social distress that results from 'hard times' and may become increasingly resistant to the government's intentions. (A similar argument has been developed by Saunders, 1980, and, in the context of American cities, by Alcaly and Mermelstein, 1977.)

To suggest that local politicians may have become increasingly frustrated by, and resistant to, central government's requests for spending cuts is not to conclude that local government expenditure as a whole has outstripped the guidelines. Some authorities overspend, some authorities underspend. The issue is what are the determinants of overspending? The above analysis has shown that differences between authorities cannot be explained either by the political complexion of the council or (in later years) by the incidence of fiscal pressure. Whether these results and observations are peculiar to the structure of local government in England and Wales, or unique to the period examined, is unknown. If the results reported have a general application, one may hypothesize that, despite sustained financial adversity, local factors and circumstances will emerge to counterbalance the impulses of fiscal pressure and the dictates of central government.

## CONCLUSIONS

This chapter has analysed the financial context of local authorities in England and Wales from 1974 to 1980. It was pointed out that the pressure on resources in this period was a result of inflation and loss of government grant. The level of fiscal pressure arising from inflation was shown to be greater than that from loss of grant, despite the wider publicity given to loss of grant. The response of local authorities was to use central government guidelines as yardsticks for local spending, and few authorities deviated significantly from them. A popular means of meeting the guidelines took the form of resource substitution, altering the source of funding away from rate- and grant-borne expenditure (to which the guidelines applied) in favour of spending financed by increased fees and charges, which was not covered by central government guidelines. Having set the new level of expenditure in accordance with government targets, local authorities then had to meet any remaining fiscal pressures arising from inflation and grant loss. This was achieved by raising local sources of income in order to provide sufficient extra income to allow the authority to practise cost compensation and a second form of resource substitution (replacing central grants with locally raised income). The response of local authorities, in other words, was to allow the guidelines to dictate (within limits) the level of expenditure that would be pursued. Having made that decision, the practices of cost compensation and resource substitution followed. As was mentioned earlier, one can only speculate on what might have happened if central government had refrained from setting any guidelines at all for volume spending. Would local authorities have made the same decisions on spending (to cut hardly at all) and taxation? It is not inconceivable that local authorities would have chosen to cut expenditures further than actually happened in order to limit taxation increases. By focussing attention upon expenditure rather than taxation the government may actually have protected expenditure.

The data analysed in the present chapter are part of a story that is still unfolding. The period covered, 1974—80, may come to be regarded as an aberration within a longer tradition of growth; alternatively, it may prove the prelude to more dramatic cuts in public spending. At the time of writing, the latter appears more likely; indeed, the Conservative government elected in 1979 proposed cuts in local government spending deeper than any reported upon here. Whether local authorities will continue to respond to the fiscal climate in the same way as they did in the years before 1980 is difficult to assess. The chances are that they will not.

The government has adopted new powers with which to control local spending. Details of these controls are provided elsewhere (SOLACE, 1980; Burgess and Travers, 1980) but the essential points are that the government provides each local authority with a centrally defined level of necessary spending (grant-related expenditure) and pays grant to each local authority according to the extent of under- or overspending. If a local authority spends significantly above the assessed grant-related expenditure, the *proportion* of grant-borne expenditure will be reduced. The implications of the grant arrangements will become apparent only through their implementation, but it is conceivable that an authority that is overspending (from the government's point of view) may actually lose grant as its actual expenditure rises beyond grant-related expenditure.

How authorities will respond to the setting of specific targets on expenditure is not clear. The Scottish experience described in the last chapter is of little guidance, for although the Scottish Office has in the past produced separate guidelines for each authority in the way that will apply to authorities in England and Wales from 1981 onwards, there were no penalties attached to breach of those guidelines. From 1981 onwards and for the first time local authorities in England and Wales (and in Scotland through a similar but cruder mechanism) will have individual guidelines underlined by potential grant penalties. The response of local authorities to these new arrangements is difficult to assess. Two conclusions, however, are difficult to escape.

First, relationships between local authorities and central government will become increasingly tense and disruptive. I have referred already to the frustrations experienced in some authorities before 1980. The government's insistence on the new grant arrangements despite widespread resistance, and the inevitable confusion and resentment as the penalty clauses are invoked, will worsen rather than improve central–local relationships. The difficulties experienced between 1974 and 1980 were manageable because local authorities were able to retain some discretion over the local balance of advantage between retrenchment and taxation. That discretion will be removed from some authorities and reduced in others. Central–local government interactions will hardly improve.

The second conclusion, and the more important, is that the importance of local government as an instrument of government has been downgraded. Faced with resistance in some authorities, and despite the close conformity of local government as a whole to the annual expenditure targets, the government has chosen to diminish the fabric of local democracy:

> The one point that can be made with certainty is that on the key issues . . . the government has chosen control and influence by central government over the individual local authorities, rather than reliance on local accountability within a national framework. This inevitably replaces local political control by new bureaucratic procedures. [SOLACE, 1980, p. 36]

Fiscal pressure, which in the short run may have strengthened the responsiveness of politicians to local conditions, may prove in the end to have resulted in a gravitation of control and responsibility to London and the demise of local government.

## ACKNOWLEDGEMENTS

The research upon which this chapter is based was financed by the SSRC. The arguments developed benefited from the critical comments made by Chris Hood, George Jones, Ed Page, Stewart Ranson, Hal Wolman, Maurice Wright.

## NOTES

1. To answer these and related questions data are taken from official publications covering local government. Frequently, data are not available for the whole of local government and analysis will rest upon information taken from a sample of twenty authorities. Some indication of the type of authorities covered along with an explanation of the choice of authorities is provided elsewhere (Greenwood, 1981).
2. The scale of grant support is often overestimated but it still reaches almost half of aggregate revenue expenditure (Crispin, 1976; see also Lynch, 1979).
3. Rate Support Grant makes up approximately four-fifths of total grant. Total grant, or Aggregate Exchequer Grant, fell over the same period by approximately 2 per cent, reflecting the shift of resources into specific and supplementary grants.
4. The potential expenditure reductions are calculated by dividing the costs of meeting pay and price increases, plus (or minus) losses (or gain) in grant, by the total expenditure of the previous financial year.
5. The size of the potential cuts noted for 1975/76 was in large part the consequence of the 'Houghton Settlement' on teachers' salaries.

## REFERENCES

Alcaly, R. E. and Mermelstein, R. (eds) (1977) *The Fiscal Crisis of American Cities* New York, Vintage Books

Blackburn, J. S. (1979) 'Presentation and interpretation by local government of White Paper on Public Expenditure' Institute of Local Government Studies, University of Birmingham.

Burgess, T. and Travers, A. (1980) *Ten Billion Pounds* London, Grant McIntyre

CIPFA (1980) *Local Government Trends* London, Chartered Institute of Public Finance and Accountancy

Crispin, A. (1976) 'Local government finance: assessing the central government's contribution' *Public Administration* Spring

Crispin, A. (1980) 'The new block grant and education — central control or national direction?' *Local Government Studies* Vol. 6, No. 6, November/December

Danziger, J. N. (1978) *Making Budgets* London, Sage

DOE (1977) *Press Notice 264* Department of the Environment

Greenwood, R. (1979) 'The local authority budgetary process' in T. A. Booth (ed.) *Planning for Welfare: Social Policy and the Expenditure Process* Oxford, Blackwell and Martin Robertson

Greenwood, R. (1980) 'The rise and falls in current expenditure' *Local Government Studies* Annual Review

Greenwood, R. (1981) *The Local Impact of Central Government Financial Instruments* Final Report to Social Science Research Council

Howick, C. (1978) 'Budgeting and corporate planning in Cheshire' *CES Review* May

Lynch, B. (1979) 'Grant dependency: how much do local authorities rely on central government support?' *CES Review* May

Newton, K. (1980) *Balancing the Books: The Financial Problems of Local Government in Western Europe* London, Sage

Peacock, A. and Wiseman, J. (1961) *The Growth of Public Expenditure in the United Kingdom* London, Oxford University Press

Saunders, P. (1980) 'A theoretical perspective on central-local state relations', paper to Conference on Comparative Intergovernmental Relations, Brasenose College, Oxford, September

SOLACE (1980) *The Local Government Bill* Society of Local Authority Chief Executives

Stewart, J. D. (1980) 'From growth to standstill' in M. Wright (ed.) *Public Spending Decisions* London, Allen and Unwin

Wildavsky, A. (1964) *The Politics of the Budgetary Process* Boston, Little, Brown

Wolman, H. A. (1980) 'Policy consequences of local expenditure restraint' *The Urban Interest*

Wolman, H. A. (1981) *Local Government Strategies to Cope with Fiscal Pressure* Washington DC, The Urban Institute.

CHAPTER FIVE

# Axeperson, Spare That Quango . . .

by CHRISTOPHER HOOD

Over the past three decades in Britain, the biggest areas of government growth in employment terms have been local government, the National Health Service and central non-departmental bodies. Whitehall itself — contrary, perhaps, to popular belief — has not been a major growth centre in staffing, because growth in some parts of Whitehall has been offset by decline in others, notably defence. There are in fact no more civil servants in Britain today than there were in the early 1950s. They just write bigger cheques, so to speak (see Hood, 1981).

So it is scarcely surprising that when hard times come for government, growth areas outside Whitehall come under pressure; and the past two chapters have discussed some of the resulting developments at the interface between central and local government. In this chapter, I look at central non-departmental bodies — another of the rapid growth areas within government in the recent past. Compared to local government and the National Health Service, central non-departmental bodies are not a large area of employment (with a total staffing of about 250,000, excluding nationalized industries) but they have attracted perhaps disproportionate political interest over the past ten years or so.

As an institutional device, they were in high fashion in the 1940s and again in the 1960s, when the Fulton Committee endorsed the idea of government growth outside Whitehall by 'hiving off' units from civil service departments to non-departmental bodies. But the fashion did not last. Enthusiasm for the growth of non-departmental bodies went decidedly sour in British politics in the 1970s. Disenchantment was not confined to the Conservative party, but it was there that the strongest attacks were made on 'quangos' (as non-departmental bodies had come to be known in popular parlance). Conservatives alleged that quangos had been recklessly multiplied by the Labour government of 1974—79, representing a creeping extension of bureaucracy and an undesirable concentration of patronage powers in the hands of government ministers (Holland and Fallon, 1978; Holland, 1979). The Conservatives came back into office in 1979 promising a drastic purge of quangos as part of a wider strategy of cutting back the public sector.

Here, then, is an interesting test case for the study of government retrenchment. Quangos might be thought to be vulnerable to attack in 'hard times' in any case, since reversing the pattern of government growth in recent decades (on the well-known 'last in, first out' basis of retrenchment) would imply striking harder at non-departmental bodies than at the core Whitehall bureaucracy. When the bureaucratic edifice of government is to be demolished, one obvious way to do it is by reversing the process by which the structure was built. But when to this general expectation is added a specific political commitment to cut back quangos, it would seem all the more likely that these animals would be in the front line for cutbacks. If ever there was to be a 'killing ground', it should have been at this point.

In the light of these expectations, it is interesting to examine the cuts that were actually made in the sphere of 'quangos' over the first year of the Conservative government elected in 1979 (normally a time in the life of a government when manifesto commitments are still strong, political energy still vigorous and action not yet crippled by internal disputes). The bulk of these cuts were announced in early 1980 following a 'searching review' of non-departmental bodies by Sir Leo Pliatzky, a distinguished former civil servant; the document announcing these cuts (*Report on Non-Departmental Public Bodies,* 1980) will for convenience be termed the Pliatzky Report. Pliatzky's survey covered 489 'executive' non-departmental bodies (broadly, those that spend money and employ their own staff, excluding the nationalized industries and the health service), 1,561 advisory bodies and 67 'tribunal systems' (comprising up to 2,000 individual tribunals).

Out of this collection, the government decided to reduce by 30 the number of executive bodies, by 211 the number of advisory bodies and by 6 the number of individual tribunals. These closures and amalgamations were said to save 3,700 ministerial appointments, 250 permanent jobs and £11.6 m. 'in a full year'. On top of this, the spending programme of the twenty 'big spenders' in the world of non-departmental bodies was to be £350 m. less than had previously been planned for 1980/81, and there were to be sales of the assets of these bodies amounting in 1980/81 to a figure 'probably of the order of £100 m.' (*Report on Non-Departmental Bodies,* 1980, p. 10). A further 'stocktaking' was promised by the Pliatzky Report; and in late 1980 the government announced that another 192 non-departmental bodies (28 executive, the remainder advisory or judicial) were to be wound up by 1983, bringing the total savings up to about £23 m. per year by 1983 (*The Times,* 4 December 1980). The bulk of this chapter is concerned with the Pliatzky cuts, but I shall briefly comment on the second round.

Did these cuts amount to 'quangocide' — the *coup de grace* for quangos — or did the quarry escape with barely a scratch? The Pliatzky cuts were perhaps not so dramatic as they appeared at first sight. Against 7 million or so employees in the public sector and public spending of roughly £70,000 m. per year, a cut of 250 permanent staff and £11.6 m. per year from closing down non-departmental bodies can scarcely be seen as a massive blow for retrenchment. It is true that the annual saving (or reductions in planned growth of spending) of over £360 m. in non-departmental bodies' expenditure was considerably larger than the figure that would be arrived at by cutting spending on a straight basis of proportionality to total public expenditure. It amounted to roughly 6 per cent of spending by non-departmental bodies as against the government's declared aim at that time of reducing overall public expenditure by roughly 3 per cent.

On the other hand, the sum of £100 m. to be raised by selling the assets of non-departmental bodies was scarcely more than proportionate to the share of non-departmental bodies in total public spending — roughly 10 per cent of the overall public sector asset sales target of £1,000 m. at that time. And the permanent staff cuts were tiny compared to the 20,000 posts that had already been lost in the civil service in the Conservative government's first six months in office (from hiring freezes), let alone the target reductions of 57,000 civil service jobs by 1982 (*Guardian,* 4 December 1979). It was less than a 1 per cent cut in the staff of non-departmental bodies as against 8 per cent in the civil service.

It is true that the government announced further cuts in late 1980, as described above. But by that time the Pliatzky cuts had been eroded by the creation of roughly thirty new non-departmental bodies. Some of these were major executive organizations commanding large budgets. The annual spending of the Urban Development Corporations created for London and Merseyside alone, amounting to £100 m. or so per year, by far outweighs the financial savings of the first and second round of quango cuts put together.

Only in some senses, then, can quangos be said to have been in the 'front line' of retrenchment, casting some doubt on the supposition that retrenchment will simply be a reversal of the process of growth. What is significant is that retrenchment was largely to be achieved by scaling down spending (and future plans for spending), not by closing down organizations. This is a theme to which we shall return in the final chapter. The cuts involved were not wholly 'cosmetic'; but a reduction of executive non-departmental bodies by less than fifty (less than 20 per cent) and a clearout of miscellaneous advisory committees, offset by important additions to the ranks of non-departmental bodies, scarcely amounts to 'quangocide'.

This chapter explores the 'practical politics' of quangocide rather than the less pragmatic, more philosophic debate about how government functions *ought* to be organized. First, I look briefly at the recent past for some indications of the tenacity of non-departmental bodies as a breed. Do they seem to be immortal or, if they die, are they typically 'reincarnated'? Second, I attempt to identify the options for retrenchment. What are the possibilities and what options were in fact taken in the Pliatzky (and subsequent) cuts?

## PAST EXPERIENCE: SOME CLUES

There was a steady growth in the numbers of non-departmental bodies in Britain at least from World War I to mid-1979, under both Conservative and Labour governments. Does this reflect 'immortality' or merely a high birth-rate?

No very firm conclusion can be drawn about this, because there is no stable and comprehensive listing of non-departmental bodies from which changes can be traced over a period of time. But the fragmentary evidence that is available (for example, Bowen, 1978, Hood, 1981) suggests a steady net increase of such bodies in recent years. Another small clue to the pattern of the past can be gained from the 1945 Fraser memorandum (an official memorandum submitted by Bruce Fraser to the Anderson Committee on Machinery of Government — 'Report on non-departmental organizations', 1945), which listed in an Appendix 184 central non-departmental bodies that had come to the notice of an official committee. Not all of these 184 were still in existence in 1945, being historical cases, and some were in effect government departments that only appeared on the list because they were formally constituted as 'boards', or something of that sort.

Of these 184, just under half (83, or 44 per cent) were still in existence in 1979 in almost unmodified form, and just over 22 per cent (42) were dead. Nearly one-third were defunct in their original form, but had either been directly superseded by other government activity or transformed (for example, by assimilation into a regular government department).

### Causes of death

If figures as rough as these can be trusted at all, they do seem to indicate a substantial amount of 'immortality' among non-departmental bodies in the recent past. But this immortality is not absolute (compare Kaufman, 1976): there *have* been disappearances. What causes quangos to 'die'? Levine (1978), in a discussion of 'organizational decline', has distinguished between political and economic or technical causes of decline in public organizations, and also between internal and external causes. These distinctions, however, are not very easy to draw in practice. Probably most of the 'deaths' among central non-departmental organizations in Britain in recent decades have arisen from external causes, though not all have been due to lack of political support.

For example, some non-departmental bodies have disappeared because their environment has collapsed. The loss of Britain's overseas empire caused the deaths of organizations such as the Imperial Shipping Committee and the Colonial Empire Marketing Board — though even in this area many bodies have survived as

Commonwealth organizations, such as the Crown Agents and the Commonwealth Institute. Similarly, bodies set up for special wartime purposes in 1939—45, such as the Boards of Control and Regional Commissioners, have also disappeared — in some cases to reappear later in a different guise, as with the regional price control machinery reintroduced in 1972—79 or the regional economic councils reintroduced in the period 1965—79.

These shade into a second of Levine's categories of organizational decline, which is the depletion of the problem for which the organization was originally set up. A clear example of this is the Decimal Currency Board, set up to effect the changeover of Britain's currency to decimal coinage in 1971. Similarly, some bodies associated with defunct taxes or forms of property holding have gone, such as the Land Commissioners and Tithe Commissioners.

A third, and particularly interesting, type of organizational decline takes place, not for any technical reason or because of large-scale changes in society, but because sufficient political support is no longer forthcoming. Examples are the National Vegetable Marketing Board (and the later Tomato and Cucumber Marketing Board), the Sugar Commission and the State Management Districts Council.

*'Reincarnation'*

In general, however, non-departmental bodies that have 'died' in the past have typically been 'reincarnated' in the sense of being replaced or superseded by other forms of government activity. Their departure does not leave a complete vacuum. Two examples from the 1940s are the Physical Training and Recreation Councils and the Council for the Encouragement of Music and the Arts — both long 'dead' in one sense, but living on in another sense in the form of the Sports Council and the Arts Council. A variant of this is what Brian Hogwood has termed the 'comet phenomenon', to denote bodies that are set up on a more or less regular cycle, blaze into activity and then disappear, only to reappear after a policy hiatus. The obvious example is the intermittent appearance of special-purpose government machinery for determining pay questions, stretching from the National Incomes Commission of the early 1960s to the 1979/80 Standing Commission on Pay Comparability.

In other cases, non-departmental bodies have been overtaken by more direct forms of government involvement, as with the various regulatory bodies formerly involved in control of the railways and of the mining industry before nationalization or with the 'Approved Societies' for the 1911 National Insurance Scheme, later replaced by direct government operation of National Insurance.

## ANTI—QUANGO STRATEGIES AND THE PLIATZKY CUTS

This brief glimpse into the past may perhaps serve to show that there is little in the way of recent historical precedent for a programme of deep retrenchment in the sphere of non-departmental bodies. So what are the possible strategies that a government might adopt in this area, and what was the actual course taken in the Pliatzky cuts? It will be argued in the following sections that the Pliatzky cuts did not amount to 'quangocide' in any sense; rather that the strategy was a mixture of cuts in spending and spending growth, of changes in personnel, of small-scale selective surgery and a degree of rather weak medicine. So far as can be ascertained at the time of writing, exactly the same argument can be applied to the second round of cuts announced in late 1980. Spending cuts were referred to in the opening section of this chapter. The next three sections will look at the other three items in a little more detail.

### Personnel changes: 'Snouts in the trough'

To the extent that governments appoint their own party camp followers to office in non-departmental bodies, opposition parties will naturally be discontented with such bodies. On a change of government, the new political masters may decide that all that is needed to bring suspect non-departmental bodies 'to heel' is an influx of new appointees sympathetic to the new government's political viewpoint, not outright abolition or other major structural solutions.

For example, the Labour government entering office in 1974 to some extent 'colonized' the Price Commission (set up by the Conservatives in 1972) by appointing to it a number of people broadly sympathetic to the Labour party's philosophy. Indeed, one

Labour MP (Michael McGuire) suggested in 1978 that Conservative party opposition to quangos at that time derived from the party's exclusion from the spoils of office rather than from deep constitutional 'principles'. In an elegant turn of phrase, McGuire asserted '. . . what really hurts the Conservatives is that some of our lads have got their snouts into the gravy train . . .' (*Daily Telegraph,* 2 August 1978).

A government opposed to non-departmental bodies as repositories of its opponents' placemen has therefore three main options open to it. The most drastic solution to the 'quango problem' is to dissolve all non-departmental bodies and the patronage attached to them. But the Pliatzky cuts could hardly be described as a 'final solution' of this type: a reduction of 3,700 ministerial appointments (the vast majority of which were advisory and unpaid) amounts to a roughly 15 per cent cut in the previous number of appointments made by ministers (Hood, 1978, p. 40). Even with the promised disappearance of a further 3,000 or so appointments in the second round of cuts, over three-quarters of the quangocracy remained untouched, and, as will be argued later, those bodies that remain are typically the most powerful ones.

Another option might have been to take the course advocated by the Outer Circle Policy Unit (1979) and others of removing at least some appointments to non-departmental bodies from the traditional system of informal old-boy-network selection and unfettered political discretion. In effect, this would mean moving towards a more meritocratic principle of selection, by rough analogy with what happened in British civil service recruitment in the mid-nineteenth century. Mrs Thatcher's government showed little sign of adopting this course. The Pliatzky Report was lukewarm about the idea of publicly advertising appointments to non-departmental bodies, although the CSD in August 1980 invited application from persons thinking themselves suitable material for appointment to non-departmental bodies, instead of the 'traditional discreet methods of trawling for suitable names by a low-key process of inquiry and name-dropping' (*The Times,* 30 October 1980). But this hardly amounts to a giant step towards meritocratic selection of appointees, in spite of the salience of 'quango patronage' as a political issue sharply raised by the Conservative party in 1978—79. Patronage, it would seem, has its uses for both Conservative and Labour governments.

Indeed, if the objection to quangos is no more than a quarrel over the party colour of the 'snouts in the gravy train' (as McGuire suggested), a Conservative government might simply substitute Tory snouts for Labour ones as jobs in non-departmental bodies come up for renewal or their incumbents resign (perhaps under pressure). There were indeed some signs of such a process taking place after the Conservative election victory in 1979. For example, ACAS (the Advisory, Conciliation and Arbritration Service) had been fiercely attacked by the Conservatives in opposition in terms of the alleged party political bias of its members, yet it emerged almost unscathed from the Pliatzky review — perhaps because personnel changes had 'tamed' the organization for the Conservatives. Similarly, having decided to retain the industrial assistance agencies set up by Labour in 1974—75 (instead of sweeping them away, as happened to the IRC after 1970), Mrs Thatcher's government replaced the chairmen of the Scottish Development Agency (appointing a businessman, Robin Duthie, to succeed a former Labour Lord Provost of Glasgow) and the British National Oil Corporation. It also replaced the entire board of the National Enterprise Board in late 1979 (following a mass resignation of Labour government appointees prompted by government decisions to remove Rolls-Royce and British Leyland from NEB control to direct control by the Department of Industry, and to issue more restrictive guidelines for NEB's operation). There would be nothing strange about such turnover of personnel on the advent of a new administration to an American observer; and, if the McGuire hypothesis is correct, such changes might go far to reconcile a Conservative government with quangos.

### Surgery: cosmetic, political and major

Of course, the mere substitution of a Tory quangocracy for a Labour one, or even a move towards meritocracy in appointments, would have fallen distinctly short of the aspirations of those Conservatives who had been calling for an outright purge. Perhaps the most prominent among these was Philip Holland MP, who considered 'The replacement of leftist academics, Trade Union leaders and ex-Labour Councillors who dominate the key QUANGO appointments by Conservative supporters is no answer . . . The malady calls for surgery rather than analgesics' (1979, p. 6).

The options for 'surgery' might be divided into three types. They are cosmetic surgery, politically selective surgery, and major surgery. Mrs Thatcher's government adopted a mixture of the first two courses in the Pliatzky purge, but not the latter.

First, 'cosmetic surgery'. Given that the 'quango numbers game' (Hood, 1981) is a highly indeterminate affair, there are many possibilities for cosmetic surgery to achieve impressive-seeming reductions in numbers by eliminating or amalgamating egregious and marginal quangos. The vast bulk of the Pliatzky cuts were in fact of this type. Many of the savings were to be achieved by amalgamations rather than by straightforward closures. Of the reduction of executive bodies by thirty, eight represented amalgamations, and even some of the twenty-two others to be closed or cut loose were to live on in some form. One example is the Personal Social Services Council: its training functions were to be passed to another non-departmental body, the Central Council for Education and Training in Social Work (*The Times,* 6 December 1979). Exactly the same applied to the second round of cuts in late 1980, where impressive-seeming reductions in numbers were to be achieved by amalgamating bodies such as the General Nursing Council for England and Wales, the Central Midwives Board, the Joint Board for Clinical Nursing Studies, the Panel of Assessors for District Nurse Training and the Council for the Education and Training of Health Visitors into a single organization.

Amalgamation presents an interesting policy issue in respect of Scotland, Wales and Northern Ireland. Given that these countries are particularly prolific in area-specific non-departmental bodies relative to population size (Hood, 1978; *Report on Non-Departmental Public Bodies,* 1980), might they be expected to have shown a higher than average casualty rate in retrenchment, for example by amalgamation of non-departmental bodies with their English counterparts? This is an issue that had been raised in relation to Scottish public expenditure generally (see HM Treasury, 1979, and *Financial Times,* 29 January 1980), but the Pliatzky Report did not in fact raise the issue in relation to non-departmental bodies. Some UK departments (the Ministry of Defence and the Department of Employment) announced their intention to amalgamate a few minor Scottish and English advisory committees, but this did not occur for Wales and Northern Ireland.

In fact, the Welsh, Scottish and Northern Ireland Offices emerged relatively unscathed from the Pliatzky cuts in terms of their associated fringe bodies, having in no case surrendered an important executive body. Even the Land Authority for Wales survived the Pliatzky review against all the odds (in view of the government's intention to abolish the function for which it was set up, namely the administration of the 1975 Community Land Act in Wales). Of the twenty-one axed bodies in the realm of the Scottish Office, four were limited-life working parties or commissions and five were licensing planning committees for the New Towns, which duplicated the work of the licensing courts and had been admitted to be redundant even by one of their own chairmen (Willie McRae, reported in *The Scotsman,* 30 July 1979, p. 7). Of the remaining twelve, eight were advisory committees.

Amalgamation, it would appear, has its uses, if only as a cosmetic, but it was not carried by the Pliatzky Report to the point where it might raise awkward questions about the entrenched administrative 'rights' of Scotland, Wales and Northern Ireland to a separate and proportionately denser structure of non-departmental bodies *vis-à-vis* their English counterparts.

Other modes of cosmetic surgery consist of the winding up of obsolete, marginal and limited-life bodies. Departmental responses to the Pliatzky purge included the dusting off of a great deal of administrative 'jumble' to be presented for 'sacrifice' — bodies that were moribund, in abeyance or had not met for several years. Typical examples were the Irish Pensions Appeal Tribunal and the Advisory Committee on Rhodesian Travel Restrictions. Similarly, the final *coup de grace* was administered to the Inland Revenue Board of Referees, originally set up to decide hard cases over the Munitions Levy (Excess Profits Tax) of 1915. Perhaps in response to such tactics, the Pliatzky Report recommended that advisory committees should in general be set up for a limited time or a specific task, and that there should be periodic 'stocktakings' of non-departmental bodies by sponsoring departments to eliminate redundant or outdated ones. The government subsequently proposed that departments should review one-fifth of all non-departmental bodies each year (so that all should be reviewed over the normal lifetime of a Parliament). But how far this exercise is likely to result in actual cuts on a large scale is a matter of judgement, given that abolition in many cases requires legislation. The Pliatzky Report shrank from anything so radical as recommending American-style 'sunset' laws, which limit the life of administrative bodies in the legislation that sets them up.

Egregious and limited-life bodies also figured largely in the 'sacrifices' offered to Pliatzky. Examples of the former include the Hadrian's Wall Advisory Committee and the various advisory committees on the Royal Parks (for bird sanctuaries, sculptures and trees). Examples of the latter include the Advisory Committee on Motorcycle Rider Training and the Committee to Examine Standards of Lawn Tennis in Great Britain. To present the latter class of cases as if they were 'cuts' was potentially very misleading since they were not destined for bureaucratic immortality in any case; and the former, worthy as they may have been, can only be regarded as token sacrifices. The second round of cuts contained similar examples.

As a symbolic activity, cosmetic surgery may well have political pay-offs so long as a government feels a need for severed heads to display on its wall. But as a tactic it is likely to be attended by diminishing political returns when these 'heads' are examined carefully. For example, a seemingly dramatic purge of over fifty of his department's quangos by the Environment Secretary (Michael Heseltine) in autumn 1979 was greeted by heavy press sarcasm, with the quality press noting that the cuts represented less than 1 per cent of the Environment Department's spending on quangos and a half per cent of its paid appointments to them. Similarly, the Pliatzky cuts in January 1980 evoked a muted response from the press and the 'quango hawks' on the Conservative back benches (*The Times,* 17 January 1980). Philip Holland repeatedly reasserted the need for 'real cuts', offering a 'death list' of 707 quangos in September 1980 (*The Times,* 25 September 1980).

Apart from the danger of diminishing political returns, cosmetic surgery has two further possible disadvantages. The first is that symbolism of this type saves very little in the way of public money and personnel (most advisory bodies are staffed by civil servants who are merely redeployed within the government machine when the bodies are wound up). Perhaps fearing this charge, the Pliatzky Report contained a prolepsis to the effect that saving money and jobs was not the 'sole objective' of the review: it had symbolic and political importance as well. The second problem is that the principle of eliminating the weakest and most marginal quangos is likely to hurt a government's own supporters as much as its enemies.

The Hadrian's Wall Advisory Committee and the advisory committees on the Royal Parks were hardly bastions of creeping socialism or sinister manifestations of the 'corporate state'.

A second possible tactic, then, is 'politically selective surgery'. If cosmetic surgery suggests striking down the obsolete and the marginal (often the least 'political' in a partisan sense), a different possibility is to use opposition to quangos to strike at particular policies that are in disfavour. The purge of special commissions, councils and boards in the early period of the Edward Heath Conservative government elected in 1970 was 'politically selective' in this sense; and surgery of this type also featured in the cuts announced in the Pliatzky Report. In fact, the Outer Circle Policy Unit (1979) asserted that Conservative attacks on quangos in 1978—79 were not really attacks on quangos as such, but attacks on particular *policies*. What was really being argued about was whether (for example) price control or business regulation were proper functions for government, not whether they should be done by quangos or not. Arguments about the scope of government had become confused with arguments about the shape of the government machine. Indeed, the same tactic can be used to attack prospective policies as well as existing ones: for example, the government in 1979 rejected the idea of setting up a national body for promotion of the Gaelic language in Scotland 'because it would be a quango'.

Of the Pliatzky cuts, the abolition of the Price Commission is perhaps the clearest case of this type of politically selective surgery (and even in that case the staff of the Commission, being seconded civil servants, did not actually face the dole queue but rather were redeployed elsewhere within the Whitehall machine). Another obvious case is the abolition of the Health Services Board, the instrument of the 1974—79 Labour government's policy for phasing out pay-beds in NHS hospitals (also staffed by civil servants). A like fate may befall advisory bodies whose advice becomes 'bad news', giving ministers counsels that they do not wish to hear. The clearest case of this in the Pliatzky Report is the Royal Commission on the Distribution of Income and Wealth (to be wound up two years earlier than originally planned). The demise of the National Ports Council (announced in mid-1980) may have been partly occasioned by a desire to avoid further talk about extending port nationalization.

Indeed, the problem of 'dissenting advisers' may be particularly marked during a time of general public spending cuts, and this may help to explain the demise of bodies such as the Central Health Services Council and the Personal Social Services Council in late 1979. These were obvious platforms for the articulation of protest against retrenchment policies, and the latter was indeed axed on the eve of publishing a report criticizing government spending cuts (*The Times,* 6 December 1979).

The same reason may underlie the reduction in numbers of disablement advisory committees from 220 to 88, which accounted for the vast bulk of the second round of cuts in 1980. The abolition of the Standing ('Clegg') Commission on Pay Comparability in 1980 was perhaps a slightly different case; the Commission had displeased the government by recommending a £640 m. pay award to teachers in spring 1980 (which was later admitted by the chairman of the Commission to have been £130 m. too much, owing to a mistake in calculation), but this is the type of body that tends to 'self-destruct' in any case, owing to the obvious impossibility of making pay comparability decisions that satisfy everyone.

The acid test, presumably, of whether objections to quangos are merely being used as a stalking-horse in attacks on particular policies, is the extent to which particular functions previously performed by non-departmental bodies are transferred to local authorities or to central government departments. The Pliatzky Report contained no major cases of functions previously performed by non-departmental bodies being returned to local authorities, although the government asked local authority associations to take on the research role of the axed Personal Social Services Council (*The Times,* 6 December 1979).

There were, however, several cases where functions formerly performed by non-departmental bodies were to be done in future by government departments, including the bulk of the advisory committees that had been scrapped. In the executive group, the major case was the scrapping of the Supplementary Benefits Commission and its counterpart in Northern Ireland, meaning a direct takeover by the social security departments of responsibility for the rules governing entitlement to supplementary benefit (*Reform of the Supplementary Benefits Scheme,* 1979, p. 2). But once again, no saving in staff or spending was involved, since the staff of the former SBC were civil servants in DHSS, and a new advisory body on supplementary benefit policy was to replace SBC.

The problems of adopting this course of action on a wide scale are discussed below, and it is perhaps not surprising that major transfers of this type are relatively hard to find in the Pliatzky Report.

After politically selective surgery, the third possible option is that of major surgery — a large-scale wipe-out of important non-departmental bodies. As we have seen, the Pliatzky purge fell very far short of this; and indeed major surgery presents serious political difficulties. To anticipate a theme that will be taken up in the final chapter, it may be less costly, in terms of political flak and negotiating effort, to impose spending cuts across a wide area than actually to close down major organizations by large-scale sackings of permanent staff (cf. Levine, 1978, pp. 316—25), as opposed to redeployment of staff formerly serving particular committees or boards. Alternatively, if closures are to be attempted, it may be politically less expensive to approach them one by one, attempting to organize a separate 'termination coalition' for each body, in order to avoid a politically dangerous build-up (by log-rolling) of concerted opposition. Over its first year in office, Mrs Thatcher's government did indeed follow a strategy of piecemeal closures rather than a single 'massacre' of many bodies at the same time (all of the important closures referred to by the Pliatzky Report had already been announced at various different points in time by the ministers involved).

That is not to say that undertaking major surgery by a cumulative series of acts of minor surgery would not itself run risks. The risks in this case can be compared with controlling public spending. As with public spending, objections to quangos tend to be directed against such bodies in the mass or in the abstract, whereas arguments *for* such bodies tend to be particularistic or case-specific ('another little quango wouldn't do us any harm'). Even Michael Heseltine, whose purge of fringe bodies controlled by the Environment Department in 1979 earned him the reputation of 'quango basher extraordinaire', subsequently set up several non-departmental bodies. These included the National Heritage Memorial Fund, spending about £3 m. per year, and Urban Development Corporations for Merseyside and London Docklands. The creation of these corporations was perhaps prompted by potential political difficulties for a Conservative government in working with local authorities in the areas involved. The Pliatzky Report itself conceded that there was a case for many non-departmental bodies, merely recommending that such bodies should not be set up unadvisedly, or in the quantity of the recent past. It is politically easy to be against non-departmental bodies in general; harder to argue that any individual case will breach some constitutional dyke.

There is a dilemma here, and it is not the only political dilemma involved in the major surgery option. A second problem is that transferring functions from non-departmental bodies to Whitehall (or to local government) may throw more pressure on other parts of the bureaucracy that government may be trying to cut back. Just as bureaucratic expansion can be 'hidden' to some extent from official statistics by channelling it into non-departmental bodies, so a mere bureaucratic reshuffle, or even an actual decline, may appear as expansion in civil service and/or local authority staffing figures. This was something that began to embarrass the Edward Heath Conservative government after 1972, when pursuit of policies such as selective assistance to private industry and consumer protection led to the administrative tasks involved being assigned to the civil service rather than to the re-creation of the non-departmental bodies that the Conservatives had swept away on assuming office, and thus meant facing the political embarrassment of increases in civil service numbers (Hood, 1978). Up to the time of writing, Margaret Thatcher's government has avoided this by keeping the bulk of Labour quangos alive (if not very well) and by not effecting closures that mean extensive staff cuts. But if 'real blood' is to be spilled this dilemma will have to be faced.

The problem of unloading quango functions on local authorities contains a further political problem, quite apart from the risk of swelling manpower and spending. As a government in Westminster moves towards its unpopular 'mid-term', local authorities will increasingly tend to be in the hands of the opposition party owing to the working of the electoral cycle, and hence to become less reliable as instruments of central government policy in a political sense. Indeed, it is just at a time when local authorities are perceived as politically hostile that Whitehall may be most tempted to by-pass them by means of non-departmental bodies. This may be why the Pliatzky Report contained no attempt to reverse the transfer of functions away from local authorities to non-departmental bodies. Indeed, government proposals to shift local authority control of building regulations to the National Housebuilders Registration Council (*The Times,* 17 December 1979) were a move in the opposite direction. Again, this is a problem of retrenchment to which we shall return in the final chapter.

### 'Medicine'

Major surgery, then, might be as politically painful to the surgeon in this case as to the patient, though other types of surgery may offer better prospects of confining the pain to the patient. Another possible anti-quango strategy is that of (nasty) 'medicine' — measures that fall short of actually killing quangos outright. This avoids dramatic 'survival struggles'; and the simplest way to do it is to achieve quango retrenchment by spending cuts rather than by large-scale organizational closures. This seems to have been the core of the Pliatzky strategy, and the same applies to the subsequent round of cuts, in which the bulk of the savings was to be achieved by cutting the budgets of organizations like the Housing Corporation, British Council and Commonwealth War Graves Commission. Beyond spending cuts of this type, there are two very different forms of possible 'medicine' for non-departmental bodies: 'cutting loose' and tighter controls.

*'Cutting loose'.* 'Cutting quangos loose' avoids immediate disband-ment of organizations by transferring them more or less as going concerns from the public sector to the private or independent sector. There are perhaps four different ways of doing this, although they are difficult to distinguish at the margin.

The first is to cut loose (on an ice-floe?) organizations formerly attached to government departments by grant or contract relationships, and hence expendable in a period of retrenchment (cf. the discussion of 'exploiting the exploitable' in Levine, 1978). Two prominent examples from the Pliatzky cuts are the Centre for Environmental Studies and the Institute for Development Studies (both politically suspect in Conservative eyes). An example from the second round of cuts is the Council for Educational Technology (facing a cut in grant of nearly £¼ m. by 1983/84).

A second possibility is to create quangos in the original sense of the term (Hague, *et al.,* 1975) — private or independent bodies carrying out government functions instead of statutory boards. Examples include proposals to hand over the building standards work of the Agrément Board to the British Standards Institution

*(Financial Times,* 3 December 1979), or the case already mentioned of proposals to hand over local authority building control regulation to the National Housebuilders Registration Council.

A third possibility — transfer of government organizations by selling them as going concerns to private enterprise — is a different matter. The 1970—74 Conservative government's attempt to do this met with little success, apart from the sale of the government brewery business and travel agency (both acquired more or less accidentally in World War I), and this appears to be a formula that will only work in a limited number of cases. Mrs Thatcher's government, by contrast, embarked on a fourth strategy, not so much of complete transfer of government bodies as going concerns to private enterprise, but rather a 'creeping capitalism' approach of selling shares in commercial public enterprise. Examples are the sale of the government's majority shareholding in BP in 1979 and the proposal to return British Airways to something like the pre-1939 Imperial Airways formula: legislation was passed in 1980 converting British Airways from a public corporation to a 'Companies Act' company, with government as 100 per cent shareholder. Similar changes of status were effected for British Aerospace and the National Freight Corporation, with the declared intention of eventually selling an unspecified proportion of the shares in these companies on the private capital market. A different kind of example is the possibility discussed in the Pliatzky Report of selling shares in development companies established by New Town Corporations (*Report on Non-Departmental Public Bodies,* p. 30). One can imagine that this approach might possibly be extended to other organizations, but this is also clearly not a device of universal application to non-departmental bodies.

*Stricter control.* A wholly different brand of medicine for quangos is greater control over non-departmental bodies by Whitehall and Westminster. For those organizations that can neither be cut down nor cut loose, a stricter regime may be prescribed, as with the much tighter guidelines laid down by the Conservative government in 1979 for organizations such as the National Enterprise Board and Scottish Development Agency (interpreted by some as in effect condemning such agencies to lingering deaths as an alternative to summary execution, although the SDA was to some extent reinvigorated by an increase of its borrowing limit in November 1980).

The recommendations of the Pliatzky Report itself, however, were somewhat less than dramatic. As far as audit was concerned, the Report confined itself to recommending the wider adoption of practices that already existed on a wide scale, such as the liability of bodies financed by government grant for over 50 per cent of their income to inspection audit by the Comptroller and Auditor-General, and the need for departmental Accounting Officers to check the fitness and management capacity of organizations receiving grant. Similarly, annual reports and accounts should be 'as informative as possible', information on salaries and expenses should at least match that required by law in company accounts, advisory committees should wherever possible be set up with a finite remit or a limited lease of life, and departments should undertake periodic 'stocktakings' of fringe bodies within their spheres. Are these the dramatically 'tougher controls' over quangos that some people had been expecting from the Pliatzky review?

The problem in practice is that tougher controls, in the sense of more detailed reporting procedures, second-guessing and double-checking at the centre, would themselves tend to expand the Whitehall bureaucracy as well as possibly aggravating the 'clearance point problem' that can arise whenever a number of administrative agencies have to work together on some item. More detailed central oversight of non-departmental bodies was called for in Bruce Fraser's memorandum to the Anderson Committee of 1945, but the atrophying of the Anderson machinery-of-government reviewing apparatus in the 1950s (Lee, 1977) is instructive. The complexities that a tough 'central control' exercise inevitably throws up can quickly dissipate the political attractiveness of the process until another dramatic *exposé* takes place. The basic financial control toolkit possessed by the Treasury and CSD means that the centre of Whitehall is inevitably involved in consultations about executive bodies with major spending implications; but to extend central involvement to the monitoring of advisory bodies and the like, or the drawing up of detailed central rules for the establishment of non-departmental bodies, is to move on to shakier political ground. Quite apart from the policing problem and the sheer intellectual difficulties of such an exercise, it touches quite basic constitutional issues over the political independence of ministers in running their departments.

Executive control over non-departmental bodies is perhaps a necessary condition for parliamentary control, unless individual backbench MPs were to be made answerable for the affairs of such bodies, as used to happen with the Forestry Commission, Ecclesiastical Commission and Charity Commission (but this has been out of official favour for many years and was not even discussed in the Pliatzky Report). But executive control is not a sufficient condition for parliamentary control; and recent discussions of Parliament's role *vis-à-vis* fringe bodies have gone beyond the scope of parliamentary audit and ministerial control.

The initiatives flowing from the Pliatzky Report, however, are likely to be very narrow. As was mentioned earlier, front-benchers of both major political parties in Britain appear reluctant to surrender any government patronage powers to backbench MPs by allowing parliamentary committees to vet some appointments in the American style. The Pliatzky Report did suggest that the fourteen departmental select committees of the House of Commons set up in 1979 could play a useful role in monitoring non-departmental bodies, but this was probably less important than it sounded. Parliamentary select committees were already in practice able to scrutinize the activities of many non-departmental bodies if they chose to take the time to do so (for example, the Arts Council and the Manpower Services Commission). Given the numbers involved, only the major bodies would be likely to come under scrutiny, even if some parliamentary committee or floor debating resources were specifically earmarked for consideration of non-departmental bodies — and the Pliatzky Report did not even go as far as this.

## CONCLUSION: RHETORIC VS. REALPOLITIK?

This brief account of cutbacks in the sphere of non-departmental bodies seems to indicate that practical politics pointed less to wholesale 'quangocide' than to a mixture of spending cuts, personnel changes, selective surgery and some degree of medicine (including the 'cut-loose-on-an-ice-floe' strategy). In spite of pre-election rhetoric, the major features of the landscape of non-departmental bodies in practice remained untouched after the Conservative government's first year in office, and the vast bulk of the sacrifices were of moribund or peripheral organizations, not bodies of major importance as executive units. The Pliatzky purge might easily be interpreted as one of those gentlemanly exercises in Whitehall gamesmanship described by Heclo and Wildavsky (1974) — rich in token sacrifices and 'fairy gold', but with little real blood being spilled. The second round of cuts was not very different.

The non-departmental body thus appears to be a remarkably tenacious form of government, even in ostensibly 'hard times' and in spite of recurrent dissatisfactions with the accountability and control of such bodies since 1918. Whatever the publicly mentionable arguments, the non-departmental body seems to be an expedient too useful for politicians to discard lightly. It offers at least four potential political uses that are not likely to disappear.

First, governments will probably always have need of 'unacknowledgeable means' or at least of bodies from which central government can distance itself in some sensitive areas, such as arms sales and cloak-and-dagger activities at home as well as abroad. Second, given that modern governments need to have a permanent administrative apparatus of some sort, there will presumably always be a value in having temporary, expendable organizations outside the permanent government service that can be discarded when circumstances permit. Third, the use of such bodies as an administrative means of by-passing other public organizations that for one reason or another politicians distrust goes back at least as far as the seventeenth century, when the task of rebuilding and refitting the English navy was assigned to the famous Special Commission of 1686—88 rather than to the Navy Board; and there are modern analogies with the use of non-departmental bodies to remove activities from local authority hands in such areas as housing, water, sport, race relations and so on. The example of the Urban Development Corporations shows the continuing attraction of this device even for a Conservative government ideologically committed to cutting back quangos and 'setting local government free'.

Fourth, the advisory committee is frequently too convenient a device for political 'window dressing' to become extinct as a form of non-departmental body. Admittedly, there is always the danger that 'heavyweight' advisory committees of prestigious individuals may have independent views and express them forcefully, even if they are contrary to government thinking. Nevertheless, as Bruce Fraser's 1945 memorandum to the Anderson Committee put it:

> When a Minister is defending a decision, it will be little help to say that it was taken on the advice of his officials; but it *may* be of political value to say that it accorded with the advice of a committee of prominent outside persons whose names may be quoted and will command confidence among those interested in the subject-matter. ['Report on non-departmental organizations', 1945, p. 6]

Advisory committees are only one manifestation of the process of government by consultation with entrenched groups (cf. Richardson and Jordan, 1979), and the major quango vehicles of this process were left almost untouched in the 1980 cuts. Indeed, at the same time that these 'purges' were being carried out, a number of important new advisory committees were set up, including the Welsh TV Advisory Committee and the Advisory Committee on Business Sponsorship of the Arts.

These are only a few examples of the *realpolitik* reasons for retaining non-departmental bodies (the issue is further discussed in Hood, 1978) and it would appear that there is a sharp contrast between the rhetoric of 'quangocide' and the reality of spending cuts and token sacrifices. Some of the themes of this chapter will reappear in the chapters in Part III, particularly the contrast between the rhetoric and the reality of government behaviour in 'hard times'.

## REFERENCES

Bowen, G. (1978) *Survey of Fringe Bodies* Civil Service Department

Hague, D. C., Barker, A. and Mackenzie, W. J. M. (eds) (1975) *Public Policy and Private Interests* London, Macmillan

Heclo, H. and Wildavsky, A. (1974) *The Private Government of Public Money* London, Macmillan

HM Treasury (1979) *Needs Assessment Study — Report* London,

Holland, P. (1979) *Quango Quango Quango* London, Adam Smith Institute

Holland, P. and Fallon, M. (1978) *The Quango Explosion: Public Bodies and Ministerial Patronage* Conservative Political Centre

Hood, C. C. (1978) 'Keeping the centre small: explanations of agency type' *Political Studies* Vol. 26, No. 1, March, pp. 30-46

Hood, C. C. (1981) 'Central non-departmental bodies and government growth' in A. Barker (ed.) *Quangos in Britain* London, Macmillan

Kaufman, H. (1976) *Are Government Organizations Immortal?* Washington, Brookings Institution

Lee, J. M. (1977) *Reviewing the Machinery of Government 1942-52: An Essay on the Anderson Committee and Its Successors* London, Birkbeck College

Levine, C. (1978) 'Organizational decline and cutback management' *Public Administration Review* Vol. 38, pp. 316-25

Outer Circle Policy Unit (1979) *What's Wrong with Quangos?* OCPU

*Reform of the Supplementary Benefits Scheme* (1979) Cmnd. 7773, London, HMSO

'Report on non-departmental organizations by the Official Committee on the Machinery of Government', 3 January 1945 (Fraser memorandum)

*Report on Non-Departmental Public Bodies* (1980) Cmnd. 7797, London, HMSO (Pliatzky Report)

Richardson, J. J. and Jordan, A. G. (1979) *Governing Under Pressure* London, Martin Robertson.

# PART III

# AREAS OF POLICY AND 'CUTS'

CHAPTER SIX

# UK Defence:
# A Case Study of Spending Cuts

by KEITH HARTLEY

Defence is one of the few British examples of a major spending
department that has a substantial history of cuts. In this context,
several major reviews of defence spending took place between 1957
and 1977. This chapter outlines the reasons for those reviews, the
philosophy behind them and the results that were actually achieved.
Consideration is given to the distribution of cuts between each of
the armed services, between weapons and manpower, and between
civilians and service personnel. For example, were the cuts
distributed equally between the Army, Navy and Air Force or on
the basis of the 'Buggins' turn' principle? Did the armed forces
respond to cuts by protecting their 'prestige' weapons projects?

Such questions are interesting because the economics of the
political market place would suggest that vote-conscious governments are likely to be influenced by domestic weapons firms as
producer interest groups. Moreover, budget-maximizing bureaucracies (in this case the Ministry of Defence and the armed forces)
have incentives to underestimate the cost of weapons projects and
to overestimate the demand for defence (for example, in terms of
the 'threat' presented by the Warsaw Pact). Bureaux can also
formulate programmes that are attractive to vote-sensitive governments in terms of their alleged social benefits, namely domestic
jobs, high technology, balance of payments and national security.
Elements such as these can affect the extent and direction of
spending cutbacks.

Indeed, there is a general problem for politicians and society, in good times as well as in hard times, in assessing the efficiency with which the Ministry of Defence and the armed forces use scarce resources. How much should the UK spend on defence and how should it be allocated among the armed forces, and between weapons and manpower? Britain's choices and solutions to these defence allocation problems are reflected in the facts of military spending. After presenting these facts, I give an account of the major Defence Reviews from 1957 to 1977. This gives insights into the 'optimality' of British military spending and provides the basis for developing a model of defence expenditure that includes political as well as economic and strategic determinants. I then analyse the effects of the Defence Reviews; and a concluding section presents some of the problems that arise in controlling military expenditure and improving efficiency.

## THE 'FACTS' OF UK DEFENCE EXPENDITURE

Table 6.1 shows the data on UK defence spending and its manpower implications. Levels and shares of military expenditure are used, since these provide indicators of both capability and burdens. Looking forward to the subject of the next chapter, the share of education in GNP is shown, both for comparative purposes and as a possible indicator of society's preferences for civil goods. Five broad generalizations are suggested by Table 6.1:

(i) In spite of the talk of 'cuts', there is no evidence of a long-run and continuous decline in the level of defence spending in real terms in a peacetime economy. Indeed, the level of spending has shown a surprising amount of stability, averaging £2,520 m. (in 1970 prices), usually within a range fluctuating between £2,328 m. and about £2,900 m. The Korean War and the re-equipment programme up to the mid-1950s were obvious exceptions, associated with substantial increases in spending. Nevertheless, the peak of 1953 was followed by even higher peaks in 1967 and 1976, with troughs in 1958, 1962 and 1969. In other words, following the end of the Korean War, it is noticeable that expenditure constantly exceeded its pre-Korean levels. This observation provides some evidence for a form of 'displacement effect', that is, a permanent shift to a higher level of spending (Peacock and Wiseman, 1967). Such an effect might be consistent with budget-maximizing or loss-minimizing behaviour by the Ministry of Defence and the armed forces. Alternatively, it might reflect the state of international tension or the cost-raising effects of technical progress in weapons. For example, a new strike aircraft now costs three times as much as its 1950's predecessor in real terms, and submarines and guided weapons are some six to seven times more expensive. Of course, such increased costs might be partly related to the type of procurement policy operated by bureaucrats.

(ii) There has been a long-run decline in the share of defence in GNP. In contrast, the share of education has generally shown a long-run upward trend, which might be a reflection of society's greater preference for social welfare spending throughout much of this period. (Similar trends are observable in the USA, and in the next chapter Maurice Kogan reflects on some of the problems that the long experience of growth in the recent past poses for cutting education spending.)

(iii) Manpower in the armed services has declined from its peak of over 850,000 in the early 1950s to 315,000 by 1979. This long-run reduction occurred in two distinct phases, separated by the creation of an all-volunteer force (AVF) in 1963. Initially, manpower reductions were associated with the end of the Korean War, the adoption of a strategic nuclear capability and the substitution of weapons for manpower, together with the planned rundown due to the abolition of conscription in 1960. Even the AVF has not been immune from cuts, and between 1963 and 1979 numbers declined by over 100,000.

(iv) Manpower reductions and a relatively constant defence budget in real terms have resulted in a long-run rise in real spending per serviceman. In 1957, when the plans to end conscription were announced, it was stated that future defence expenditure would not fall by as much as the armed services' manpower. This was expected because of the increasing complexity of modern weapons, the higher costs per man of regular forces (in terms of pay and accommodation) and the greater use of civilians (Ministry of Defence, 1957). In fact, since this 1957 forecast, manpower has more than halved, whereas real spending has increased by £221 m. For policy-makers it is necessary to discover whether the rising trend in defence spending per serviceman reflects relatively more expensive inputs in terms of labour or of weapons, and the implications of these changing inputs for military productivity (for

TABLE 6.1
UK DEFENCE EXPENDITURE, 1948—79

| Year | Defence expenditure Current prices (£m) | Defence expenditure Constant prices (1970=100) | Annual change in real defence spending (£m) | Defence spending as per cent of GNP | State education spending as per cent of GNP | Services manpower (000's) | Real defence spending per serviceman (1970=100) (£) |
|---|---|---|---|---|---|---|---|
| 1948 | 740 | 1737 | | 7.1 | 2.8 | 846.9 | 2051 |
| 1949 | 770 | 1754 | +17 | 6.5 | 2.9 | 769.9 | 2278 |
| 1950 | 820 | 1814 | +60 | 6.6 | 3.0 | 689.7 | 2630 |
| 1951 | 1090 | 2211 | +397 | 7.9 | 3.1 | 826.7 | 2675 |
| 1952 | 1450 | 2690 | +479 | 9.8 | 3.2 | 872.0 | 3085 |
| 1953 | 1540 | 2775 | +85 | 9.7 | 3.1 | 865.6 | 3206 |
| 1954 | 1551 | 2745 | −30 | 9.2 | 3.1 | 838.9 | 3272 |
| 1955 | 1523 | 2581 | −164 | 7.9 | 3.2 | 802.9 | 3215 |
| 1956 | 1625 | 2621 | +40 | 7.8 | 3.4 | 761.3 | 3443 |
| 1957 | 1551 | 2416 | −205 | 6.9 | 3.7 | 702.1 | 3441 |
| 1958 | 1541 | 2328 | −88 | 6.7 | 3.8 | 615.0 | 3785 |
| 1959 | 1561 | 2344 | +16 | 6.4 | 3.9 | 566.1 | 4141 |
| 1960 | 1614 | 2398 | +54 | 6.3 | 4.0 | 519.2 | 4619 |
| 1961 | 1725 | 2478 | +80 | 6.3 | 4.1 | 474.4 | 5223 |

| Year | | | | | | | |
|------|------|------|------|-----|-----|-------|------|
| 1962 | 1840 | 2358 | −120 | 6.4 | 4.6 | 442.3 | 5331 |
| 1963 | 1892 | 2557 | +199 | 6.2 | 4.7 | 426.2 | 6000 |
| 1964 | 1990 | 2605 | +48  | 5.9 | 4.8 | 422.8 | 6161 |
| 1965 | 2105 | 2628 | +23  | 5.9 | 5.0 | 422.6 | 6219 |
| 1966 | 2206 | 2651 | +23  | 5.8 | 5.3 | 417.3 | 6353 |
| 1967 | 2410 | 2829 | +178 | 5.9 | 5.6 | 415.7 | 6805 |
| 1968 | 2441 | 2733 | −96  | 5.6 | 5.8 | 398.7 | 6853 |
| 1969 | 2295 | 2439 | −294 | 4.9 | 5.9 | 380.0 | 6418 |
| 1970 | 2462 | 2462 | +23  | 4.8 | 6.1 | 371.1 | 6634 |
| 1971 | 2777 | 2538 | +76  | 4.8 | 6.2 | 368.0 | 6897 |
| 1972 | 3071 | 2618 | +80  | 4.8 | 6.5 | 371.4 | 7049 |
| 1973 | 3470 | 2711 | +93  | 4.7 | 6.5 | 360.8 | 7514 |
| 1974 | 4085 | 2751 | +40  | 4.9 | 6.1 | 345.3 | 7967 |
| 1975 | 5164 | 2799 | +48  | 4.9 | 6.9 | 338.4 | 8271 |
| 1976 | 6207 | 2888 | +89  | 4.9 | 6.5 | 336.6 | 8580 |
| 1977 | 6859 | 2754 | −134 | 4.8 | 6.2 | 330.5 | 8333 |
| 1978 | 7493 | 2768 | +14  | 4.6 | 6.1 | 320.7 | 8631 |
| 1979 | 8149 | 2637 | −131 | 4.4 | 4.8 | 315.0 | 8371 |

*Sources: Statement on the Defence Estimates* London, HMSO; *The Annual Abstract of Statistics* London, HMSO; *National Income and Expenditure* London, HMSO. The constant-price figures are based on the Retail Price Index. The defence share figures differ slightly from those quoted in the official statements referred to in the text, which are based on NATO definitions.

example, in terms of the 'hitting power' achieved per unit of expenditure).

(v) Annual changes in real defence spending have usually been under £100 m. Major reductions occurred between 1953 and 1958, between 1967 and 1969 and after 1976. Recently, the impression has arisen that UK defence spending has been subjected to 'drastic cuts' and a general belief has grown up that *all* military spending changes have been in a downward direction. What Table 6.1 shows is that, for the whole period, the number of annual increases in fact greatly exceeded the number of cuts. The cuts of the late 1960s were followed by annual increases in spending until by 1976 the defence budget exceeded its 1967 level! Since the establishment of the AVF in 1963, cuts have been associated with Labour governments.

Significantly, the defence sector appears to be more responsive to increases than to decreases in actual expenditure. All the annual cuts have been substantially less than the yearly increases of some £400 m. or more during the Korean War. Such differences in the magnitude of annual changes in expenditure might reflect contractual commitments and the costs of changing such commitments. Usually, contracts for both weapons and manpower exceed the life of a Parliament. For example, a new combat aircraft requires ten years from initial design to delivery, and manpower commitments to the voluntary force often extend to more than twenty years. At any given moment, then, past decisions account for over 90 per cent of expenditure on major weapons figures; even over the life of a typical Parliament about 80 per cent of weapons spending will be governed by past decisions.

The differences between increases and decreases in spending might also provide some casual empirical support for the idea that the Ministry of Defence and the armed forces behave as a budget-sensitive bureaucracy, resisting cuts and negotiating long-term contracts. Or, it might be argued that a distinction has to be made between changes in planned and in actual expenditure, and that emphasis on the latter underestimates the true magnitude of the cuts, particularly in recent years. Nevertheless, variations in defence spending provide valuable insights on the 'optimum' size of British military outlays. Spending cuts reveal society's preferences towards, and valuations of, military and civil goods, and some indications of the circumstances under which defence budgets have been regarded as 'too large'.

## THE MAJOR DEFENCE REVIEWS: DOES THE UK SPEND TOO MUCH OR TOO LITTLE ON DEFENCE?

To economists, the optimum size of the defence budget can be arrived at by a standard application of cost—benefit analysis. In practice, such applications are both controversial and problematic. As far as costs are concerned, it seems that the employment contract in the armed services does not provide inducements for military commanders to respond to economic incentives and to substitute capital for labour as manpower becomes relatively more expensive. Instead, the contract is incomplete, so allowing individuals to be opportunistic, to hoard or distort information and generally to pursue discretionary behaviour (Williamson, 1975). On the other side of the equation, the benefits calculation is particularly difficult since it requires society to make judgements about the valuation of human lives in a situation where individuals are unable to express a preference for different amounts of defence (because of the limitations of the voting system), where there are incentives to 'free ride' under a defence 'umbrella' provided by others, and where difficulties arise for any government trying to aggregate individual preferences.

In the face of such difficulties, various pragmatic criteria have been used to determine the 'optimum' defence budget for the UK. These include the extent to which the UK is involved in wars (such as Korea, Cyprus, Indonesia, Northern Ireland), its commitments and the state of international tension, as well as its economic performance and comparisons with allies. Many such criteria have some economic logic in a cost—benefit framework, but there are potential confusions. In particular, the question of whether the UK spends 'too much' on defence can result in a misleading emphasis on defence inputs (such as numbers of aircraft, ships and tanks) and expenditures, and in a confusion of such inputs with the final outputs of the defence sector.

Ultimately, the point at which defence spending becomes 'too high' or an 'excessive burden' depends on its price in terms of the sacrifices of a government's other policy targets. Obviously, governments of different political philosophies will differ in their tastes and preferences for, and hence in their relative valuations of, defence against civil goods, including other public sector services. In fact, by observation we can quantify the upper bounds or maximally acceptable levels of military spending, and these were reflected in the Defence Reviews of 1957, 1965—68 and 1975.

## The 1957 Review

By the mid-1950s, Conservative government policy aimed to ensure that the cost of defence 'whether in terms of manpower, materials or money, does not overload the economy' (Ministry of Defence, 1956, p. 6). Accordingly, in late 1955 it was decided to reduce military manpower to about 700,000 by early 1958. The aim was to release resources for expanding industrial production. Continued worries about the increasing costs of defence in relation to the UK's economic performance, together with advances in military technology led to the 1957 Defence Review. Defence spending had been absorbing some 10 per cent of GNP and the 1957 Review announced that such a share was 'too high'. The 1957 cuts were expected to release skilled labour, especially scarce scientists and technicians, for employment in civil industry with associated favourable effects on capital investment and exports (Ministry of Defence, 1957). The 1957 Review also reflected major changes in military technology and strategy. It announced the substitution of nuclear weapons, rockets and missiles for large-scale conventional forces and manned aircraft. Conscription and certain reserve forces were to be abolished and replaced by a relatively small AVF of 375,000 personnel to be achieved by the end of 1962. An economics-of-politics approach would explain the abolition of conscription as a clear potential vote-winner, so that the two main parties had an inducement to adopt similar policies favouring an AVF (Hartley, 1977). But it is harder to explain precisely why the 375,000 force figure was decided upon (perhaps it was thought that two conscripts equal one regular soldier?).

## Reviews of 1965—68

The next major Defence Reviews occurred between 1965 and 1968 under Labour governments. In the early 1960s, the Conservative government had regarded 7 per cent as the upper limit for the share of defence spending in GNP, but this was too high for the new

Labour administration. During 1965/66, the Labour government planned to reduce the share to about 6 per cent, or a target of £2,000 m. (1964 prices) to be achieved by 1969/70. In other words, real defence spending in 1969/70 was to be restricted to its 1964 level and this involved cuts of £400 m. (1964 prices) compared with the plans of the previous Conservative government. Once again, economic factors, especially the balance of payments, were dominant.

An indication of potential inefficiency in weapons procurement emerged when it was claimed that cuts of over £200 m. (1964 prices) had been achieved 'without reducing our ability to carry out the present scale of military tasks' (Ministry of Defence, 1966, p. 1). But further changes were required to reduce the 'excessive' foreign exchange costs of Britain's overseas defence commitments as well as the 'over-stretch' of military manpower caused by the UK's worldwide role. Thus, the 1966 Review recognized that there would have to be some sacrifice of the UK's commitments overseas, especially outside Europe (Aden and the Mediterranean). These changes had major implications for weapons, force structures and inter-service competition. Land-based RAF aircraft were to replace naval carrier-borne aircraft; US aircraft, with varying amounts of British work-sharing, were to replace British projects (TSR−2, P1154, HS681), and UK-based troops were to be substituted for overseas garrisons.

Although the 1966 Review aimed at outlining defence policy for the 1970s, other Reviews followed in 1967 and 1968. Both were responses to the UK's continued balance of payments problems, with defence cuts being used to reduce overseas spending directly and also to contribute to the deflationary policies required to 'correct' the international payments deficit. The 1967−68 Reviews announced further reductions in the UK's overseas defence commitments, with the withdrawal from East of Suez by the early 1970s. Manpower was to be reduced by some 75,000 servicemen (20 per cent) and by 80,000 civilians. It was expected that military spending (in 1964 prices) would be £1,860 m. in 1969/70 and some £1,600 m. by 1973.

The philosophy of the Labour government's reviews of 1965−68 was that 'there is no military strength . . . except on the basis of economic strength' and it planned further to reduce defence spending to 5 per cent of GNP by 1972/73 (Ministry of Defence,

1968, p. 1). This policy was modified by the subsequent Conservative government of 1970—74, which declared that defence policies should not in the future be under constant threat of financial retrenchment (Ministry of Defence, 1971, p. 1). Thus, defence spending was in fact some 5¾ per cent of GNP in 1973/74, compared with Labour's 5 per cent target.

## The 1975 Review

There were further changes in 1974—75, with the election of a Labour government pledged to achieving substantial cuts in defence expenditure. Equity played a large part in the argument. It was argued that Britain's NATO and worldwide commitments imposed 'an extra burden which none of her European allies and trading competitors was bearing' (Ministry of Defence, 1975, p. 1). The cost of maintaining the 1974 size and structure of forces and commitments was expected to rise (at 1974 prices) from £4,000 m. in 1975/76 to an annual average of £4,450 m. between 1979 and 1984: an annual increase of 11¼ per cent, mostly reflecting advances in weapons technology. The 1975 Defence Review determined that 'resources must be released for investment and improving the balance of payments', and that '. . . the burden of defence expenditure should be brought more into line with that of our major European Allies' (Ministry of Defence, 1975, p. 2). The 1975 Review purported to start from 'clear strategic priorities', unconstrained by an arbitrary financial limit; but it specified a lower target for defence of 4½ per cent of GNP and a level of real spending of £3,790 m. (1974 prices) to be achieved by 1984. Indeed, from a strategic standpoint, the rationale for determining the UK's optimum size of defence budget on the basis of some arbitrary share figure related to that of its European allies is a somewhat debatable one. For example, there are international differences in the definitions of defence and GNP, and many countries use 'cheap' conscripts. Moreover, the essential issue is the UK's perception of a threat (that is, from a potential *enemy* rather than allies) and whether its citizens believe that it is worth spending more or less on defence (Hartley and Lynk, 1980).

Britain's 1975 Defence Review resulted in further changes in the size of forces and commitments. Britain was the only European member of NATO with contributions to all areas of the Alliance (both geographically and in terms of nuclear and conventional forces), as well as worldwide commitments. Whilst future emphasis was to be placed on NATO, it was proposed to reduce some of Britain's European commitments as well as many of those outside NATO. General-purpose forces were to be used to meet uncertainty, but it was announced that the UK Labour government would not introduce a new generation of strategic nuclear weapons. A commitment was made to retain a BAOR of 55,000 troops plus a tactical air force in central Europe, and naval forces in the Eastern Atlantic and Channel areas. But reductions were to be made in certain specialist reinforcement units for NATO, especially on the southern flank (such as amphibious and joint airborne task forces). For the RAF, which suffered the greatest manpower cuts, there were major reductions in the transport fleet, and the Navy was to experience a decline of one-seventh in some of its combat ships: these changes reflected the withdrawals from Britain's worldwide role and the Mediterranean. In total, manpower was expected to fall by 38,000 servicemen and 30,000 civilians by 1979. In addition, numbers employed in defence industries on MoD contracts were expected to fall by about 10,000 by 1979.

## WHAT DETERMINES UK DEFENCE EXPENDITURE?

The level of UK defence spending over the period 1948—73 can be explained by a model containing economic, political and strategic factors, although these categories are not mutually exclusive. This model is described in Hartley and MacLean (1978). Economic factors can be represented by GNP, per capita income, the balance of payments and unemployment rates. Political determinants are portrayed by the party complexion of the government (Conservative or Labour) and in the choice between defence and private and public sector civil goods. Strategic factors include the involvement of the UK in wars, the behaviour of allies and potential enemies and advances in military technology.

This model, when tested by econometric techniques, provided a satisfactory explanation of the facts in the sense of accounting for over 90 per cent of the variations in the level and shares of UK military expenditure, most of the significant correlations having the expected signs (Hartley and MacLean, 1978, p. 290, Table 2).[1] Non-economic factors had substantial quantitative effects on defence spending, such as the Korean War and the party complexion of the government (Conservative governments are associated with higher real defence spending of over £100 m. per annum in 1963 prices). Advances in weapons technology appear to have an effect in raising military spending, but the abolition of conscription did not appear to have any effect. Perhaps surprisingly, spending data did not conform to simple expectations of incremental budgeting, whereby this year's budget equals, or exceeds, last year's (Davis *et al.,* 1966).

The Appendix to this chapter presents some further tentative evidence concerning trade-offs between defence spending and various public and private expenditures. The relationships between the dependent variables and the share of defence spending in GNP are, in most cases, negative, implying that other items of spending act as substitutes for defence, rising when defence spending falls and vice-versa.

These results should be treated with some caution, since there were estimation difficulties (serial correlation) that reduced the reliability of the equations. Given these reservations, it can be seen that the shares elasticities for state social welfare programmes were substantially less than one (that is, the percentage rise in the share of these items in GNP is less than the corresponding fall in the share of defence spending in GNP, and vice-versa). For private expenditures, the comparable elasticities were higher and approximately unity, with the negative sign for investment supporting the standard policy argument for cuts in defence spending (that is, that cuts will produce higher investment). But there was no evidence of any *additional* and independent effect of Defence Reviews on private investment (a dummy variable for Defence Reviews added to the investment equations produced no significant coefficients). In view of the debate about 'trade-offs', it is interesting that *public* investment gave a significant, but positive, coefficient — rising when defence spending rises rather than vice-versa. Elsewhere, the positive coefficients for the time trend ($t$) in the public sector equations might be interpreted as evidence of society's changing preferences in favour of state civil and social welfare spending. Rather more tentative is the evidence that defence spending had a positive effect on votes in this period.

## THE EFFECTS OF THE DEFENCE REVIEWS

In analysing the Reviews, consideration has to be given to the definition of 'cuts', their implementation and effects on the military—industrial complex, the response of the armed forces and the efficiency of the results. Some attention will be given to the 1975 Review, since its plans are well documented. The resulting choices provide insights into government preferences, the behaviour of bureaucracies and the extent of inter-service competition or collusion.

### How are cuts in spending defined and were the cuts implemented?

Cuts are defined as announced reductions in actual or planned expenditure. But this definition is not without its problems. Presumably, defence budgets (and all budgets) are cut annually by the Treasury in the annual review of public spending, in that the armed services will bid for more funds than they are allocated; but this is not documented. Doubts also arise about the meaning of savings based on reductions in *long-term* spending *plans* (this is the well-known phenomenon of 'fairy gold', which we encounter elsewhere in this book — see Chapters 1 and 8). For example, Table 6.2 shows that the 1975 Labour government was able to announce annual 'savings' on its predecessor's 1984 programme; but this assumes that the plans would have been implemented. In this context, defence choices are made under uncertainty and plans can be affected by unexpected changes in, say, technical progress or international tension.

A comparison between the targets of the Defence Reviews and the data in Tables 6.1 and 6.4 confirms that, in terms of directions of change, the manpower and spending plans were broadly achieved. Such comparisons are more easily undertaken for manpower, whereas spending is complicated by relative price effects and variations in base years. However, the cuts were not always fully implemented. The 1957 policy announcing the end of manned combat aircraft was modified by 1959 (TSR—2). This change could have been the result of a new policy formulated in a world of uncertainty, or the outcome of pressure from established interest

TABLE 6.2
SAVINGS FROM THE 1975 DEFENCE REVIEW (£m, 1978 PRICES)

| | 1973/74 | 1974/75 | 1975/76 | 1976/77 | 1977/78 | 1978/79 | 1979/80 | Annual average 1980—84 |
|---|---|---|---|---|---|---|---|---|
| Pre-1975 Defence Review programme | 7633 | 7728 | 7818 | 8003 | 8232 | 8532 | 8721 | 8992 |
| 1975 revised budget | 7569 | 7055 | 7226 | 7256 | 7017 | 6963 | 7249 | 7634 |
| Total reductions | 64 | 673 | 592 | 747 | 1215 | 1569 | 1472 | 1358 |

groups, namely, the RAF and the UK aerospace industry. Similarly, the effects of the 1965—68 Reviews were modified by the 1970 Conservative government; and the spending plans of the 1975 Review were revised *upwards* in 1977 as a result of a NATO agreement to increase real defence budgets by 3 per cent per annum. This NATO agreement is an example of external constraints on a UK government's ability and willingness to cut defence spending.

*The adjustment period: how long does it take to achieve major cuts?*

Table 6.2 confirms that defence expenditure is not susceptible to large-scale cuts in the *short run*. A four—five-year adjustment period is required before the largest annual cuts are achieved ('fairy gold' again, or present is preferred to future consumption). Significantly, expenditure rose in the years immediately following the 1975 Review and by 1979 was expected to exceed the 1975 revised budget!

*The military—industrial complex: which industries were affected by the Reviews?*

Both the armed services and defence firms constitute a major interest group, accounting for over a million jobs in 1979. Vote-conscious governments are unlikely to ignore such interest groups (Hartley, 1977). For example, the armed services have employment and multiplier effects through their decisions on the location and closure of bases. In an era of cuts, they can use their expertise and discretion, threatening to close bases in marginal constituencies or to sacrifice major weapons projects located in high unemployment areas ('sore thumbs' and bleeding stumps' — tactics discussed further in Chapter 8). Cancellations are likely to be resisted by producer groups. Industries such as aerospace, electronics, shipbuilding and ordnance are major suppliers of defence equipment (firms such as British Aerospace, British Shipbuilding, GEC, Rolls-Royce, Royal Ordnance Factories, British Leyland, Ferranti, Plessey, Westland). The existence of such a state-supported domestic weapons industry represents an additional constraint on defence choices.

Governments have claimed that cuts release scarce resources, especially labour, for use in the civil sector (see also Appendix). Hence, employment functions were used to test for any *labour* effects of the Reviews of 1965—68 and 1975. The results showed that, within engineering, only instrument engineering, the tractors—motor cycles group and possibly shipbuilding 'lost' (released) labour following the Reviews.[2] Similarly, only a few industries seemed to acquire labour, namely the insulated wires, cables, electronics, computers and radar group, together with electrical machinery and electrical engineering. Surprisingly, the Reviews had no separate *employment* effect on the defence-intensive aerospace sector: this might reflect the substantial rise in the industry's proportion of output exported (from 20 per cent in 1965 to 38 per cent in 1969).

### The response of the armed forces

The optimal size of a country's defence budget is also associated with the selection of the 'best' allocation of the expenditure between weapons and manpower, nuclear and conventional forces, as well as army, navy and air forces and their geographical distribution. If choices reflect preferences, then the force structures of the late 1970s were an indication of the 1974 Labour government's preferred outcomes. Table 6.3 shows such outcomes and their costs in terms of the sacrifice of alternative defence capabilities.

Since the 1966 Review, there has been a substantial rise in the share of the defence budget allocated to European Theatre ground forces (NATO). Substantial changes have also taken place within the broad expenditure heads shown in Table 6.3. For example, destroyers, frigates and submarines have become relatively more important within the Navy, as have strike aircraft within the Air Force. Similarly, the cuts and changing commitments have been reflected in the declining importance of the Army's non-NATO role, of amphibious and carrier forces for the Navy, and of air defence and transport aircraft in the RAF. Nevertheless, the budgetary shares of the Army, Navy and RAF have been relatively unchanged. This relative stability has occurred despite Defence Reviews and technical progress that might have been expected to result in changing comparative advantages for each of the armed services. The resulting stability in shares has been explained in terms of the UK's desire to maintain 'balanced forces' (Smith, 1980,

TABLE 6.3
FUNCTIONAL COSTING, EXPENDITURE AND
UK FORCE STRUCTURES

| Programme | Fiscal year | | | |
|---|---|---|---|---|
| | 1966/67 | | 1979/80 | |
| | £m | % | £m | % |
| 1. Nuclear strategic forces | 105 | 4.8 | 126 | 1.5 |
| 2. Navy general-purpose combat forces | 309 | 14.2 | 1,131 | 13.2 |
| 3. European Theatre ground forces | 264 | 12.2 | 1,496 | 17.5 |
| 4. Other Army combat forces | 121 | 5.6 | 81 | 0.9 |
| 5. Air Force general-purpose forces | 364 | 16.8 | 1,462 | 17.1 |
| 6. Reserve formations | 37 | 1.7 | 148 | 1.7 |
| 7. R & D | 275 | 12.6 | 1,151 | 13.4 |
| 8. Training | 188 | 8.6 | 777 | 9.0 |
| 9. Production and repair facilities in UK | 153 | 7.0 | 590 | 6.8 |
| 10. War and contingency stocks | 38 | 1.7 | 160 | 1.9 |
| 11. Other support functions | 301 | 13.8 | 1,481 | 17.3 |
| Total expenditure (current prices) | 2,172 | 100 | 8,558 | 100 |

p. 112). It could, of course, reflect pressures from established service interest groups, each insisting upon 'equal misery' in cuts.

However, in an era of defence cuts, the most disturbing trend concerns the share of combat forces in the military budget (programmes 1—6 in Table 6.3). Combat forces accounted for almost 52 per cent of total expenditure in 1979/80, compared with over 55 per cent in 1966/67. This declining share has been associated with an equivalent *increase* in the proportion of the budget allocated to 'other support functions' — pensions and personnel services, which reflect some of the costs of recruiting and retaining an all-volunteer force. Of course, the crucial issue concerns the effects of the cuts on defence output. Since 1968, there has been a downward trend in the numbers of troops and combat units (such as vessels, regiments, aircraft squadrons). But the effect on defence output depends on the productivity of manpower and weapons, together with the age and operational availability of equipment (including spares).

TABLE 6.4
DEFENCE MANPOWER CUTS

| | 1965 | | 1965—71 | | | 1974 | | 1974—79 | | |
|---|---|---|---|---|---|---|---|---|---|---|
| | No. (000s) | % | Reduction No. (000s) | % | % share of reduction | No. (000s) | % | Reduction No. (000s) | % | % share of reduction |
| *Services* | | | | | | | | | | |
| Navy | 95 | 23.3 | −16 | −16.8 | 30.2 | 78.3 | 22.4 | −5.8 | −7.4 | 16.9 |
| Army | 187 | 45.9 | −18 | −9.6 | 33.9 | 171.7 | 49.2 | −15.5 | −9.0 | 45.2 |
| Air Force | 125 | 30.7 | −19 | −15.2 | 35.8 | 99.2 | 28.4 | −12.9 | −13.0 | 37.6 |
| Total | 407 | 100.0 | −53 | −13.0 | 100.0 | 349.2 | 100.0 | −34.2 | −9.8 | 100.0 |
| *Civilians:* | | | | | | | | | | |
| Non-industrial | 108.1 | 28.6 | +3.7 | +3.4 | | 128.5 | 40.8 | −7.9 | −6.2 | 27.5 |
| UK-based (industrial and non-industrial) | 278.3 | 73.5 | −24.8 | −8.9 | 40.5 | 267.1 | 84.9 | −19.4 | −7.3 | 67.6 |
| Locally engaged | 100.2 | 26.0 | −36.4 | −36.3 | 59.5 | 47.5 | 15.1 | −9.3 | −19.6 | 32.4 |
| Total | 378.5 | 100.0 | −61.2 | −16.2 | 100.0 | 314.6 | 100.0 | −28.7 | −9.1 | 100.0 |

*Manpower cuts.* It takes about five years to adjust manpower *downwards* to new planned levels. Table 6.4 shows the effects of the cuts on service and on civilian manpower. Both groups were subject to similar percentage cuts, although the aggregates conceal wide variations. For the armed services, the 1965—68 Reviews appeared *equitable* (an 'equal misery' approach), in that each contributed about one-third of the manpower cuts. But the 1975 Review resulted in a different sharing system, with the Army and the RAF bearing most of the manpower reductions. Neither the 1960's nor 1970's Reviews supported the *fair shares* rule, whereby each service's manpower is cut by its percentage of the total force (meaning, for example, that the RAF, with 28 per cent of manpower, would have borne 28 per cent of the manpower cuts). Also, in both Reviews, the RAF fared worse than average in terms of percentage manpower reductions. However, manpower is only one input into the military production function. The RAF as a capital-intensive service is likely to prefer cuts in manpower rather than in weapons, whereas the Army as a labour-intensive force will wish to retain its soldiers.

A similar analysis can be applied to civilians, including non-industrial civil servants. Locally engaged civilians have borne the greatest percentage manpower cuts, especially after 1965 and the UK withdrawal from East of Suez. As with servicemen, there was no evidence of a 'fair shares' rule applying as between UK and locally engaged civilians. Table 6.4 shows that non-industrial civil servants appear to have been relatively protected from the manpower cuts (reminiscent of the theme of Whitehall saving itself at the expense of other parts of the public sector, which is discussed elsewhere in this book). Admittedly, there have been job reclassifications from industrial to non-industrial status. Nonetheless, it is noticeable that in an era when the number of troops and combat units have declined, there were more non-industrials in 1979 than in 1965. Employment functions were estimated, but no statistically significant relationships were obtained between the numbers of non-industrial or industrial staffs and measures of defence output (i.e., total military outlays and their share in GNP).

*The 1975 Review and the effects on equipment.* The 1975 Defence Review provides further insights into the armed forces' response to expenditure cuts. In addition to manpower savings, there were to be substantial *future* reductions in the share of new equipment. By

1983/84 (nine years later), new equipment was expected to be 39.6 per cent of the defence budget compared with the previous plan of almost 45 per cent. The Navy responded partly by the premature disposal of older ships and partly by adjusting new construction programmes. For example, it sacrificed 50 per cent of its amphibious ships and 30 per cent of its 'other vessels', as well as nine new destroyers and frigates from its forward plans. However, the Navy protected its plans to build new anti-submarine cruisers with their fixed-wing aircraft capability (it may be recalled that the 1966 Defence Review planned the abolition of carrier-borne aircraft).

The Army protected its major asset — manpower — by offering economies in headquarters staff, training, logistic and support services, as well as in new equipment. Expenditure on new equipment was to be reduced by 30 per cent. Since Army equipment is relatively cheap, there are only limited possibilities for economies through cancellation or postponement of major new weapons. Thus, the required equipment economies affected a wide range of items, involving a mix of reduced numbers, postponements and cancellations.

The RAF sacrificed 50 per cent of its transport fleet, 25 per cent of its maritime patrol aircraft and 25 per cent of its support helicopters. There were also economies in training, communication and general support aircraft, as well as the withdrawal from some twelve bases. There was, however, no change in the numbers of combat aircraft, nor were the major new aircraft programmes cancelled: these involved the Jaguar and Tornado aircraft, both of which were international collaborative projects. Significantly, following the experience with TSR—2 (cancelled in the 1965 Defence Review), both the RAF and the UK aerospace industry believe that one of the 'benefits' of collaborative programmes is that they are much more difficult to cancel!

### The efficiency of the cuts

Cuts need not necessarily be disastrous. Indeed, to the extent that bureaucracies may tend to produce 'too large' an output, a budget cut might represent a desirable change. But bureaucrats are experts in the military production function and they can respond to cuts by offering 'token' savings in manpower or weapons (depending on their preferences). The cuts of the 1960s and 1970s were achieved by 'sacrificing' Britain's worldwide role, much of it involving relatively old equipment, whilst NATO was regarded as a 'binding' commitment and constraint. There is also support for the view that, during the cuts, the armed forces succeeded in protecting their prestige weapons projects (such as aircraft carriers). These can be defined as weapons that are expensive solutions to obtaining military 'protection' or that buy 'too much' striking power (over-insurance). Often they are high-technology gadgets, giving prestige and personal satisfaction to their users. Guns, missiles, minesweepers and spares are less glamorous than tanks, strike planes, aircraft carriers and new equipment. After all, employment contracts for bureaucrats and servicemen provide no inducements to respond to economic incentives; they do not share in any savings, so that there is every incentive to spend. In the circumstances, it has been suggested that increased efficiency in the military sector requires major budgetary cuts, possibly of the order of 50 per cent. It is argued that only massive cuts will compel the armed forces to re-think the cost-effectiveness of their missions and shock them into increased efficiency.[3]

## CHOICES FOR THE 1980s

Hard times and choices are not confined to a period of cuts. The Conservative government elected in 1979 planned to increase annual real defence spending by 3 per cent to 1984. But even with increased spending, choices cannot be avoided. Moreover, economic and demographic factors suggest that some difficult and searching choices will arise between 1985 and 1996. Technical progress will increase the costs of maintaining present forces (by some £270 m. per year in 1979 prices) and there will be a substantial decline in the male population aged 15−19. The result is likely to be a smaller AVF in 1990 (say, 250,000), which will require a reappraisal of existing commitments and a search for lower-cost solutions. Four possible options are as follows:

(a) To fill the manpower gap, civilians and women could replace servicemen, and reserves could be substituted for regulars. Conscription might seem a cheap solution, but it is costly, inefficient and inequitable servitude.

(b) Weapons can be substituted for manpower, but technical progress means that equipment is becoming costlier. Economies could be achieved by sacrificing traditional commitments (such as the UK's strategic nuclear deterrent) or by using lower-cost weapons and competitive procurement policies (for example, buying from abroad rather than from UK producers). Predictably, such policies would encounter opposition from established interest groups, with claims about the loss of jobs and technological capability, and of undue dependence on the USA (Hartley, 1974).

(c) Commitments might be reduced. A smaller AVF will require a reappraisal of labour-intensive commitments (such as BAOR) and the possibility of substituting aircraft, ships and nuclear weapons for part of BAOR. Such a reappraisal might also require the UK armed services to specialize by comparative advantage, so abandoning the doctrine of 'balanced forces'.

(d) The efficiency of the armed forces might be increased. The non-competitive environment and the employment contract in the armed services are unlikely to provide strong incentives for individuals and groups to minimize costs, as has been pointed out. Efficiency might be improved through more experiments with increased competition involving rival services, other state agencies and a greater use of private markets in fields such as training, transport and repairs. It might be objected that competitive bidding of this type would result in monopoly and 'hostages to fortune'. But this is a strange objection: after all, the current situation is monopolistic, and contracts could be for limited periods, on the principle of the franchises given to independent TV companies.

Ultimately, an emphasis on defence *output* and a recognition of substitution possibilities will encourage policy-makers to be less concerned with any specific manpower figure.

## CONCLUSION: SOME PROBLEMS

Two major issues dominate debates about defence policy, in good times and bad. First, how can society control military expenditure? To do so would require the specification of a clear, unambiguous objective function for defence, reflecting community preferences and minimizing opportunities for discretionary behaviour. Supposing that such a function could be specified (!), governments would still have to ensure compliance. Possible solutions to that would include bargaining about budgets, changing senior personnel and organizations, the use of promotions policy, a modified employment contract (that is, more complete, reducing the scope for discretion) and new information systems (Kanter, 1979).

The second major issue is the question of how society can introduce incentives for efficiency into the military sector. How do we determine what is a military 'need'? Whose interpretation of need is being used in defining operational requirements? Can a weapon be said to be 'needed' regardless of cost? Four of the issues raised by military 'needs' are discussed below.

First, the definition of defence needs is produced by the Ministry of Defence and the armed forces, each of which is a monopoly supplier of information and of defence services. Given the present allocation of 'property rights' in defence (with the Army specializing in land forces, and so on), there is no competition from rival forces and hence no alternative sources of information. Indeed, the present system might encourage collusion and log-rolling. In contrast, free entry and competition from rival services, other state agencies and the private sector could be used as a policing/monitoring mechanism. In this way, competition could result in beneficial, rather than wasteful, rivalry and duplication.

Second, budget-maximizing tactics mean that the armed services aim to re-equip their existing force levels: this becomes the definition of need. In contrast, the government as a buyer of defence services lacks the specialist knowledge to monitor and assess such decisions.

Third, need often tends to be desire — that is, what is preferred by a specialist professional aiming at complete protection in a world of no resource constraints. We might all like a Rolls-Royce car but, for most people, the sacrifices are too great so that a Datsun or Mini has to be chosen.

Fourth, and finally, budgets do not provide effective resource constraints. Monopoly bureaux can use their specialist information to 'buy into' new weapons programmes, using criteria of 'need, vital and essential'. And each service is likely to support its rivals (collusion or log-rolling) in the queueing and bidding hierarchy. New programmes also attract support from producer groups (firms and unions) as well as budget-conscious civil servants. Later, the armed services can either demand a higher budget to maintain defence output or use their specialist knowledge and discretion to reduce defence output in *their* preferred areas. Such reductions in output might then be used to argue for a larger military budget, on the grounds that the country's defences are weak! Essentially, the problem is to confront the armed services with fixed budgets, output constraints and fewer opportunities for discretionary behaviour, and to provide politicians and society with information on what the defence trade-offs actually are. But this requires the measurement of defence output.

The problems of measuring 'need' and of making cuts in a sector where service-providers have a high degree of discretion in how they organize and allocate resources is not confined to the world of defence, of course. These matters figure equally large in the area of education, which is considered in the next chapter, and to which the phenomenon of 'hard times', in terms of spending cuts and falling demand, is a relatively new experience.

## ACKNOWLEDGEMENTS

This is an SSRC-financed study of defence cuts and it is part of the Public Sector Studies Programme at the University of York. Thanks are due to Ted Lynk and Pat MacLean as Research Fellows on the project; to Chris Hood for comments and suggestions; and to the Ministry of Defence for advice and data. The usual disclaimers apply.

## NOTES

1.  An example is:
    $$D = \text{constant} - 128.5\overset{**}{U} - 0.2\overset{**}{B} + 134.0\overset{**}{P} + 396.9\overset{**}{W} + 65.1\overset{**}{t}$$
    $$- 0.3\overset{*}{S}$$
    $$\bar{R}^2 = 0.92$$

    where $D$ = level of defence spending; $U$ = UK unemployment rate with a one-year lag; $B$ = current account of balance of payments; $P$ = political variable with 1 = Conservative governments and 0 = Labour; $W$ = dummy for Korean War with 1 = 1952−54; $t$ = time trend, 1948−73; $S$ = expenditure on substitutes (private investment).

    All expenditure data in 1963 prices; ** significant at 1% level; * significant at 5% level; $\bar{R}^2$ is adjusted for degrees of freedom.

2. A standard employment function was estimated and a dummy variable was used to measure any separate and independent effect of the Reviews — i.e. $N = N(Q,t,N_{t-1},D)$, where $N =$ employment; $Q =$ output; $t =$ time trend 1959-76; and $D =$ dummy variable (1,0) for Reviews.

3. The existence of a substantial amount of organizational slack does not mean that broad efficiency criteria are never used by decision-makers. For example, if the allocation of funds between the armed services were determined solely by the economics of politics and bureaucracies, the RAF might never have been formed; up to the 1930s, its interest group was relatively small. The subsequent development of the RAF might suggest that decision-makers were influenced by notions of a military production function where investment in an air force was worthwhile. Or is this an example where efficiency criteria and interest group explanations coincide?

## REFERENCES

Davis, O., *et al.* (1966) 'A theory of the budgetary process' *American Political Science Review* September

Hartley, K. (1974) *A Market for Aircraft* Hobart Paper 57, London, IEA

Hartley, K. (1977) *Problems of Economic Policy* London, Allen and Unwin, chs. 3 and 11

Hartley, K. and MacLean, P. (1978) 'Military expenditure and capitalism; a comment' *Cambridge Journal of Economics* September

Hartley, K. and Lynk, E. (1980) 'The political economy of UK defence expenditure' *RUSI Journal* March

Kanter, A. (1979) *Defence Politics* London, University of Chicago Press

Ministry of Defence (1956) *Statement on the Defence Estimates* Cmnd. 9691, London, HMSO

Ministry of Defence (1957) *Outline of Future Policy* Cmnd. 124, London, HMSO

Ministry of Defence (1966) *The Defence Review* Cmnd. 2901, London, HMSO

Ministry of Defence (1968) *Supplementary Statement on Defence Policy* Cmnd. 3701, London, HMSO

Ministry of Defence (1971) *Statement on the Defence Estimates* Cmnd. 4592, London, HMSO

Ministry of Defence (1975) *Statement on the Defence Estimates* Cmnd. 5976, London, HMSO

Peacock, A. and Wiseman, J. (1967) *The Growth of Public Expenditure in the UK* London, Allen and Unwin

Smith, D. (1980) *The Defence of the Realm in the 1980s* London, Croom Helm

Williamson, O. E. (1975) *Markets and Hierarchies: Analysis and Anti-Trust Implications* New York, Free Press.

## APPENDIX

TABLE 6.A
DEFENCE SUBSTITUTES AND VOTES

| Dependent variable | Coefficients of: | | |
|---|---|---|---|
| | Log $D/Y$ | $t$ | $R^2$ |
| 1. $\log \dfrac{SST}{Y}$ | *−0.16 (0.06) | **0.02 (0.002) | 0.96 |
| 2. $\log \dfrac{E}{Y}$ | **−0.17 (0.04) | **0.03 (0.001) | 0.99 |
| 3. $\log \dfrac{NHS}{Y}$ | **−0.51 (0.10) | | 0.51 |
| 4. $\log \dfrac{G\text{-}D}{Y}$ | *−0.23 (0.09) | **0.01 (0.002) | 0.89 |
| 5. $\log \dfrac{GI}{Y}$ | **0.38 (0.11) | **0.02 (0.003) | 0.69 |
| 6. $\log \dfrac{PI}{Y}$ | **−0.85 (0.13) | | 0.63 |
| 7. $\log \dfrac{C}{Y}$ | **−0.83 (0.16) | **−0.06 (0.004) | 0.93 |
| 8. $\log V$ | *0.27 (0.10) | | 0.58 |

NOTES:
(i)    All equations included a constant term.
(ii)   $D/Y$ is the share of defence in GNP. Data from the annual *Statement on the Defence Estimates* were used in equations 1, 2, 3 and 7 and from *National Income and Expenditure* in the remaining equations.
(iii)   $\frac{SST}{Y}$ is the share of social services including transfers in GNP.
(iv)   $\frac{E}{Y}$ is the share of education in GNP.
(v)   $\frac{NHS}{Y}$ is the share of health services expenditure in GNP.
(vi)   $\frac{G-D}{Y}$ is the share of government civil expenditure in GNP.
(vii)   $\frac{GI}{Y}$ is the share of government public investment in GNP.
(viii)   $\frac{PI}{Y}$ is the share of private investment in GNP.
(ix)   $\frac{C}{Y}$ is the share of consumption in GNP.
(x)   $V$ is percentage of total votes for the previous governing party in the election year ($t$). The elections were October 1950 — June 1970 ($n = 7$).
(xi)   $t$ is a time trend 1948—73.
(xii)   ** = significant at 1% level; * = significant at 5% level.
Standard errors are in brackets.

CHAPTER SEVEN

# Education in 'Hard Times'

by MAURICE KOGAN

We encounter two problems in trying to trace how patterns of government behaviour in the education sector change at a time of radically altered policies on public spending. The first is common to all studies of 'government in hard times' and arises from the well-known difficulty of identifying and documenting changes in bureaucratic behaviour, particularly within British central government departments. Much of what can be said must be based on surmise. If the observer is fortunate, he may be able to build up an account from statements by major actors within the bureaucracy; but these actors may not always be aware that their behaviour is an important element in creating the policies that they administer.

The second difficulty is perhaps more particular to the education system. The institutions and individuals who 'deliver' educational policy are deliberately endowed with a degree of discretion (that is, freedom to decide within limits). Such discretion may partially cut across the mechanisms for controlling and deciding spending; the result is a system that is particularly rich in the multiplicity of points of service delivery and of decision-making.

It may well be that this picture of the education system is a product of the growth era, and things may change if a prolonged period of hard times is in prospect. The discretion with which service-providers are endowed may be reduced as a result of changes in the financing of the service. I shall return to this point in a later section of this chapter. Unlike the world of defence considered in the last chapter, the education system has not been subjected to a long period of cutbacks; but certainly in the cuts of 1979/80 the

152

institutional fabric of the education system seems to have had a life of its own, a degree of autonomy that reduces the ability of ministers under spending pressures to change it at will.

To explore the government of education in hard times, this chapter is divided into four main parts. I shall begin by looking at the idiosyncratic aspects of the education service — what makes it different from other government services. To make the subject manageable, the chapter concentrates on the public sector of education in Britain, mainly at school level: the financing of universities is not discussed. In the second section, I give a brief account of the cuts that have been attempted in this sphere up to 1979/80. The third section attempts to interpret the impact of reduced spending levels on institutional structures and behaviour. The final section offers some speculative comments on what might happen next if 'hard times' for education continue.

## EDUCATION: WHY IS IT DIFFERENT?

In order to understand the operation of the cutback process in education, it is necessary to grasp some of the distinctive features of the service. First, education has idiosyncratic aspects as a local authority-provided service. There is a set of linked assumptions about what constitutes education as a task and about the working relationships that are involved. In Britain, the task of education is construed in terms of encounters between individual teachers and pupils. This has important consequences for our later discussion, because it means both that there is a high degree of discretion at the point at which education is 'delivered' to its clients and that education is a highly manpower-intensive process. A second important feature of the service (which has already been mentioned in the last chapter) is that it has a history of massive expansion from World War II to the 1970s, a point that has obvious relevance when it comes to sudden cutbacks. Third, though there is a good deal of 'discretion' in one sense, as I have already noted, this is not a service that can be turned on or off at will: education is hedged about with virtually immutable statutory commitments to provide certain services. Fourth, unlike defence, education is characterized by long institutional linkages in the creation and delivery of policy.

All of these characteristics affect the ability of central government to make radical cuts in education spending. For example, manpower is easily the largest element of cost and it is not readily hireable and fireable to balance the books: even before legislative measures extending formal job security over a wide range of employments, teachers and many ancillary staff of local education authorities had security of tenure. This means that natural wastage of staff is the main hope of securing savings, and this is not instantly achievable: local authorities must plan any reduction that they want over a long period of time.

To talk of planned reductions, of course, relates to another characteristic of education as a service that was mentioned earlier — namely the fact that education has steadily expanded over a long period until the very recent past, meaning that assumptions of continuing growth have become deeply embedded. These assumptions are difficult to remove suddenly, and indeed there is no logical point at which educational expansion ceases to be desirable. Even now, despite the enormous expansion of the education system since 1945, a number of policies and aspirations remain unfulfilled, and a good case can be made for further expansion. For example, Britain's recruitment levels of students for higher education are still dramatically lower than those of the USA or of such comparable European countries as Sweden. Similarly, there is still an unfulfilled commitment on the statute book to provide compulsory part-time education for pupils between the ages of 16 and 18. Again, there is still unsatisfied demand for places for pupils of nursery school age.

Much of the expansion of education in the recent past has been fuelled by rising aspirations and new conceptions of the benefits that education might convey, as well as by demographic factors (the increase of the school-age population as a result of the various 'baby bulges' after 1945). A belief developed that education could create a richer and more productive economy, creating an expansionist ethos reflected in such grandiose phrases as 'half our future' (the title of the 1963 Newsom Report on secondary education). It would take the skills of an historian rather than of a political scientist to explain how expansion of the education service became accepted as a goal of policy, and what part was played in that process by social expectations and professional arguments. However it came about, the assumption that educational expansion was a 'good thing' and likely to be productive was strong enough to affect not only Ministers of Education but also Chancellors of the Exchequer and the officials who advised them. It is an astonishing story of public, political and administrative commitment to, or at least acceptance of, the expansion of a service whose products are wholly indirect and invisible, and the effectiveness of which is largely immeasurable. Expansion extended as far as the 1972 White Paper (*Education: A Framework for Expansion,* 1972) produced by Margaret Thatcher, cumulatively creating a greatly expanded institutional network embracing a large number of entrenched stakeholders.

Equally puzzling as an historical question is the swift subsequent deceleration in the growth of the system, and the erosion of confidence in education's social and productive functions in the 1970s. The deceleration in spending growth is demonstrated in Table 6.1 (p. 128), which contrasts state education spending with defence spending as percentages of GNP between 1948 and 1979. This table shows that state education spending doubled as a percentage of GNP between the early 1950s and the late 1960s and overtook defence spending in terms of the proportion of GNP involved. Since the early 1970s, education spending remained more or less on a plateau, absorbing a relatively constant proportion of GNP until 1979, when a sharp decline can be observed.

Loss of confidence in education in the 1970s was not just something taking place in the minds of Conservative politicians; it also extended to client groups such as potential undergraduate students (for example, there has been a fall in recruitment rates for higher education from 13 per cent to 11.8 per cent). The rise and fall of the ethos of educational expansionism raises the same sort of questions about the interplay between social expectations (perhaps linked to rising unemployment from 1971 onwards), ideas in good currency and policy development as those discussed by Maurice Wright for public spending generally in Chapter 1.

It is one thing to move from a pattern of spending growth to a plateau, as happened to education spending in the 1970s. It is another thing to move off the plateau in a downward direction. Government's ability to do so is restricted by such factors as its statutory commitment to provide full-time education for all pupils between 5 and 16 years old, and to all who present themselves voluntarily for education until the age of 18. All students accepted for advanced work in higher education are eligible for financial support from government. It is true that once one moves outside the zone of compulsory schooling, the scope for changes in policy is in principle greater. But it has become part of the conventional wisdom, since the Robbins Report (*Higher Education,* 1963), that higher education will be governed by the mis-named principle of 'social demand', which states that all qualified candidates will find places. It is difficult to judge what might be the political consequences of going back on this, by limiting provision so that some qualified candidates might fail to find places in higher education. But no vote-conscious government would take such a step lightly.

It is important to distinguish those cuts in education spending that are mainly due to falling numbers and fall in social demand, from those that arise from changes in the norms affecting the *quality* of education provision. The latter are more affected by hard times than the former, where government's ability to make drastic cuts in education spending is hedged about with statutory restriction. I shall be returning to this point.

Even in the case of changes in norms reducing educational quality, central government is limited in its room for manoeuvre by the institutional fabric of the system. The largest area of the educational sector, that of publicly provided primary and secondary schools, constitutes a multi-level system. A 'level' can be defined as the point in a system that brings its own values into decision-making and has authority to pursue policies and practices largely based on those values (Becher and Kogan, 1980, Chapter 10). In this sense, each school is part of a system that has authoritative levels at the tiers of central government, local authority and school; within the school each individual teacher constitutes a further level, and he or she may also work within an intra-school level of a department or a tutorial house.

Thus local authorities are legally responsible for creating and controlling school curricula. But these powers and responsibilities are delegated — in law to the school governors, but in practice to the head teacher. In his turn, the head teacher increasingly shares his authority to create the curriculum with members of the teaching staff through various collegial decision procedures. These delegated matters — curriculum and the administration of teaching — are, of course, prime determinants of how resources are used, of how demands for different educational services are generated, and of the ways in which each school interacts with its clients and political milieu, including parents, employers, higher educational institutions and local government voters.

Discretion over service delivery is therefore strong at a number of levels in the system. Policies and the underlying assumptions about what constitutes education, its curriculum and other arrangements, are made incrementally and by amalgams of practices developed at all of the different levels. Moreover, central government recognizes and accepts this state of affairs. Though the Department of Education and Science (DES) and the Welsh Office have recently attempted to give a lead on the creation of a core curriculum and on the self-monitoring of standards, their statements reaffirm that a strong element of discretion should remain at the working levels (see Department of Education and Science and Welsh Office, 1980).

In this section, I have stressed the factors that limit government's scope for imposing cuts on education spending. But education is not just an immovable object. Large-scale changes do in fact occur, created by ministerial fiat. The discretion exercised by teachers and schools is compassed by large and context-setting decisions such as raising the age at which children are legally allowed to leave school, increasing the length of the training period required for teachers and expanding the higher education system. The assumptions and institutional relationships resulting from such decisions are not made in Heaven, but are accidents of history, some of it quite recent. Schools remain to a large extent hierarchically dependent on central authorities, although serious attempts to decentralize the education system have been made in many countries in the recent past (see OECD, 1980). And there are obvious questions to be asked about how discretion and current patterns of institutional relationships are likely to develop in response to the phenomenon of hard times. I shall be addressing this question later in the chapter; but I shall first look at the cuts of the recent past.

## RECENT CHANGES IN EDUCATION SPENDING AND DECISION PROCESSES

Between 1953 and 1973, the total increase for all educational spending in Britain was 265.6 per cent, at constant prices. The average annual rate of increase was over 7 per cent between 1953 and 1964, fell slightly to 5.6 per cent between 1964 and 1970 and rose again to 6.7 per cent between 1970 and 1973. Between 1973 and

1978, educational spending remained on a plateau, with an average increase in real spending of less than 0.1 per cent. (During this latter period, the average annual rise in total public spending was 2.2 per cent at constant prices, with health and social services averaging 2 per cent and defence −2 per cent annual growth — see *The Government's Expenditure Plans 1979/80 to 1982/83,* 1979, Table 12, p. 20). The system thus moved from growth to standstill in the 1970s. The next stage was reached in 1979, when the government for the first time tried to push education off its real spending plateau, as we shall see.

From the mid-1970s, then, the 'mood' on educational spending began to change. The DES began to consider more closely which areas of educational provision it thought to be absolutely essential and to reduce activity in areas deemed to be marginal. This change of mood was not, of course, confined to education: it applied to the whole range of local government services, as we have seen in earlier chapters, and was reflected elsewhere in attempts by central government departments to confront priorities of spending more sharply. So far as education is concerned, the essence of the story can be told from the Expenditure White Paper of November 1979 (*The Government's Expenditure Plans 1980/81,* 1979). Current spending on education by local authorities in Great Britain was estimated to have been £7.7 bn. for 1978/79; it was expected to be £7.8 bn. for 1979/80; and the planned figure for 1980/81 was £7.4 bn. A general reduction of 2 per cent was thus prescribed, in line with that prescribed for the public sector as a whole.

Throughout the periods of expansion since World War II, education spending, as in other policy areas (Heclo and Wildavsky, 1974) was controlled by bargained changes at the margin rather than by any process of synoptic or wide-sweep rational planning. Moreover, in bargaining for extra spending or defending itself from spending cuts during financial squeezes, the DES was not only facing the Treasury; it also had a complex task of 'demand articulation' for education spending in negotiation with the local authority and teacher associations and with other bodies such as the University Grants Committee.

The last point is important. Throughout the expansionist era, the process of expenditure negotiation began deep in the womb of the educational consultative system; in fact, long-term consultations helped to formulate the expansionist programmes to which I have referred. The public spending decisions with their consequences in Rate Support Grant and other grants-in-aid could be seen as a formal outcome of norms that were negotiated within the educational world. The fabric of consultation was preserved more or less intact when education spending moved from growth onto a plateau (in terms of proportion of GNP) in the 1970s; but the public spending allocations of 1979, attempting to move education spending off that plateau, constituted a major challenge to the traditional consultative process.

One has to look a long way back to find parallels to this development. Possibly the 'Geddes' axe' of the 1920s was the last clear case of government moving straight out of a bargaining relationship and into unilateral decisions on policy interlinked with public expenditure decisions. Given the novelty of this experience for those involved in 1979, we might have expected a degree of conflict when 'inertia commitments' meet unusually pre-emptive demands for spending cuts. It is therefore particularly interesting to observe the decisions made in 1979, after the change in government from Labour to Conservative and the demand for further public spending cuts.

The decision process continued — outwardly, at least — to be collaborative or at least consultative. Through the mechanism of the Expenditure Steering Group for Educational Services (a committee of the Consultative Council on Local Government Finance), the DES and local authority representatives jointly considered how cuts in education spending of 2½, 5 or 7 per cent might work out. On the basis of the figures given in *The Government's Expenditure Plans 1979/80 to 1982/83* (January 1979), the education service was required to produce spending cuts of £300 m. (out of a total of £600 m. for local government as a whole).

The alternatives discussed, and the reactions to them, help to illustrate the way in which the discussion was limited by conceptions of what was educationally and politically desirable. For example, one possibility was to reduce staffing levels in primary and secondary schools, leading to considerable savings but also to redundancy for 45,000 teachers. Not surprisingly, this course was not taken. Instead, ministers looked for items that seemed more 'marginal' to the education system, on the basis of their political judgement as Conservative politicians. What they decided was to relieve local authorities from their statutory obligations to provide free or wholly subsidized school meals, school transport and nursery classes.

In fact, these items turned out to be far from politically marginal, in terms of the forces that mobilized against the proposals; indeed, in attempting to break out of statutory restrictions on spending cuts, the government was treading a path full of pitfalls. I shall come back to this point; but it is also interesting to notice the possibilities for spending cuts that do not seem to have been seriously considered at this time. For example, making staff redundant would have meant breaking contracts of employment, as was explained earlier, involving heavy compensation payments, which might push spending up in the short term. The 'natural', or least painful, way of making staff savings is to freeze posts when people retire or leave, and this tends to mean that some of the first in are likely to be the first out, in contrast to the traditional 'last in, first out' formula for labour cutbacks in industry.

Far more politically attractive than large-scale redundancies is the idea of making administrative costs bear the brunt of spending cuts. But this also turns out to be not such an easy answer as it might seem at first sight. This issue will be discussed further, in the context of cuts in social services generally, in the next chapter. As far as education is concerned, of the 1 million people employed in the service by local authorities in Britain, less than 30,000 are administrators in town halls. Moreover, between 1973/74 and 1978/79 administration's share of the total education budget fell by £40 m. from 4 per cent to 3½ per cent. Many local authorities had already suffered from earlier changes in Rate Support Grant and had had a hard look at medium-term methods of reducing costs through rationalizing school meals services, cutting down on heating systems and failing to replace administrative staff, even though the duties of such staff had in fact grown in response to increasing pressures for more open politics and government in education. The proliferation of open forums, consultative documents and more activity by school governing bodies, means more rather than less administration. Far from bureaucracy being a rich potential source of cuts, the sums to be saved by further cutbacks in this area were likely to be relatively trivial.

If redundancies and administrative cuts are difficult or expensive, politicians might expect the fall in school rolls (which began in the late 1970s as a result of a declining birth rate) to make the work of spending cuts easier. But the education system does not shed staff and accommodation automatically in response to falling school rolls; in spite of a prospective reduction of 750,000 pupil places, nothing like a proportionate reduction in the use of school accommodation has taken place (Lady Young, 1980). The DES had hoped that 475,000 places in temporary accommodation and 275,000 in permanent accommodation would disappear by 1982 (from a cost-cutting point of view, it was in some ways particularly desirable to eliminate temporary classrooms since they cost five times as much to heat as permanently built rooms). But schools were reluctant to lose their temporary or old-fashioned buildings, no matter how under-used they were. Nor have staffing reductions automatically resulted from falling school rolls. This can be explained partly in terms of local political pressures against school closures and amalgamations and partly in terms of the institutional strengths, to which I have already referred, that make high-level decisions difficult to implement at the working level.

Drastic changes do not come naturally in the mainstream of educational activity because such activity is continuous. Unlike, say, defence or construction projects, educational activities have no clear beginning or end. Since they follow a repetitive cycle, changes have to be planned well in advance. It is true that projects in bricks and stone can be cancelled or postponed, but the scope for savings here is fairly small, since less than 5 per cent of annual education spending is on capital goods. Similarly, the scope for savings by eliminating one-off items of spending (such as the Centre for Educational Disadvantage, which was axed as part of the 'Pliatzky purge' described in Chapter 5, though Labour local authorities subsequently tried to keep it alive) is relatively small in this field. Real cuts essentially mean getting rid of people and of the buildings they inhabit. But the traditional consultative process is hardly geared to making quantum cuts of this type.

## SOME INTERPRETATIONS: THE IMPLICATIONS OF SPENDING CUTS FOR CENTRAL—LOCAL RELATIONSHIPS

The ways in which the 2 per cent cuts described above were achieved indicate changes in intentions and style rather than in the mechanics or underlying relationships between central government and local authorities in education. It was not new for the central authorities to earmark areas for cuts or extra spending within educational budgets (for example, the 1979 Expenditure White Paper (*The Government's Expenditure Plans 1979/80 to 1982/83,* 1979) had assumed that there should be 85,000 more nursery places and that it was necessary to have a margin of 9,000 teachers beyond that needed to sustain pupil—teacher ratios). But local authorities did not participate in the decision that £600 m. might be saved from their spending: they were not invited to demonstrate whether they could do without that sum or not. That judgement came from somewhere in the higher levels of the political system and was taken as a given. Quite apart from the way that such aggregate figures were plucked out of the air and what they implied in terms of reduced levels of local authority services, the local authorities objected to the way that the November 1979 expenditure White Paper earmarked savings. They feared that it might create the impression that no reduction in service need take place in any area where savings were not explicitly earmarked (or hypothecated) in central government's spending White Paper, thus making the political management of cuts more difficult for local authorities and reducing their scope for manoeuvre.

Other departures from the previous pattern may be noted. Central government was for the first time aiming at an absolute reduction in expenditure — thus cutting into 'base-spending', in the well-known incremental budgeting jargon. Moreover, whereas the specification of extra nursery places and a margin of teachers are hypothecations well within the limits of consensus between central government and local authorities, charging for school transport and the other earmarked cuts was of an entirely different order. A further departure was the plan to introduce a new grant scheme for financing local authorities, incorporating penalties for local authorities that exceed stated levels of rate-borne expenditure. This was discussed in Chapter 4, and has important implications for the traditional pattern of discretion over service delivery in education.

Up till now, the technical data amassed by DES as a background to bargaining on educational spending at the centre of government (identifying separately the resources required to maintain standards from those needed to improve standards) have not changed very much. But cutting a service hitherto accustomed to expansion inevitably leads to a change in the atmosphere in which negotiations take place. Whenever spending cuts are in prospect, fantasy statements variously and picturesquely known as 'sore thumbs' and 'bleeding stumps' will be produced, exaggerating the potentially disastrous effects of proposed cuts or suggesting that cuts will have to be made in areas where they are least likely to be accepted (tactics that are discussed further in the next chapter). Statements such as these help to establish the boundaries of reality within which the real discussion might take place. For example, those outside the DES—local authority negotiations in 1979/80 (and particularly those inside the teacher associations) might be more frightened that teachers would be made redundant or that nursery classes would close, than those who studied at first hand the cuts that central government negotiators were proposing. A more obvious and realistic case was the set of statements made by university vice-chancellors in 1979/80 about the likely effects of rises in fees for overseas students on various self-proclaimed centres of excellence in higher education.

Other effects of expenditure standstill or reduction are less dramatic than the closures or redundancies emphasized in 'sore thumb' portrayals of the process. Items of importance to schools may be disregarded in central negotiations because they are marginal in spending terms. Book allowances, sabbatical leave and in-service training for teachers, a reduction in postal communications with parents and others or school outings, are examples of items that are well within government's statutory limits of manoeuvre; they may seem too trivial for ministers or their officials to defend, but they are central to the quality of education. Their restriction does more to squeeze the operating discretion given to individual teachers than such larger-scale reductions as the removal of a teaching post. But in a political climate of tax revolts and hostility to public spending, cries of anguish about 'marginal' items of this kind may not be listened to. Indeed, if they are heard, they may be taken as evidence that policies of public spending cuts are beginning to work. The same process of reduction that is seen by some as painful and debilitating amputation is seen by others as healthful pruning or slimming.

Apart from the familiar 'sore thumb' argument and the sacrifice of items perceived at the centre to be marginal or trivial, one might expect the onset of pressures for spending cuts to bring out 'fairy gold' arguments, to the effect that spending now will create savings later. After all, the whole case for increasing educational spending in the past was based on the argument that a stronger economy based on a more qualified and better motivated work force would result. But ultimately such arguments require supporting facts to carry conviction; and in fact there are virtually no examples that educational lobbyists can produce to show that spending now would mean savings later (this could apply to teacher redundancies, of course, but that is hardly an argument likely to be advanced by educational lobbyists). Attempts to demonstrate that better staffing ratios in schools produce better learning, or reduce juvenile delinquency, or make people more productive, have always been at the level of impressions gained by those involved, rather than of data hard enough to convince the Treasury sceptic. There is no analogy in education to the arguments successfully produced by some health authorities to the effect that transferring revenue costs into capital spending, by modernizing old plant, will lead to considerable reductions in maintenance costs.

## Effects on central administrators

The effects of the change from expansion to cutbacks on central administrators involved in education might be supposed to be dramatic in the short term, but they can only be surmised here. It is difficult, though, to match observation with the assumptions contained in a number of American economic theories of bureaucratic behaviour, such as that of Niskanen (1971), to the effect that bureaucrats (usually successfully) seek to maximize their personal utility in the form of budgets and payrolls. The determinant influences on the cuts I have been describing seem to have come from ministers, not officials. Whilst officials worked on the cuts, tested their feasibility and influenced the outcomes, the decisions about what was central and what was marginal were made by ministers. As we have seen, they decided, as part of an overall political strategy, that places in nursery classes, cheap school meals, free milk and transport were less desirable than (say) reductions in personal taxation or government grants to assist able students to attend private schools.

Indeed, there are two possible ways of explaining why it is difficult to apply American theories of bureaucratic behaviour to the process of cuts that I described earlier. First, it may well be that the

centre at present, and it is not surprising that resistance is being put up at the working levels. But changes in social expectations may come to affect all levels of the system in the course of time.

Thus the onset of hard times for education led to negotiations of 'irreducible minima' in levels of service that should be protected from cuts; the fall in school rolls even led to allowances for extra costs or diseconomies of scale that might occur as a result of operating with smaller pupil numbers in some cases. But what is defined as 'irreducible' is not necessarily immutable, and it is interesting to note how educational norms can change in response to different economic assumptions. Just as in the period immediately after World War II university teachers could be found as many as nine or ten to a room — hardly the stereotype of academic tranquillity in book-lined studies (Becher and Kogan, 1980, Chapter 2) — so today, step by step, higher education teachers are becoming used to less generous assumptions about staffing ratios. Similarly, there used to be a conventional wisdom that a secondary school should contain between 800 and 1,200 pupils if an adequate range of courses was to be provided. A range of smaller school sizes is now thought to be acceptable. Both central government and those running the services at local authority level yielded to changed demands for education in two ways. They shared in the adjustment of norms among teachers and practitioners, to the effect that 'small is beautiful' for educational establishments — partly, no doubt, a product of bleaker economic times. Similarly, they accepted that the irreducibles could be reduced a bit further, if the alternative was politically too unpleasant to contemplate (for example, in terms of teacher redundancies).

In reaching a different level of service provision, there is interplay between political norms and technical calculations. For example, once two important political decisions had been taken in 1979 — that there should be neither reduction nor improvement in staffing ratios and that diseconomies of scale have to be allowed for (that is, schools need more resources per head as pupil numbers decline), both decisions greatly reducing the scope for savings — the DES was able to calculate the teacher numbers required to meet the needs of a greatly reduced school-age population and the financial savings that could be made. Similarly, having taken the political decision to forgo the 'improvement factor' that had been built into DES calculations about educational provision at least since the time of the 1965 National Plan, it became a technical calculation to estimate what the resulting savings would be. How far even the technical task of educational planning is affected by changing social and political norms cannot be assessed here, though there is an increasing general tendency for policy analysts to consider the value implications as well as the technical feasibility of policy proposals (cf. Wildavsky, 1980).

In the interplay between norms and technicalities, the political impact of changed conditions may take time to be felt. It may be quite easy to accept a standstill statement to the effect that: 'We will not cut your resources as against the work that you must do, but we will allow for no improvements in conditions either' when the statement is first made, perhaps at a moment of crisis. But the lack of change or improvement will become increasingly noticed in a service where improvement has until now been taken for granted as a continuous process: over the last thirty-five years teachers have become used to steady enhancement of staffing ratios, of salaries and of the building stock.

Does the interplay between political norms, practitioner norms and technical factors (adjusting to changes in the school-age population and different rules of the spending game) mean that a change in institutional relationships in the education world has already taken place? On present evidence, highly fragmentary though that is, it appears that no large-scale change in the working of the system has taken place so far. In 1971, Edward Boyle (in Kogan, 1971) could say that educational policy is largely decided as a result of pressures inside the education world. It would appear that that statement remains largely true. Much of what happens now is a projection of historical commitments: the protection of staffing ratios, for example, implies that what teachers have always had, they will continue to have. But nothing need be for ever, as the attack on free school meals as a 'marginal' service has demonstrated: quite well-entrenched institutional positions can be overturned in hard times. In the final section of this chapter, therefore, I try to sketch some of the consequences that continued reduction in scale might have on the political and institutional structure of the education world.

CONTINUING 'HARD TIMES':
WHAT MIGHT HAPPEN?

I shall discuss possible effects on educational politics and institutions of continuing hard times at three levels. First, I shall discuss the subjective nature of educational norms. Second, I shall consider changes well away from the centre of government, within schools and local authorities. Third, I shall consider possible changes at the centre itself.

I have already suggested that assumptions such as what constitutes the optimum size of school, or the appropriate staffing ratio in higher education, begin to bend as pressure of demand from clients diminishes, political support wanes and spending reductions are imposed. Change in political norms is, of course, a process subject to sudden reversals. An attack on a marginal position may all at once convert it into an irreducible, as when Conservative peers and backbench MPs revolted in early 1980 against their own government's decision to charge for school transport. It is a long time since school buses have been so eloquently defended in terms of their contribution to education.

Unexpected reversals on marginal issues are understandable enough. But the larger question of what constitutes the marginal as opposed to the essential and irreducible may have to be reopened if hard times continue. One of the leading assumptions in the cutbacks so far, as we have seen, was that in most cases there would be 'no redundancies'. Even at the time of writing, that promise of continued employment is beginning to weaken as local authorities dismiss school dinner ladies and as more teachers more willingly accept early retirement.

The power of educational institutions has traditionally been strongly geared to the ability of their incumbents to assume permanent tenure. Though cuts in money terms have not directly attacked the tenure of teachers so far, the closure or amalgamation of schools certainly has; and continuing hard times may well make the unthinkables and the irreducibles both thinkable and reducible, particularly as those outside the education service contemplate the drastic reduction in employment prospects for those leaving school or higher education. Ultimately, what is irreducible depends on the balance of political forces and on the economic environment, not on any unavoidable logic of the professional task or of institutional relationships in education.

The second issue concerns changes within school and local authority institutions. Even apart from central government's attempts to cut educational spending, demography has seriously upset the certainty with which schools used to work. To lose 750,000 clients in the schools and to experience slackened rates of demand among potential clients and falling absolute numbers in higher and further education are demoralizing elements, the impact of which is keenly felt in individual institutions. When it comes to closure, institutional and political behaviour may change markedly. One case study of school closure (Wood, 1980) shows how, as closure approached, the head of a school moved from the role of the leading professional — managing an institution, helping to control pupils and working responsibly with the local authority — to that of leader of an articulate pressure group resisting the decisions being made by those above him in the political and managerial system. Local authority leaders who had been used to a consensual acceptance of policies while the educational system was expanding (and even when major changes, such as the amalgamation of selective schools into comprehensive schools, were taking place) found themselves facing almost unmanageable levels of dissent and conflict.

Closure is, of course, the exception. The majority of schools will survive, but with far smaller numbers. Many of them will have to enter into consortium arrangements with other schools, and this type of change may significantly alter the nature of schools as institutions. Traditionally the school has always been the basic institutional unit in education: within its boundaries tasks and priorities have been settled, and it has acquired a distinctive personality and set of political and working relationships of its own. But if schools enter consortia with other schools, the centre of organizational and political gravity will rise above the single institution and lodge somewhere within the governing mechanisms for the consortium. Client groups will therefore become more scattered *vis-à-vis* producers, the authority of head teachers will be diminished and the institutional allegiance of individual teachers may change if (to take a hypothetical example) a teacher is partly employed in a school and partly in a sixth form centre that is the result of a consortium of schools. Within schools themselves, the atmosphere may change. In the years of expansion, there has been a prodigious growth in posts at middle and senior level, so that quite young people have become heads of teaching departments, deputy heads or even heads of houses. But as the system contracts, the familiar phenomenon of the 'age block' will develop. Promotion opportunities for teachers below the relatively youthful incumbents of middle and senior posts will be sharply reduced, creating intergenerational divisions among teachers in schools, which may well affect their mode of working and are likely to find their way into educational politics.

Turning now to the third issue, what might be the impact of changes such as these on the decision process within DES? That, again, is likely to depend more on politics than on any ineluctable logic of the educational system. So far, the response of the analytic machinery within DES to the onset of 'hard times' for education has not been dramatic. There have been qualitative analyses of the effects of demographic change and of a range of policy options for handling reductions, and there have also been analyses of curriculum and associated organizational problems. But, interestingly, there have been no analyses of the institutional and career consequences of change. An analytic system that has been accustomed to handling incremental growth over a long period can perhaps go into reverse without too much difficulty when growth becomes decremental; but quantum cuts are another matter and if that is what is in prospect for education, a knowledge base and analytic capacity rather different from that used in the past may be needed. Indeed, as Maurice Wright's remarks on policy planning systems in Chapter 1 indicated, central government may need to increase rather than decrease its analytic capacity when it is attempting to disengage from commitments to activities and services. For example, the DES is unlikely to jettison its main statutory commitments to educational provision, but continuing hard times might well lead to increased central monitoring of the actions taken by field authorities, not simply as an advisory service but for the purpose of more authoritative central prescription and control of the education system.

This chapter has been concerned primarily with the impact of financial duress on educational government. As yet, the basic institutional relationships of the educational world do not seem to have changed drastically as education begins to move off the spending plateau of the recent past. It may well be that the discretion traditionally accorded to the operating levels of schools and teachers will remain entrenched even in a continuing period of hard times, since it can plausibly be argued to stem from the basic nature of the teaching—learning process as that is conventionally conceived. But I have also indicated some of the threats to that system that may develop in hard times — by central government pressures to control local government spending more tightly (as discussed in Part II), the possible development of stronger central monitoring capacity, the chipping away of extra-statutory marginal spending items that results in less discretion, and so on. 'Nothing is for ever.' And in this case, as was mentioned earlier, the hard times of the title involve falling demand as a result of demographic changes as well as of economic difficulty, meaning that the system is threatened on two fronts. The position of education in hard times thus involves some rather special circumstances; but sacred cows run the risk of being deconsecrated in other areas too, as the next chapter on social service spending (echoing several of the points made here) will show.

## ACKNOWLEDGEMENTS

This chapter includes material from 'Falling rolls and their impact on schools as social institutions', a paper given at the Annual Conference of the National Association of Head Teachers, Oxford, September 1979. I am grateful for considerable help given by Richard Jameson of the DES and by Rita Hale of the Association of Metropolitan Authorities.

## REFERENCES

Becher, T. and Kogan, M. (1980) *Structure and Process in Higher Education* London, Heinemann

Department of Education and Science and Welsh Office (1980) *A Framework for School Curriculum: Proposals for Consultation by the Secretaries of State for Education and Science and for Wales* London, HMSO

Downs, A. (1957) *An Economic Theory of Democracy* New York, Harper and Row

*Education: A Framework for Expansion* (1972) (Mrs Thatcher's

White Paper) Cmnd. 5174, London, HMSO

Heclo, H. and Wildavsky, A. (1974) *The Private Government of Public Money* London, Macmillan

*Higher Education* (1963) Cmnd. 2154, London, HMSO (Robbins Report)

Klein, R. (1976) 'The politics of public expenditure: American theory and British practice' *British Journal of Political Science* Vol. 6, Part IV, October (also R. Klein, 'A Reply', ibid.)

Kogan, M. (1976) 'The politics of public expenditure by Rudolf Klein: a comment' *British Journal of Political Science* Vol. 6, Part IV, October

Kogan, M. (with E. Boyle and A. Crosland) (1971) *The Politics of Education* Harmondsworth, Penguin Books

Newsom, J. H. (Chairman) (1963) *Half Our Future,* A Report of the Central Advisory Council for Education (England), London, HMSO

Niskanen, W. (1971) *Bureaucracy and Representative Government* Chicago, Aldine Atherton

OECD (1980) *Review of Swedish Educational Reform* Paris·

*The Government's Expenditure Plans 1979/80 to 1982/83* (1979) (Expenditure White Paper) Cmnd. 7439, London, HMSO

*The Government's Expenditure Plans 1980/81* (1979) (Expenditure White Paper) Cmnd. 7746, London, HMSO

Wildavsky, A. (1980) *The Art and Craft of Policy Analysis* London, Macmillan

Wood, T. (1980) 'Falling rolls and the pathology of closure: a study of two schools', MA dissertation, Brunel University

Young, Lady (1980) Speech to Conference of Local Authorities on 'Renewal of Primary Schools', London, July.

CHAPTER EIGHT

# Social Service Spending in a Hostile Environment

by HOWARD GLENNERSTER

Since World War II, social service administrators in Britain have become accustomed to having more resources to allocate year by year. There have certainly been cuts and squeezes from time to time; but these have normally taken the form of cuts in capital programmes or of standstills in recurrent expenditure, which could be seen as temporary phenomena — part of the normal Treasury 'crisis package' produced in response to balance of payments crises. Over the long run, spending on the social services has formed a rising share of public spending, which was in itself taking a rising share of incomes. Table 8.1 demonstrates this point. Until the mid-1970s, this trend was largely made possible by the reduced share of government spending taken by defence and by foreign affairs. Britain's declining world role was used to finance improved standards of social provision — or at least more expensive standards.

The rising cost of social services, however, should not blind us to the fact that the amount of extra real resources that programme managers and local officials have had at their disposal is not as great as the raw expenditure figures might suggest. Social services are manpower- (or, more often, woman-power-) intensive. The impact of the 'relative price effect' in public spending (which was discussed in Chapter 1) is particularly important in the manpower-intensive sectors of health, personal social services and education. Its effect is uneven between one year, or run of years, and the next; but, over

TABLE 8.1
GENERAL GOVERNMENT EXPENDITURE, 1951–1978 (UK BASIS)

| Purposes | 1951 % | 1961 % | 1971 % | 1975 % | 1978 % |
|---|---|---|---|---|---|
| Social security | 12 | 16 | 17½ | 16½ | 22 |
| Health and personal social services | 10 | 10½ | 11½ | 12½ | 12½ |
| Education | 7 | 10 | 12½ | 12½ | 12 |
| Housing | 7 | 5½ | 5 | 8 | 7 |
| *Total social services* | 36 | 42 | 46½ | 49½ | 53½ |
| Defence and external relations | 24 | 18 | 13 | 11 | 13 |
| Other spending | 40 | 40 | 40½ | 39½ | 33½ |
| Total government expenditure | 100 | 100 | 100 | 100 | 100 |
| Use of resources by the social services as a % of GDP | 9.9 | 9.5 | 12.4 | 15.1 | 13.1 |
| Current grants to the personal sector as a % of personal income (pensions and other cash benefits) | 6.0 | 7.5 | 10.0 | 11.4 | 12.5 |
| Total social service spending as a % of Gross Domestic Income | 16 | 17 | 23 | 27 | 28 |

Source: *National Income and Expenditure Blue Books* 1952–1980, London,
        HMSO

the long run, public salaries and wages have kept pace with those in the private sector. Other factors affecting the relative price effect in these sectors have included higher levels of interest rates and land and construction costs. One recent survey suggests that over the period from 1950 to 1978 social service spending as a whole grew by 3.7 per cent per year on average, with social security growing at 4.9 per cent, education at 4.4 per cent, health at 2.6 per cent, personal social services at 5.7 per cent, and housing at 3.7 per cent (Gould and Roweth, 1980). By far the biggest rate of increase relative to the national income took the form of transfer items, such as pensions and other cash benefits and subsidies, which effectively transfer purchasing power from some groups in the population to others. These items, too, are affected by a comparable inbuilt escalator clause. As earnings of the working population rise, so political pressures arise to allow welfare beneficiaries 'to share in the rising national prosperity'. Benefits rates have in fact followed rising earnings fairly closely since the 1950s. Thus the scope for extending the range of benefits or for including more groups has been more limited than the figures might suggest. The significant extensions have been benefits to the disabled and to those who look after them, extra as-of-right benefits to single parents, and the extension of child benefits to parents (to include the first child). Indeed, the latter measure, costly as it appeared at first sight, was less a new departure in public spending than an exercise in shuffling tax allowances and benefits, for the new child benefits replaced tax allowances formerly enjoyed by tax-paying parents.

Nevertheless, even when all these qualifications have been made, the period up to 1976 was one of fairly steady incremental real growth in social service spending in Britain. The period since 1976 has been very different. The Labour government of 1974—79 planned to lower the rate of growth in health and personal social service spending to about 2 per cent per year, and both education and housing were to fall in absolute terms. In the end there was a very substantial fall in housing expenditure, a smaller fall in education spending, but a major increase in social security expenditure, partly reflecting higher spending on unemployment benefit and partly the switch from tax allowances to cash benefits for children. The subsequent Conservative government, in its Public Expenditure White Paper of March 1980 (*The Government's Expenditure Plans 1980/81 to 1983/84,* 1980) envisaged further major falls in housing expenditure, small increases in net spending on health and personal social services after taking account of increased revenue from user charges, a modest rise in social security spending (though this included real reductions in the levels of short-term benefits) and some further absolute decline in education spending. These changes are summarized in Table 8.2 and are further discussed in Glennerster (1980). How will this new resource climate affect social administrators and social planners?

TABLE 8.2
SOCIAL SERVICE SPENDING IN 1975/76, 1979/80, 1983/84
(GB BASES, 1979 SURVEY PRICES)

| Programme | 1975/76 (actual) £m. | 1979/80 (actual) £m. | 1983/84 (planned) £m. |
|---|---|---|---|
| Social security | 15,378 | 18,890 | 19,600 |
| Health and personal social services | 8,620 | 9,067 | 9,500 |
| Education | 9,757 | 9,654 | 8,670 |
| Housing | 6,299 | 5,372 | 2,790 |

Source: *The Government's Expenditure Plans 1980/81 to 1983/84* (1980)

## THE PRESUMPTION OF GROWTH

A recurring theme of this book is that the presumption of growth in a relatively stable economic and political environment is deeply embedded, not merely in administrative and budgetary practice, but in the framework of ideas that political scientists have used to analyse resource decisions. Against this background, Conservative politicians in particular argue that cuts will be good for the public sector; and indeed the notion that cuts may be beneficial for government performance has been put forward by academic commentators both in Britain and in the USA (see, for example, Wright, 1980, and Charles Levine's symposium in *Public Administration Review,* 1978). The argument is that public authorities faced with a tight financial situation will be forced to adopt more efficient appraisals of their spending.

Thus Stewart (1980) suggests that the management process can no longer focus on the increment. Consensus through bargaining is reduced because there is less to bargain for. Organizations will respond, Stewart says, by stressing the need to make choices and will reappraise their existing activities — a process more liable to produce conflict and hence clearer lines of authority. Writing on 'zero-based budgeting' begins from very similar premises. Indeed, politicians making cuts in public spending typically argue that the outcome will be greater efficiency: 'toning up' and 'cutting the fat' are the typical phrases. The more stern the financial climate, the more rationally organizations will react.

Do actual results match these expectations? Later sections of this chapter will question this view. Possible evidence in support of the 'cut-the-fat hypothesis' is provided by Hinings *et al.* (1980), reporting studies of the ways that local authorities responded to financial constraints in the 1970s. These authors suggest that fewer resources will make local authorities adopt a wider and more 'rational' review of the budget base. They produce a rationality index that lists a number of budgetary and analytical procedures that constitute, in their view, a rational mode of procedure for organizations under financial stress. These include: a strategic analysis of expenditure (classification of estimates into base and other items); manpower forecasts; a strategic analysis of demands for services; an explicit statement of objectives; and policy or issue analysis.

They conclude that in the mid-1970s more authorities acted in ways defined above as 'rational', and hence that '. . . a contraction in the supply of resources widens the parameters of budgetary review *and* introduces a greater measure of rationality . . . budgetary famine, at least for a time, decreases the likelihood of incremental budgeting'. On the other hand, Wright (1980) comes to the opposite conclusion about the process of public expenditure planning in Whitehall. He contrasts the rational planning ideals originally set for PESC against more recent developments that appear to reflect 'incrementalism' rather than 'rationality' — the emphasis on cash limits and on the next financial year rather than a longer time-horizon.

My own view of what in practice has been happening to social service planning is more in line with Wright's conclusion than with the results claimed by Hinings *et al.* But more fundamentally I believe that the whole antithesis between *more* and *less* rationality is unhelpful. My suggestion in this chapter is that it may be useful to try to distinguish between different kinds of rationality that different actors or interests may follow. The ideal type of rationality defined by Greenwood *et al.* (1980), by Hinings *et al.* (1980) and by Wright (1980) represents the view of the 'strategic coordinator', in Lindblom's phrase. But other actors have a different view of 'rational' action. Politicians or bureaucrats in charge of spending departments may see things differently, as may service professionals and other employees organized in professional associations or trade unions.

Consumers and their watchdog organizations have interests that suggest a different perception of rational behaviour.

We can therefore distinguish at least four different types of rationality: what I shall call 'strategic' rationality, similar in kind to that discussed by Wright and by Greenwood *et al.*; political rationality; professional rationality; and consumer rationality. My hypothesis is that in a period of relative economic abundance some *modus vivendi* is possible among these different approaches to resource allocation. This was reflected in the social planning systems that emerged in the 1970s. But in a period of restraint there is increasing conflict about how to allocate resources and growing incompatibilities among the differing forms of rationality. Which mode dominates will depend on the power-relations in particular contexts, but in general the strategic coordinator mode is likely to be overwhelmed by the others. In developing this view, I shall confine myself to social welfare planning and resource allocation.

## COMPROMISE IN AN ERA OF GROWTH

Resource allocation for all the social services in Britain begins with the PESC system. PESC procedures were originally designed to ensure that the demands made by the public sector did not interfere with broader economic interests. The *quid pro quo* for spending departments was an assurance that their programmes would not be continually chopped and changed. The spending department politicians and their senior officials were given rules of the game in competing for a limited overall increment. They used and orchestrated the demands made on them by the professional organizations involved in service delivery, by the client organizations, or by their watchdogs like the 'poverty lobby'. The rational—comprehensive methodology that was originally envisaged for PESC was watered down and evolved into a set of rules and procedures that enabled these competing interests to bargain in a more informed way within an extended time-horizon. Once a slice of the budget was gained, a department was assured in principle that the *volume* of resources agreed upon in the previous PESC round would be maintained despite price increases (Glennerster, 1974).

In the early 1970s, after what appeared to be the relative success of this strategy up to about 1970, various attempts were made to

extend the process within spending departments and down into the
local authorities and into public agencies like water authorities, the
Manpower Services Commission and the National Parks. More
than twenty separate planning systems of one kind or another were
developed. Many of them, concerned with expenditure planning,
were essentially extensions of the PESC cycle (Glennerster, 1979).
They had a time-scale tied to PESC, a three- or four-year operational
programme, sometimes paralleled by a ten- or fifteen-year strategic
plan where major capital schemes were involved. Such systems
entailed exactly the same kind of compromise trade-offs. Financial
'guidelines' were set by central government that had the effect of
bringing local spending expectations into line with the national
expenditure targets. In return there was some promise that this
level of resources would be available in the long run to give some
basis for forward planning. Discussion between the authorities and
interested client groups or professional organizations could be
conducted within a 'realistic' framework and a general process of
mutual education could begin. The publication of and debate on
the document *Priorities for Health and Personal Social Services*
(DHSS, 1976) and the modified version published a year later (*The
Way Forward,* DHSS, 1977) were good examples of the way in which
the DHSS sought to ration the potentially limitless demands of
health care (Booth, 1979). A similar process had begun with housing
investment programmes and social service department planning
statements.

This approach to social planning, however, was very dependent
on some measure of stability in the outcome of the PESC rounds;
and, as the economic crisis deepened and its fluctuations grew in
scale, any attempt to insulate the public sector increased the burden
of adjustment the private sector had to bear, and that became
unacceptable. Wildavsky has summarized the problem:

> Budgeting by volume is, first of all, an effort by elements of the
> public sector to invade the private sector. What budgeting by
> volume says in effect, is that the public sector will be protected
> against inflation by getting its agreed level of services before
> other needs are met . . . To the degree that price changes are
> automatically absorbed into budgets, a certain volume of
> activity is guaranteed. To the degree agencies have to absorb
> inflation, the real level of their activity declines. Multi-year

budgeting in cash terms diminishes the relative size of the public sector, leaving the private sector larger. [1978, p. 502]

The real issue is the size of the public and private sectors, and their capacity to operate effectively in the context of inflation.

With the coming of the cash limit regime for public expenditure control, the emphasis of the public expenditure cycle has shifted more heavily to its control function and away from its original planning role (Wright, 1980). What effect might this change in climate have upon the way social welfare institutions allocate resources and determine priorities? Let us first examine the case advanced by the strategic coordinators.

*Strategic rationality*

If we abstract the ideal components of strategic rational planning advocated in the National Health Service planning system, the housing investment programmes and the personal social services, they can be seen to consist of five major elements:

(i)   A comprehensive assessment of the needs and demands of different client groups.

(ii)  An appraisal of medium- and long-term service priorities within the context of 'realistic' resource guidelines set by central government.

(iii) The allocation of central government resources among geographical areas according to their relative needs, 'objectively' determined.

(iv)  The coordination of plans for service provision among agencies concerned with the same client groups or where activities are interrelated.

(v)   The translation of such forward planning into a set of consistent operational plans, capital programmes, staffing requirements and revenue budgets.

Rarely, if ever, was this ideal achieved; but logically neither a standstill budget nor even a reduced budget invalidates such an approach. Indeed, the harsher the constraints, the greater may be the logical case for each element, as is suggested by some of the authors referred to earlier. Demands for improvements in service provision tend to arise in a fairly haphazard way: from a new research study, a public scandal about a subnormality hospital or a bad case of child battering. Where growth is in prospect it is reasonable, if not optimal, to meet each demand as it comes, in the knowledge that other groups' turn will come when the political timing is right. On the other hand, if a service is to be cut, the logic and justice of reviewing all needs afresh is more compelling. This is the case for zero-based budgeting. Contraction may encourage strategic coordinators to ask precisely what each programme is intended to achieve. It may provide an occasion for identifying current activities or institutions that can be phased out; the 1979 NHS study of acute beds in London is a good example (DHSS, 1979). The lower the central government funds available, the stronger the case for ensuring that such funds go to those authorities with the greatest social problems. Similarly, the case for shifting the responsibility for care from high-cost provision, such as hospitals, to lower-cost care in the community becomes more compelling and so, therefore, does the case for greater cooperation between local authority social service departments and the National Health Service.

Finally, it is much more important in a period of financial constraint to make sure that the revenue consequences of capital programmes are fully taken into account. In periods of regular annual growth in the budget, problems arising from miscalculation — or no calculation at all — can be met by shelving some other planned growth. With nil growth or cuts, the result of such a miscalculation may mean an empty hospital or old people's home — a public monument to administrative cock-up. Thus all five elements in the foregoing list of good planning practices logically seem to be more important in a period of restraint.

This is the kind of view expressed by people in 'strategic coordinator' roles in local and health authorities and central departments. It is, however, only one way to view a 'rational' response to a harsh economic climate. Politicians who have to undertake the unpleasant task may react rather differently. In the section that follows, I attempt to extract from the experience of 1976—80 the main political strategies involved in cutting public spending.

*Political rationality: opening gambits*

We may suppose that national politicians committed to cuts in public spending will wish to make the maximum cuts with the minimum of unpopularity for their party nationally and for themselves as departmental heads. Past studies of how politicians and civil servants in Whitehall behave in such a context (notably Heclo and Wildavsky, 1974) are based on a financial climate rather less hostile to government spending than that of 1979/80. But they can help us some of the way, in identifying a range of well-tried moves based, in the first instance, on the assumption that the cuts will be a passing phase. Six of these are listed below.

*Fairy gold* — or making cuts in the future rather than in the present. Particularly in the early 1970s, ministers in spending departments and their advisers agreed to reduce programme spending two years ahead or more, hoping that the financial climate would have changed by the time the future arrived — as indeed was the case in the mid-1970s. To some extent this also happened with the 1976 cuts, and this is a theme that we have encountered elsewhere in this book.

*Sore thumbs.* This is the time-honoured practice (also described by Heclo and Wildavsky, 1974) by which spending departments, when asked to suggest spending cuts, offer up their most popular projects or ones that would cause much political embarrassment if they were cut, in the hope that some other department will lose its programme instead. This is such a familiar stratagem that its mileage may be limited; and, if the Treasury is determined enough, the counter-strategy is to accept such offers at face value and thus inflict the maximum pain on the offending department. Notice, however, that both tactics are the very reverse of a rational consideration of social priorities in a strategic coordinator sense.

*Sell your assets.* Faced with the difficulty of making sufficient 'real cuts', ministers may agree to cosmetic arrangements like the sale of New Town sites. These have short-term attractions, but 'pawnshop' tactics of this kind may cut off future income flows while only postponing the evil day as regards cuts in current spending. Their 'rationality' in a long-run economic sense is therefore highly debatable.

*Charge.* Public spending figures are expressed and bargained about in *net* terms — i.e. after user charges have been deducted. If a spending department wishes to preserve the 'real fabric' of a service, it will look to any existing charges it levies for its services to see how far they can be increased, or to any possibility of extending user charges. There is a long history to this approach in the Health Service, dating from 1951 to the tactics followed by the DES and DHSS in their initial responses to the Conservative government elected in 1979. In the latter case, the NHS budget and the priorities of the 1974—79 Labour government, as embodied in previous documents, emerged relatively unscathed from the Public Expenditure White Papers of late 1979 and early 1980 (*The Government's Expenditure Plans 1980/81,* 1979; *The Government's Expenditure Plans 1980/81 to 1983/84,* 1980). But this was achieved at the price of a significant rise in prescription and dental charges. School meals prices, charges on school transport and overseas students' fees were the DES equivalent. Because the 1974—79 Labour government had avoided increasing these charges for a number of years previously, the savings in the first year were useful. It is not a trick, however, that can be repeated to such effect. Charges form a very small proportion of revenue. The old, children and the poor, who are usually exempted from charges, form a high proportion of those affected — over 40 per cent. Thus over half the prescriptions are still free. Moreover, if the charges became really penal or extensive, the 'real fabric' of the service is affected and its very rationale is undermined (Parker, 1976, 1980; Maynard, 1979).

*Cut capital, not current spending.* Here we move nearer to real results. Deferred building programmes do save real money now and will result in lower debt charges. They are certainly easiest to make in political terms, since no one need be sacked and few people will notice. The heaviest burden of cuts in 1976 fell on capital account; and similarly capital spending took the brunt of the Conservative government's cuts of 1979/80. However politically rational this tactic may be, it is not necessarily the strategically rational thing to do. Inefficient plant and old geographical patterns and uses are preserved.

*Protect the base.* The first instinct of any service manager or spending department minister is to protect what exists now. Since the Public Expenditure White Papers have always included costed provisions for new programmes or for improvements to existing ones, it has been possible to achieve significant reductions in these planning totals by abandoning or postponing improvements — not as a sham, as in the 'fairy gold' tactic, but for real. Most of the 'cuts' in the February 1976 White Paper (*Public Expenditure to 1979/80,* 1976) were of this kind. The readjustment called for in service providers' expectations was real enough, but all that was being envisaged was a standstill in spending in real terms. As a short-term expedient, this is reasonable enough. As a long-term strategy it would greatly reduce the effectiveness of an organization by ossifying it.

So far, I am suggesting that many of the opening gambits used by participants in the budgeting process have been likely to confuse rather than to further an objective appraisal of options from a strategic perspective. However, most of these tactics are also unlikely to produce any lasting or significant results, and the years of 1976 and of 1979/80 give us an opportunity to observe a further stage of political strategy when spending cuts are for real.

### Political rationality: real cuts

*Equal pain for all.* The strategy that causes least political cost to ministers around the Cabinet table or council chamber is to be even-handed and call for a 5 or 10 per cent cut all round. Certainly this does happen, but rarely in a pure form. Indeed, experience in 1976 and later suggests that in practice politicians often are prepared to accept a differential set of priorities among departments. Such judgements may be fairly crude, but they can be made.

*Rough justice.* The scale of cuts imposed on the different social policy departments in February 1976 reflected the differing demographic demands being put on each (Glennerster, 1977). This meant that education suffered absolute cuts, even with real spending per pupil being maintained (in fact, the DES was able to show that falling school rolls increased costs per pupil, and secured some concessions as a result). The DHSS, on the other hand, using their programme budget, were able to show the cost consequences of an ageing population and the growing demands it put on services. This helped to give DHSS a relative advantage (Banks, 1979). Similarly, the political priorities in the Conservative spending plans of 1979/80 were also fairly clear, with defence and law and order given clear preference over other services. It may be that local authorities have responded to a demand for real cuts by more strategic appraisal, as Greenwood *et al.* (1980) report. But such an impression might well be gained by examining plans cast in volume terms and the publicly stated intentions, rather than by looking at the outcomes, or at the less obvious strategies that are pursued to make spending cuts stick.

*Cut bureaucracy.* Naturally, administrative costs will be first on the agenda of any politician faced with the reality of cutting real spending. But he soon discovers that they form a disappointingly small percentage of the budget and are difficult to achieve in reality. The most vulnerable often turn out to be the bureaucrats whom bureaucrats do not like — the planners and research staff. Niskanen's (1971) account of the logic of bureaucratic production would suggest that in a period of cuts the core bureaucracy will remain unscathed, putting up good grounds for its own existence but responding more readily to the need for more distant sacrificial offerings — quangos first, or area health authorities. If the bodies concerned are actually offering informed criticism of the bureaucracy and its political masters they are likely to be high on the list for cuts — the National Institute for Economic and Social Research, or the Centre for Environmental Studies, for example. This is a theme we have already encountered in the discussion of culling quangos in Chapter 5.

*Cut someone else's budget, not your own.* In recent years, the major target for central government economies has been local government. For Whitehall politicians this has the great advantage that they take the credit for reducing tax burdens and attacking the extravagance of others, but leave the real pain and unpopularity to fall elsewhere. Between 1974/75 and 1980/81, local government spending is planned to have fallen by 14 per cent in real terms. Central government, on the other hand, has allowed its own spending to rise by 7.7 per cent.

*Cut by cash limit — or let inflation do the work.* The cash limit regime was intended to remove one of the major reasons for slippage between PESC plans and outcomes in the pre-1976 system. So long as the price estimates in the cash limits were realistic and wages did not outrun the incomes policy guidelines, the system was consistent with the longer-term expenditure and service planning in PESC. However, the first cash limits were fixed below the level of price increases that actually occurred. For that, and other reasons, public expenditure *fell* in real terms by 2.5 per cent, though it had been expected to rise. It was a cut of £1,800 m. in 1979 prices. Actual expenditure in 1977/78 was well down on planned spending for many reasons, but the cash limits cannot be blamed. The pay and price increases that occurred in 1977/78 were in line with the cash limits (HM Treasury, 1979). But the lessons for politicians engaged in spending cuts were instructive. The explicit cuts in volume terms, extracted with much pain, public debate and acrimony, had been surpassed through unannounced cash limit squeezes with very little or no public debate.

The use of cash limits rather than cuts in volume terms as a convenient political vehicle for spending cuts is a theme we have encountered in earlier chapters of this book. Cash limits have been used as a weapon for cutting spending rather than simply for control. For example, the budget speech of June 1979 announced that the government would deal with pay claims in the public services in general by setting cash limits at a level such that 'substantial offsetting economies will have to be found' (*Hansard,* 12 June 1979).

It is this that has made planning even in annual terms so difficult for local and health authorities. For example, when the new Rate Support Grant Order was announced in November 1979, the cash limit attached to it was based on an estimated increase in pay and prices of 13 per cent. But a number of pay awards from the Standing Commission on Pay Comparability were on their way at that time. An addition to the cash limit for this purpose raised it to 17¼ per cent above the base figure — which seemed unlikely to meet the cost of these pay awards or of other price increases. This attempt to avoid responsibility for the cuts is perfectly rational in political terms, but it plays havoc with any attempt to plan service provision even a year ahead.

In defence of cash limits, it is often argued that such a regime merely puts the public sector under the same 'discipline' as the private sector, which receives no automatic public subsidy to make up for inflation. The comparison is not an entirely fair one. Private firms have the option, which they frequently adopt, of raising prices rather than achieving productivity increases overnight or suffering major disruption to their production process. Local authorities have had some way out through their capacity to raise rates, but at the time of writing the government is planning to restrict this option.

The political results can also be perverse. Local authorities are unlikely to take this kind of squeeze lying down and authorities controlled by the party in opposition at Westminster (particularly when it is the Labour party) will wish to make it clear where the political responsibility lies. They may well decide to be more bloody-minded and less ready to economize as a result. Making cuts becomes party betrayal. The behaviour of Lothian region, discussed in Chapter 3, is a case in point; and we shall return to this point in the next chapter.

*Shift public burdens on to private costs.* Clearly, a general shift to a selectivist strategy in social policy is one likely result of the spending restraints currently in force. That is too big an issue to discuss in detail and opens up a broad political debate. One strategy that has the same effect may be less obvious. The idea of community care, whatever its theoretical therapeutic advantage over institutional care, appears to cost less money. That is, it costs the government less money; but this saving is achieved in large part by redistributing the costs of dealing with some types of dependants from the wider community to the families concerned. Of course, that may not be in the least irrational from the strategic coordinator point of view, so long as the results are desired, measured and anticipated; but it is not in the interests of the rational politician making spending cuts to make such consequences explicit. Another example of the same strategy is the proposal to shift responsibility for paying sickness benefits from government to private employers in the first few weeks of sickness. Both cash and the hidden administrative costs are then transferred to the private sector. A similar process has already taken place with occupational pension schemes.

The conclusion to this section, then, is that spending ministers and their departments are capable of making spending cuts using analytic or strategic rationality as well as pure political opportunism. But the temptation to shuffle off responsibility and leave inflation to do the work is very great. If this happens, it results in service managers working in a very volatile financial and political climate.

They must abandon notions of a settled strategy and play a game against chance and multiple opponents. It could well be argued that all these political responses are still short-run responses typical of a phase of adjustment to hard times — withdrawal symptoms. In the longer run, as Glassberger (1978) has argued, when politicians begin to accept that a harsh financial climate is here to say, they may adopt a 'calculated risk strategy'. Defending the budgetary base will become unattractive. Political reputations will be made by the tough-minded chairman or minister prepared to prescribe harsh medicine. Observing the early behaviour of the Conservative government elected in 1979 appears to reveal a case of a government that is dedicated to harsh medicine using strategies that seek to avoid direct political responsibility for cuts as far as possible.

### Professional and bureaucratic rationality

*Defend professional demarcations.* Just as it makes political sense to pass the difficult decisions about what is to be cut to others, so it makes sense for administrators simply to squeeze the budgets or staffing complements that professional workers in the field have available and let *them* do the rationing. The task of refusing an old person a place in a home falls on the field worker, or on the teacher or clinician in comparable cases. Just as the local politician wants to avoid unpopularity by making it clear to his public that it is not his fault, so the professional worker wants to make it clear that falling standards or inability to help is not his fault. So traditional trade union attitudes and practices have begun to replace professional and welfare values. Extra duties, after hours clubs, filling in for absent colleagues and the like, begin to be seen as disloyal rather than as unprofessional. Any attempts at redeployment or rationalization come to be viewed as inherently wrong and to be fought on principle.

Because incumbent professionals and other workers are now well organized, most local authorities are pursuing a 'no redundancy' policy, which makes it much more difficult for the service or organization to respond flexibly to changing needs. Resources become 'silted up'. This tendency is increased by other factors. Agencies begin to become intellectually constipated as they recruit fewer younger staff with different perceptions and enthusiasms. Agencies working with fewer resources will be less ready to take on difficult clients and those in greatest need. Morale is low as promotions and extras disappear. In short, although politicians often talk about cuts as 'achieving greater efficiency' or 'cutting out the fat', the effect in a social service organization can be precisely the reverse — less is achieved from the same staff. The values and professional standards of the organizations are felt to be under attack and the response is defensive.

*Professional restrictive practices.* Writing on incrementalist budgeting suggests that the growth of the public sector has been largely the product of gradual extensions of service provision so that the volume of state activity has steadily grown, and grown faster than in the private sector. It is therefore instructive to look at the national income figures, which show the expenditure on government-purchased goods and services in constant prices. If we take total general government final consumption (i.e. central and local government spending on current goods and services) we find that in 1957 it formed 16.5 per cent of GNP at market prices and in 1978 20.9 per cent. But if we express that expenditure in 1975 prices, we find that if the relative price of public services to private in 1957 had been what it was in 1975, the share of GNP taken by government consumption would then have been not 16.5 but 23.4 per cent — that is, higher than it actually was in 1975 or 1978. The rising share of real resources bought by government is, on this analysis, more than accounted for by price rises in public sector services relative to private goods. Moreover, most of that increase is accounted for by the relatively high labour-intensity of the public services.

If government wants to hold the public sector share of resources constant or reduce it, it must do one of three things. First, it might break the link between public and private sector incomes — not merely temporarily, but continuously, so that public sector workers fall further behind in comparative incomes. The abolition of the 'Clegg' Commission on Pay Comparability in 1980 and the attempt to impose tight pay curbs on the public sector may have some significance here; but to follow such a course is bound to affect recruitment both in quantity and in quality. Second, government might attempt to reduce the labour-intensity of public services and lower the cost of the labour input — for example, by substituting ancillary workers for fully trained professionals, in social work, medicine and teaching (Judge, 1978). Third, government might reprivatize public services like health, education and the care of the elderly.

The option that would be least damaging to public services would be the second, but a period of restraint in which public sector workers' jobs and their relative incomes are under attack is precisely the time when they are least likely to agree to such a reappraisal of their tasks. To pursue the first option is bound to provoke conflict with public sector unions and intensify the trade unionization and restrictive practices of professional bodies. The most likely end result is therefore the third option. The overall result must be to make any kind of professional involvement in service planning very difficult to achieve, and if more services come to be provided by private bodies the task of coordination may become even more complex, as attempts at health planning in the USA have shown.

*Beggar-thy-neighbour.* Although it is often suggested that organizations may cooperate in situations of scarcity where mutual assistance can be beneficial, contrary tendencies are at work in social service agencies. They are catering for a range of clients, some of whom are much more costly and burdensome to professionals than others. Where resources are shrinking, a department's natural desire is to unload its difficult or expensive cases on to another agency, especially if they are considered peripheral to the traditional professional core of that service. In harsh times, organizational or professional altruism tends to disappear. Groups like the handicapped, elderly and disabled are a case in point. They have always been peripheral to the medical profession's view of its task. Hence, in hard times health authorities are eager to shed responsibility for such groups as fast as they can, but local authority social services departments are correspondingly more reluctant to accept financial responsibility. Indeed, in their turn the latter are keen to transfer their more burdensome cases and more reluctant to accept new difficult ones. Evidence for this trend is impressionistic and derived from interviews, but it would be an entirely rational response. If there were some 'price system' or set of incentives, trading or collaboration among agencies might produce an efficient outcome. In practice, there are few incentives working against 'beggar-thy-neighbour' activities. Even the provision of extra finance may not achieve this, since local authorities have become increasingly reluctant to take the bait of short-term financial gains if it means carrying long-term additions to their budgets.

*The presumption of organizational immortality.* Least of all have administrators fully faced up to the implications of public authorities ceasing to perform functions traditionally seen to be their responsibility. In inner-city and rural areas, education departments have been forced to learn the art of school closure. But cutback management is still at the stage of institutional closure rather than of abandoning traditional functions or of eliminating organizations. The account in Chapter 5 of the attempt to cull quangos in 1979/80 brings out this point. When a private concern goes bankrupt, some other body has to pay the social costs — government (unemployment pay), private individuals or other organizations. But government is not yet bankrupt in this sense (we shall be looking at the concept of 'political bankruptcy' a little more closely in the next chapter). Its responsibilities for local communities or individual employees are more extensively defined or more directly appreciated. Closure therefore ends up as a much more costly exercise than in the case of private firms. Often the functions of an agency being shut down are merely merged with those of another continuing agency. Thus it is entirely doubtful whether the elimination of Area Health Authorities in their present form will achieve savings even in the medium term. Yet if public authorities and their duties never die but merely work on reduced funds, their effectiveness must suffer.

In brief, then, it is possible to argue that the result of nil growth or worse is to make inter-agency and inter-professional cooperation less likely, to make the caring professions less caring and the organizations they work for less responsive to client needs — especially to those whose needs are most demanding.

### Consumer rationality: hold what you have

Faced with a reduction in their services, how are the consumers to react? They have least reason to be motivated by long-term rationality. It has always been difficult to interest the consumer in the long run. If he is being consulted about a better future, he may have some interests. But if he is consulted about which local hospital or school to close, there is little he can answer except 'Not ours'. Moreover, the more notice consumers are given of closure or cuts, the more opportunity they will have to mobilize opposition.

The story of the Lambeth, Southwark and Lewisham Area Health Authority in 1979 is a case in point. Faced with rising costs in the newly built teaching hospitals in its area, and very poor facilities and social conditions elsewhere in the area, the AHA overspent its budgetary allocation for 1978/79, and in mid-1979 it also looked as if the 1979/80 budgetary allocation would be overshot by over £5 m. However, in July 1979 the AHA refused to reduce levels of patient activity below that for 1977/78 and rejected specific proposals for cuts put forward by the Authority's permanent staff. Five days later, the Health Minister (using emergency powers under the 1977 Health Services Act) sacked the AHA and appointed five Health Commissioners to take over the Authority's functions and to implement spending cuts. Cuts were rapidly imposed, including a hospital closure undertaken without consultation with the Community Health Council. (In fact, the government's action was later successfully challenged at law and the AHA members reinstated, though the Minister's power to order spending cuts was not in question.)

The point of the story is that the strategy adopted by the minister's Health Commissioners in this case — cut quickly and don't consult anyone — must be a rational response by administrators under pressure for spending cuts. Indeed, it may be the only rational response of an authority faced with a costly and protracted battle. Many have been surprised by the extent of local support for even the most outdated facilities. This may not be as perverse as it seems. Local informal community networks are people's prime sources of information about where to go to seek help or care. Familiarity also helps to break down the barriers at the point of entry to a system of care. For example, it takes a long time for a community to get used to a hostel for the mentally handicapped. But if in the end it is accepted, a family finding that they have a child who needs to be looked after may be able to turn to such an institution with less fear or felt stigma than would otherwise be the case. Instinctive consumer reactions may not be as illogical as they may sometimes seem to administrators.

## WHERE NOW?

Regardless of any macro-economic or political advantages to be gained by cutting public spending, it would, on the previous analysis, be spurious to argue that such cuts necessarily provoke more efficiency or rationality. I have argued that different sectional interests, each pursued rationally in their own terms, pull in opposite directions. Other cases could certainly have been chosen to add to the examples and categories of alternative strategies sketched out above. We need closer observation and more evidence of organizational practices, especially at local level, before these initial hypotheses can be taken further. But a few tentative things may be said at this stage. There are perhaps three main points.

First, one of the most counter-productive forms of economy in terms of 'strategic rationality' is cutting spending by unrealistic cash limits. It will probably undo most of the attempts to produce considered priorities over the medium term that were begun in the 1970s. But it is important to bring home to public sector managers and politicians the full resource costs of their decisions, including the high relative price of the services they provide. One way of doing this is to make a reality of budgeting in cost terms in the PESC round and in local authorities. Each department should have to pay in programme terms for any relative price increase that any given service suffered in the previous year, and conversely it would benefit from any relative price decline that it achieved. This would give services a financial incentive to appreciate both the full cost of salary settlements and the advantages of using expensive labour more effectively. To be feasible, such a system would depend on some form of pay policy and realistic cash limits.

Second, social service planning must come to terms with greater uncertainty and abandon long-term targetry. Incremental planning methods should be used instead. These are more appropriate to a world of economic crisis in that they put a premium on robustness and flexibility and on access to consumer criticism.

Third, since services will be less prepared to plan for coordination without the potential reward of increments in resources to be shared, other financial incentives must be provided to induce concerted activities. One such way would be to force services and departments to pay a 'shadow' or notional price for the services of other departments on which they rely. For example, if social services departments were made wholly responsible for the care of the elderly, disabled and mentally handicapped on the basis of the budget devoted to these groups at present by both the NHS and local authority social services departments, the latter would then be free to provide care themselves or to purchase it, either from the NHS or from voluntary agencies; or alternatively to pay families to look after relatives. This would give a financial inducement to seek out the most cost-effective care; and this is surely a matter that deserves some attention in a period of hard times.

## REFERENCES

Banks, G. T., (1979) 'Programme budgeting in DHSS' in Booth (ed.)

Booth, T. A. (ed.) (1979) *Planning for Welfare: Social Policy and the Expenditure Process* Oxford, Blackwell and Martin Robertson.

DHSS (1976) *Priorities for Health and Personal Social Services in England* London, HMSO

DHSS (1977) *Priorities in the Health and Social Services: The Way Forward* London, HMSO

DHSS (1979) *London Planning Consortium, Acute Hospital Services in London* London, HMSO

Glassberger, A. (1978) 'Organizational responses to municipal decreases' *Public Administration Review* Vol 38, pp. 325-32.

Glennerster, H. (1974) *Social Service Budgets and Social Policy* London, Allen and Unwin

Glennerster, H. (1977) 'The year of the cuts' in K. Jones (ed.) *The Year Book of Social Policy 1976,* London, Routledge

Glennerster, H. (1979) *Social Planning in England and Wales,* paper for SSRC Seminar, Bristol, 19 March

Glennerster, H. (1980) 'Public spending and the social services: the end of an era?' in M. Brown (ed.) *The Year Book of Social Policy 1979,* London, Routledge and Kegan Paul

Gould, F. and Roweth, B. (1980) 'Public spending and social policy: the United Kingdom 1950—77' *Journal of Social Policy* Vol 9, Part 3

Greenwood, R. *et al.* (1980) 'Incremental budgeting and the assumption of growth' in Wright (ed.)

Heclo, H. and Wildavsky, A. (1974) *The Private Government of Public Money* London, Macmillan

Hinings, C. R. *et al.* (1980) 'The organizational consequences of financial restraint in local government' in Wright (ed.)

HM Treasury (1979) *Public Expenditure 1977—8: Outturn compared with Plan* Treasury Working Paper No. 11

Judge, K. (ed.) (1978) *Rationing Social Services* London, Heinemann

Levine, C. H. (1978) symposium on 'Organizational decline and cutback management' *Public Administration Review,* July/August

Maynard, A. (1979) 'Pricing, insurance and the National Health Service' *Journal of Social Policy* Vol. 8, Part 2

Niskanen, W. (1971) *Bureaucracy and Representative Government* Chicago, Aldine Atherton

Parker, R. (1976) 'Charging for the social services' *Journal of Social Policy* Vol 5

Parker, R. (1980) 'Policies, presumptions and prospects' in K. Judge (ed.) *Pricing the Social Services* London, Macmillan

*Public Expenditure to 1979/80* (1976) (Expenditure White Paper) Cmnd. 6393, London, HMSO

*The Government's Expenditure Plans 1980/81* (1979) (Expenditure White Paper) Cmnd. 7746, London, HMSO.

*The Government's Expenditure Plans 1980/81 to 1983/84* (1980) (Expenditure White Paper) Cmnd. 7841, London, HMSO.

Wildavsky, A. (1978) 'A budget for all seasons' *Public Administration Review* November/December

Wright, M. (ed.) (1980) *Public Spending Decisions* London, Allen and Unwin

# PART IV
# CONCLUSION

CHAPTER NINE

# From Decrementalism to Quantum Cuts?

by CHRISTOPHER HOOD and MAURICE WRIGHT

## 'HARD TIMES' FOR GOVERNMENT: A PASSING PHASE?

In the last chapter, Howard Glennerster's comments on social service spending in hard times returned us to some of the general themes of government behaviour in a time of cutback that have recurred in this book. Indeed, it is becoming a commonplace that much of the familiar wisdom about the behaviour and good management of the public sector has been built up in a context of government growth. Examples are the idea of incremental budgeting (each agency holds on to its established 'base', with arguments concentrated on increases at the margin); the idea of forward planning (for more resources, better and more integrated services); the idea of staff consultation and public participation in the affairs of public agencies (in the context of more and improved public services); the idea of training and incentive systems (manipulating public service personnel in exchange for promotion or extra responsibilities); the idea of structural reorganization, often in the form of complex coordinating systems (to accommodate new tasks and control a denser structure of agencies); the idea of political trouble-shooting by 'levelling up' and throwing dollars at problems; and so on.

What happens to ideas like these when growth stops or goes into reverse? Perhaps we shall need different interpretations and ideas for politics in an age of austerity — 'who gets how much less, when, how', with apologies to Harold Lasswell. Can we envisage decremental (or even quantum cutback?) budgeting simply by putting the well-known incremental mechanisms into reverse gear: 'bad news' planning (planning ahead for cutback and austerity); staff consultation and public participation for less and worse public services; motivations for public service personnel to upgrade their skills and maintain high commitment to their work without prospects of promotion; reorganization for static or contracting responsibilities; politics 'on the cheap' (by outright redistribution rather than levelling up?); and so on? What changes in political processes and ideas would be required for a transition to more austere times?

Such questions are scarcely worth pondering if you believe that the current faltering in the pace of government growth is only a temporary political phase, to be quickly replaced by a return to the post-1945 politics-as-normal path of steady growth. Clearly, this is one possible scenario. Like the postal order long awaited by Billy Bunter (greedy and mendacious schoolboy anti-hero of British boys' fiction), something may turn up to relieve the public spending problems faced by most Western governments. After all, nobody predicted the European economic miracles of the 1950s.

Indeed, the 'Billy Bunter theory' (the postal order will arrive) has an obvious political attractiveness in Britain, if for postal order you read 'North Sea oil revenues'. Government revenues from oil production in Britain will rise to about £15 bn. per year by the mid-1980s on fairly conservative assumptions about prices and output (Riddell, 1980). This may present politicians with a resource to be used — according to ideological convictions or putative election pay-offs — either to maintain and increase public spending or to cut taxes and interest rates. Whatever the economic wisdom *sub specie aeternitatis* of using a once-for-all asset to buy a few more years of politics-as-normal, 'rational' politicians *à la* Glennerster would want to look hard at the possibility of playing this card as an election winner.

But on conventional assumptions, North Sea oil revenues would not buy much more than another decade of 'politics-as-normal' in this sense, with hard times then returning in an even sharper way. And Billy Bunter's postal order never actually *did* turn up. So the alternative possibility — that 'hard times' for government are here to stay in one form or another — deserves thinking about. And if the phenomenon *is* here to stay, we may be facing not only a challenge to our understanding of how public organizations can be managed, but a rather wider 'crisis of government' analogous to that identified by historians for the mid-seventeenth century, when the cost of government rose sharply, but the ability of governments to obtain the resources that they required did not.

This chapter will first discuss what happens to the organizational structure and operation of government in hard times, in so far as British experience to date reveals any clues. This is the theme of our earlier chapters. In conclusion, we shall raise some wider questions about the implication of hard times for the relationship between government and citizens, and the possibility of 'political bank-ruptcy'.

## WHO GETS HOW MUCH LESS, WHEN, HOW?

In a business recession, contraction of activity displays some relatively well-known features. Usually, the first firms to suffer are the capital goods producers, with consumer goods producers hit only later and often not so badly by a downturn in demand. In a general atmosphere of cost-cutting, competition may intensify; marginal and least profitable firms go bankrupt; sub-contractors used by big firms to 'take up the slack' when business is booming are dropped off the hook; firms lay off employees and introduce short-time working until demand turns up again; and so on.

A 'government recession' is different. The whole process is a political one. But one might plausibly expect there to be some analogies. For example, one might suppose that local government and agencies on the fringe of central government would be singled out for bearing the brunt of contraction, for the reasons explained in Chapter 5. Michael Lee's chapter stressed the tendency for retrenchment to exacerbate centre—periphery conflicts in the public service, and Howard Glennerster's discussion of 'beggar-thy-neighbour' tactics would also suggest that the core apparatus of central government will have a corporate interest in saving itself at the expense of other parts of the public sector less well placed to influence central government politicians. As Dr Bernard Donoughue (policy adviser to James Callaghan during Callaghan's period of office as Prime Minister) puts it: '. . . it seems absolutely human and understandable that if cuts are imposed, those who decide where the cuts should be implemented decide "they should be on anybody else but us" . . .' (*The Times,* 2 April 1980).

Although this idea seems plausible enough and fits to some extent with what has happened to local government (as described in Chapters 3 and 4), it is not the whole story. The corporate influence of Whitehall in resisting cuts to its own organization may be strong (as Kellner and Crowther-Hunt, 1980, tell us), but it is not necessarily invincible. Even a government making cuts based on pure *realpolitik* — that is, hitting hardest at its enemies and at political weaklings — will not necessarily find that Whitehall itself is entirely sacrosanct. Indeed, it may not always be in Whitehall's corporate interest to resist all cutbacks, for such cutbacks may give Whitehall's mandarins a heaven-sent opportunity to dump policy commitments that have been foisted on to the bureaucracy against its will. In the local authority context, Hinings *et al.* (1980, pp. 57—8) have described how some authorities took advantage of cutbacks to discard corporate planning mechanisms that had been unwillingly adopted a few years before.

There is a further difficulty with the general hypothesis that organizational death and decline are likely to occur more at the periphery than at the centre. The experience of 1979/80, as described in Chapter 5, seems to indicate that there are difficulties in radically weeding non-departmental bodies, in spite of what one might have expected from a government with a strong ideological bias against quangos and of what one might have supposed about Whitehall's preference for putting such agencies into the front line of retrenchment and so cushioning government departments themselves from the axe. The analogy with sub-contractors in a business recession does not seem to fit at all in this case.

Indeed, it seems that there are as many differences as similarities when one compares government contraction with other features of business recession. Total close-down of individual agencies — the analogy with firms going bankrupt — is comparatively rare (we shall be discussing the general idea of 'government bankruptcy' at the close of this chapter). Savings of staff tend to be made by 'natural wastage' and shedding part-time workers rather than by short-time working or by laying off those who have most recently joined the organization. Retrenchment may intensify competition among agencies in some ways, but there are also likely to be pressures for rationalization that reduce competition.

The analogy between 'capital' and 'consumer' goods is, of course, difficult to make in the public sector. Capital spending invariably takes the brunt of spending cuts in the first instance, conveniently throwing a large part of the burden of adjustment on to the private construction industry. (An era of hard times may thus be less likely to generate *folies de grandeur* like the Concorde aeroplane or the other 'great planning disasters' of the 1960s and 1970s as chronicled by Hall, 1980, unless unemployment prompts government to undertake big construction projects for work-creation purposes.) But capital spending squeezes are not necessarily linked to organizational shut-downs. Even in education — the source of trained manpower and in that sense perhaps analogous to a 'capital goods producer' — where a major reduction in demand is signalled for the medium-term future, bankruptcies have been rare. Teacher training colleges and schools are closing, but no university or polytechnic has been closed down, in spite of much sabre-rattling talk about the Education Department's 'hit list' of universities and polytechnics to be axed. Instead, generalized cash cuts have 'shared out the misery'. This is another theme that has frequently appeared in earlier chapters.

## Cut clean or share the misery?

As Howard Glennerster observed in the last chapter, an apparent preference for cutting back government by 'sharing the misery' — that is, relatively unselective percentage cuts throughout government rather than picking out a few areas for drastic cuts — is often put down by critics to political cowardice or even to irrationality. It is seen as reluctance by politicians or bureaucrats to face up to sharp choices. A more rational approach, such criticisms imply, is to examine all agencies and programmes, old and new, and to identify what should be the main killing grounds suitable for deep selective cuts. This means taking down some trees and leaving the rest intact rather than ineffectively lopping some branches off every tree in the forest. It is the difference between the quantum cutback — terminating specific programmes and closing down organizations — and the decremental cut, which squeezes government spending generally by a given percentage.

As Glennerster pointed out, however, the equal misery approach may have a very strong element of rationality about it in some circumstances. Consider first the time factor. It takes much longer to carry out a searching review of government activities as a prerequisite for selective incisions or quantum cuts than to impose general budgetary cuts (cf. Greenwood *et al.,* 1980, p. 28). The foreign bankers may not be prepared to wait that long. 'Ministry moles' and pressure groups have time to mobilize more effective opposition to cuts. Selective cuts or total shutdowns of particular organizations may mean legislation, reallocation of responsibilities and the like — a process that is politically and legally accident-prone and has a strong potential for delay built into it. Recent examples of the pitfalls of this approach are Glennerster's case of the Lambeth, Lewisham and Southwark Health Commissioners in 1979 and Kogan's case of the government's defeat in Parliament in early 1980 over cuts in free school transport. On the other hand, unselective spending cuts on a crude non-analytic 'slash and burn' basis (Garrett, 1980, p. 191) can be introduced at any time. One can always 'cut and come again' on this basis, as Mrs Thatcher's Conservative government has demonstrated.

Similarly, the 'searching review' to find areas for cuts can easily come to grief at the level of bureaucratic politics. As Wildavsky (1980) has remarked, bureaucratic man is not self-evaluating man, a theme emphasized by Keith Hartley in Chapter 6. The information necessary to evaluate the activities of any agency is largely and inevitably monopolized by its own staff, who are *ipso facto* in a strong position to weaken the impact of reviews. The recent history of Whitehall (Programme Analysis and Review (PAR), PESC, 'Pliatzky', and so on) is that insiderish reviews typically produce 'disappointing' results, tending to the conclusion that all parts of the bureaucracy are indispensable. Bureaucrats are hardly likely to break ranks in the face of a common threat; and, as Michael Lee points out in Chapter 2, the old 1940s' idea of centralized 'technocratic' evaluation of the government machine (briefly revived in the 1970s) is all but dead. Not only does the centre lack the analytic capacity to make this idea a reality; central control is also being undermined by unionization and bureaucratic politics pushing the management of government bureaucracy into something approaching a 'plant bargaining' model. Both of these obstacles to central evaluation may intensify in a period of retrenchment. So the rational cost-cutter who wants to throttle back quickly may very well come to choose an unselective strategy of cuts rather than a selective one.

Relatedly, if selectivity in cuts means shutting down some organizations to prevent others from feeling any draughts at all, it may cost more in the short run for government to shut one of its own organizations than to keep it going. Mass sackings in particular government 'plants' are likely to be much more expensive than the unselective general hiring freeze, which relies on normal staff turnover to reduce numbers of employees.

Unemployment in general makes government more expensive, because it entails loss of income tax and extra cost in unemployment benefits, means-tested family benefits and statutory redundancy payments. For example, in November 1980 it was estimated that a newly unemployed worker on average cost government about £5000 per year in lost revenue and higher benefit (*Sunday Times Business News,* 16 November 1980, p. 60); though this sum will be slightly reduced by plans to abolish earnings-related unemployment benefit (whereby for the first six months of unemployment, government paid up to 85 per cent of an individual's former income). Moreover, when government is sending one of its own workers to the dole queue, the process is likely to be more expensive still. Average earnings in the public sector in 1980 were £6708 per year (as revealed in the April 1980 *New Earnings Survey,* reported in *Department of Employment Gazette,* October 1980, p. 1092, Table 2). This means that for government to 'break even' financially within a year in dismissing an employee on average wages who failed to get another job, it would have to negotiate an extra-statutory redundancy payment of considerably less than £2000 (and even that figure would have to be heavily discounted, since government would have to pay it in a lump sum rather than spread over time).

For some types of employees — notably young and short-service staff — this is probably attainable. But it is likely to be a different matter if government contemplates closing down labour-intensive organizations containing large numbers of long-serving, middle-rank, highly unionized employees — characteristics that apply to a large proportion of government establishments. For a labour-intensive organization, realizable asset values are likely to be low relative to the year-to-year running costs, and in such a case real savings will only be obtainable from shutdown in the long run. Politicians, however, have to think in the short term, because deferring immediate gratification for long-term benefits may simply mean that their political enemies will reap the benefits of their sacrifices. There is nothing 'irrational' about this.

A further general point is that the specifically political costs of a selective approach have to be carefully weighed, apart from the financial costs pure and simple. As Dahl and Lindblom long ago argued (1953), political system-maintenance may have to be traded off to some extent against maximally resource-efficient choices. To be specific, a total shutdown of an agency mobilizes everybody in that organization and turns them *all* into enemies of retrenchment — often with the desperate fervour of a life-and-death struggle, similar to the various industrial work-ins that took place in collapsing companies in Britain in the early 1970s, and to the school closure study referred to by Maurice Kogan in Chapter 7.

The decremental approach is not necessarily less drastic in its overall financial effects than the quantum cutback. But the former, using general spending cuts rather than the 'surgical' threat of closing down entire organizations, has at least two political advantages. First, it avoids specifying the precise victims of such cuts (indeed, Page, 1980, argues that the shift from piecemeal grants to general grant financing of local authorities by central government in Britain is partly explained by the greater political ease of cutting general grants). Second, it has a better chance of dividing the members of the organization in question rather than of uniting them against closure. Indeed, if generalized cost savings can be presented as the price of survival for the bulk of the members of the organization, this may well be accepted even in the context of high unionization and industrial militancy (as happened at the British Leyland motor works in 1979, in sharp contrast to the Upper Clyde Shipbuilders' struggle of a few years earlier). Richard Rose (1980b, p. 28) writes of 'the politics of reprieve', when actual outcomes are less bad than has been expected or threatened. Moreover, the hope may be held out — however spurious it may be — that expansion will eventually return when the time of troubles is over.

Typically, the cutback process is a multi-stage one. As we have seen, the choice between decremental cuts and quantum cutbacks is not only faced at the centre of Whitehall; it is also faced by organizations subjected to overall spending cuts by central decisions.

Thus, a decremental cut in an organization's overall finances may be translated into quantum selective cutbacks within that organization (as happened, say, in the case of the Manpower Services Commission in 1979) or by decremental cuts across the whole of an organization's activities. Commonly, the political process within organizations may lead the 'decremental' approach to be preferred for as long as possible over the selective quantum cutback approach of closing down specific departments and sub-units, for exactly the same reasons that apply to Whitehall.

We might therefore suppose — paradoxically, perhaps — that there is a case for an argument based on the tortoise and the hare principle when it comes to selectivity in cuts. An ostensibly soft approach of generalized cuts may in some circumstances deliver quicker and more reliable results than a highly discriminatory approach relying on selective massacres of particular agencies and programmes — which runs a much higher risk of delay and of political banana-skins.

There is a species of political logic and rationality about this. But decremental cuts are not a panacea. Just as they are quick and easy to impose, they are rapidly and effortlessly reversible. As we have seen in several places in this book, decremental cuts imposed on tomorrow's spending have a habit of never actually materializing. By the time tomorrow comes, it is yesterday again. Quantum cuts, once embarked upon, are by their nature final and harder to reverse. Also, to the extent that decremental cuts are 'real', the choices avoided by higher decision-makers in blandly passing cuts down the line must at some point be faced. There is always a level at which decrementalism has to be translated into specific 'quantum' decisions; and the organizational level of this transition rises the deeper the decremental cuts that the centre imposes. Finally, however attractive decrementalism may seem to the harrassed 'cutback manager' in Whitehall, awkward questions are raised about what such a 'primacy of politics' approach may do to the operational efficiency of the government machine in delivering policies (a consideration that Michael Lee asserts to have been more in the forefront of decisions about the government machine thirty or forty years ago than it is today). After all, a forest of tree trunks without limbs is not a very useful asset.

## CUTS AND SQUEEZES –
## BUREAUCRATIC DISEASES?

In this book, we have seen two somewhat contrasting views of the effect of cuts on the efficiency of government operations. Economists conventionally assume that administrative efficiency ('*X*-efficiency', as they term it) falls as organizations grow larger, and one might plausibly argue from this that contraction in government will produce 'leaner', more efficient delivery of public services. Thus Keith Hartley in Chapter 6 puts forward the view that cuts in the public service will tend to force greater efficiency because, faced with fewer overall resources, government will be compelled to choose between the essential and the inessential. The pressure grows to discard luxuries in order to concentrate on essentials, to do away with needless 'bureaucracy', and so on. Hartley draws from this the neat paradox that the efficiency of military forces will tend to rise as a result of the intendedly anti-military policies of Labour governments, and to fall as a result of the intendedly pro-military policies of Conservative governments. Such a view relies, of course, on mechanisms for effective choice coming into play.

It was precisely by denying that last assumption that Howard Glennerster drew exactly the opposite conclusion about the effect of cuts on government efficiency in Chapter 8. He argued that spending cuts may actually bring about a reduction in efficiency. This is because the course of retrenchment is fatally distorted by bureaucratic preferences that will not necessarily lead to more resource-efficient outcomes and may well have the reverse effect.

This argument has several strands. As we have seen, the expectation and desire that government contraction will result in a reduction in bureaucracy (the 'tail' as opposed to the 'teeth', in military parlance) is a perilous one. As a slogan for mounting cutbacks, this has obvious political appeal, but in reality it may be as problematic to translate into action as the massacre of quangos at the expense of other parts of the public sector.

The reason for this may be partly tactical. As in the case of the 'rational' public service strike, which aims to do maximum harm to the public in order to force government to yield, bureaucracies and politicians seeking to resist cuts may choose to concentrate those cuts in the places where they will most hurt the outside public, be most easily noticed, and thus court the maximum political unpopularity for the government. Such actors may actively help to orchestrate the chorus of protest against 'inhuman' cuts (cf. Greenwood *et al.,* 1980, p. 28). Hence (to put it vulgarly) the pressure for closing down the flower gardens rather than reducing the town hall bureaucracy, for cutting down on school books rather than on educational administrators, and so on. Sometimes there really is no choice but to act in this way — as when, after voting down the 1979 EEC budget, the first thing that Euro-MPs discovered was that their own salaries and expenses had been cut. Far more commonly, there will be scope for bureaucratic choice. Thus in 1980 the Public Record Office chose to meet a requirement for a 10 per cent budget cut in the following year by closing down its central London public search rooms, thus making the cuts highly visible to its clientele and subjecting its London-based clients (who may include some 'influentials') to maximum inconvenience (*The Times,* 23 June 1980). Similarly, the Scottish Development Agency was coming under fire in mid-1980 for concentrating its cuts on money given away to companies rather than on its own organization. This is the 'sore thumbs' and 'bleeding stumps' tactic, referred to by Kogan, Glennerster, Hartley and others.

Quite apart from the paradoxical effect of tactical considerations like these, a declining organization may actually generate relatively more bureaucracy for other reasons. Both Maurice Kogan and Michael Lee make this point. Cutbacks have to be 'administered'. More stringent central controls may be operated over such matters as expenses, use of resources and equipment; people with fewer prospects for promotion may have to be goaded into satisfactory work by the bureaucratic stick rather than by the carrot of self-interest; and so on. Such parts of the bureaucracy as do disappear, as Howard Glennerster points out, may in reality be planners or technical analysts rather than bureaucrats in a traditional sense. Moreover, as organizations contract, the number of bureaucrats needed to run them may not fall proportionately. This is the reverse side of the coin of economies of scale in bureaucratic overheads — so often advanced as a justification for large-scale organization. Both of these bureaucracy-enhancing effects may come about during a period of hard times for government, before we need to start making any assumptions about the degree to which bureaucrats are well placed successfully to pursue strategies to ensure their own survival or expansion at the expense of operational units; and this may help to explain why 'cutting the bureaucracy' often turns out to be a chimerical path to government retrenchment, as we have seen in earlier chapters.

There is a second possible factor militating against government becoming 'leaner' and more efficient during hard times, and that is the desire to preserve jobs. The most recent experience of large-scale job losses in government service in Britain was when roughly 700,000 people (about half of its employees) were shed from the civil service after World War II. This was done without major difficulties, but it is not really an accurate parallel for the 1980s. First, those who were demobilized were temporary recruits without the traditional tenure rights attaching to bureaucratic (and academic) jobs, and they were leaving in a context of comparatively low general unemployment by present-day standards: there were civilian jobs at hand. Second, as Michael Lee points out in Chapter 2, heightened politicization, unionization and industrial militancy in the government service make it far less a neutral and technical problem to be discussed and manipulated (as the metaphor of the 'machinery of government' implies), and more a question of power-politics in which the protagonists use whatever weapons come conveniently to hand. The post-1945 experience of demobilization is therefore probably very misleading, since the economic and political atmosphere surrounding the release of manpower was quite different.

Pressures for job-saving in the public service were discussed in the last chapter as conditioning the way in which cuts take place. For example, the abolition of ninety Area Health Authorities in England, announced in mid-1980 as a dramatic cut in bureaucracy, was to be done largely through 'natural wastage'. In circumstances like these, the jobs that are retained may become meaningless, non-existent or impossible. Pressure for saving jobs may be the key to understanding many of the 'funny stories' about the quirks of the cutback process, such as the xerox copy sent to individual members of DOE exhorting economy in xeroxing (*Guardian,* 4 June 1980) or the retention of careers advisory services in areas where there are no 'careers' to be had and job-seekers do not have any effective choice. Similarly, trading ancillary equipment and the like for the retention of jobs (a tendency that has become familiar in many parts of the public sector) may mean that the jobs that are retained are done with even lower efficiency than before, even if demand is falling. The many stories of schools retaining teachers but cutting back on heating or on books, are cases in point — such as the Northamptonshire secondary school where each science textbook was said to be shared between ten children (*Sunday Times,* 13 April 1980) or the Solihull secondary school 'forced' to ask parents to contribute £10 each towards books (*Guardian,* 24 June 1980). Pressures for saving jobs may also lead to stronger resistance to the introduction of labour-saving devices.

Peter Self (1980, p. 126) paints an optimistic picture of public sector operations in hard times, arguing that increased competition for jobs and promotion will drive up standards. But in a nil — or low — recruitment and promotion era, these pressures may not work so well. And if there are strong pressures to avoid sackings by relying on natural wastage (resignations and retirements) to reduce manpower, a very lop-sided pattern of resource use may develop. Critical skills disappear; the most talented or enterprising members may leave the declining agencies and sectors without a corresponding influx of bright young recruits, creating age blocks in the bureaucracy and leaving behind a steadily ageing pool of discontented lower-quality people. Indeed, when it does come to redundancies, government is more likely to dismiss its low-paid, short-service or relatively youthful workers without dependants (because these are cheapest to fire in terms of redundancy pay and means-tested family benefits, as was explained in the last section). This means that longer-serving 'dead wood' is not likely to go from the middle ranks; that services are reduced primarily at the 'sharp end'; and that youthful talent is even less plentiful. All this is another possible formula for a spiral of *falling* effectiveness, efficiency and innovativeness analogous to that originally traced for public transport by Hirschman (1970).

Any system of controlling government spending by specifying the input but not the output is potentially extremely vulnerable to such processes. The device of cash limits on government spending (cash limits having priority over targets set in volume terms) is precisely such a control system; and, as we have seen in earlier chapters, cash limits have been widely used as the actual instrument of retrenchment since 1976. A system such as this is bound to mean that contracts are inadequately specified, in Keith Hartley's language. Hence the powerful logic of the need to supplement mere cash control by outside management reviews of cost-cutting exercises to monitor the decisions taken and to evaluate the resulting effectiveness of each agency. Similarly, there is a logical need for a counterweight to the beggar-thy-neighbour tactics so tempting to bureaucrats as cutback devices, the need of a facility for giving careful thought to the extent to which making cuts in one place just loads extra costs somewhere else in the public sector (as with the closure of job creation programmes and the like). But the precedents for waste-cutting exercises in Whitehall are not very encouraging, if Leslie Chapman's (1978) cautionary tales are to be believed. Indeed, part of the attractiveness of cash limits as an instrument for cuts, as far as politicians are concerned, is that someone else has to make the hard choices about how the antiseptic figures are to be translated into concrete changes in bureaucratic activity.

Perhaps the difference between Hartley's view and Glennerster's view is the difference between what is technically possible and what is institutionally likely to happen. Or it may reflect a difference between labour-intensive and cash- or equipment-intensive public services. Labour-intensive services will be particularly vulnerable to inefficiencies of the type identified by Glennerster, because of promotion blockages and pressures for 'no redundancy' policies. Cash- or equipment-intensive services, on the other hand, may not be shackled in quite the same way, allowing the 'Hartley effect' to operate more freely. This is pure speculation, but it does fit with Hartley's view of the effect of cuts on the defence sector and with Kogan's picture of the Department of Education and Science as a small cash-intensive department with no necessary bureaucratic stake in an ever-expanding educational system. Just as happened in the growth era of the past, contraction primarily affects those parts of the education system outside Whitehall. It would not need fewer DES officials to write smaller cheques, as it were.

A further possible way of reconciling Hartley's views with those of Glennerster might be to argue that they depict different stages along a time-path. 'Equal misery' approaches, combined with 'no redundancies' and minimal agency 'deaths', are among the natural first responses to calls for immediate spending cuts. But with each successive wave, such responses may produce such a distortion of resource that eventually sharp choices *do* have to be faced in a later round of quantum cuts, producing the 'Hartley effect'. This has a common-sense logic about it, and it squares both with Greenwood *et al.*'s description (1980) of local authority responses to central government demands for cuts from the middle 1970s and also with Hartley's own account of how defence cuts in Britain changed from an original 'equal misery' pattern to something rather more selective. If that is so, education and social services may be expected to enter a second stage of response as the cutback process 'matures' (indeed, there are already some straws in the wind that might suggest this, such as proposals to close down specific university departments and teaching hospitals).

### 'Fungibility' and cutbacks

A further element determining whether the result of cuts will really be a public sector slimmed down to the more effective pursuit of government's tasks, is what might be called the 'fungibility factor'. This unlovely but necessary term refers to the ability of organizations in receipt of grants to defeat the objectives of the grantor — that is, responding to grant changes by reshuffling elements of their budget not under the grantor's control. It is the inevitable consequence of the modern trend towards government by cheque-book rather than by direct provision of services, since money (unlike services, programmes, laws and the like) is 'fungible', or usable for a wide variety of purposes (cf. Rose and Peters, 1978, p. 25).

For example, the award of grants to organizations as an attempt to increase the grantee's spending on a particular item may not in fact result in any net spending rise on the item in question, because a possible response by the grantee to the grantor's initiative is to release discretionary spending from that particular item to other areas of expenditure. Exactly the same thing can happen when grants are cut. 'Fungibility' is a problem commonly arising in multi-level grant or subsidy schemes. It ranges from EEC grants to member governments, for example on regional aid (EEC money has in the past been simply substituted for national government spending in Britain without increasing the net regional aid expenditure above what it would otherwise have been), to job-creation subsidies offered by governments to employers (with the obvious danger that government-subsidized 'created jobs' may be substituted for unsubsidized jobs by employers, with nil net employment creation).

Fungibility is important because much of government growth

over the past few decades has been concentrated in institutions outside the direct control of Whitehall, particularly with the growth of local government services largely financed by general grants from central government. A quarter or so of public spending is under the direct control not of Whitehall, but of local authorities that have access to sources of income other than central grants (rates, fees and charges). The implications of this for central government's ability to keep local government spending on target in hard times were discussed by Midwinter and Page and by Greenwood in Part II. Under the traditional system of control, Greenwood sees 'resource substitution' (switching expenditure to rates and charges when government grants are cut) as an important 'escape route' for local authorities in evading the full force of central government pressures for cuts — but only at times of modest inflation, when local spending levels can be maintained by rises in the property tax sufficiently small to be politically acceptable.

Hence a large element of uncertainty is built into the whole system of control over public spending. Central government may be happy to countenance the variations in local spending described in Chapters 3 and 4, so long as its overall targets are met — even the dramatic spending 'rebellions' by Scottish districts on particular items, as described by Midwinter and Page, can be ignored on the *de minimis* principle, so long as the big-spending regional authorities do not follow suit. But if major resistance develops to central pressures for cuts, different tactics of control are needed and blunt instruments may be wheeled out. Control may become much more discriminatory, as in the case of retrospective grant reductions for particular 'delinquent' authorities, breaking the previous pattern of technocratically determined 'formula' grants. Similarly, local spending may be cut back according to whatever administrative weapons come conveniently to hand (such as the moratorium on local authority housing starts imposed by DOE in October 1980). A more ambitious and interesting change of tactics is the change to a 'block grant' regime for local authorities in England and Wales, as mentioned in several of our chapters. The essence of this is that central government uses the local political system as the mechanism of control by publicizing before local voters what government considers to be the 'reasonable rate-borne expenditure' for each council and fixing grant levels only *after* local tax levels have been set. This contrasts with the previous system, which was aimed at the financial decisions of councillors and did not tap directly into the political system (see Dunsire, 1980).

A further uncertainty is constituted by the discretion that local authorities have over the allocation of their budgets among particular items — and, as Page and Midwinter show in Chapter 3, wide variations can be observed for some services, particularly those less exposed to union pressures and countrywide standards. So in the context of a régime of general grant finance of local authorities, it is perfectly possible (for example) for the DES or the DOE to lose a battle in the Cabinet over spending cuts, only to win the battle at the point of policy delivery as local authorities switch money about.

All this exposes cutbacks imposed by central government to the bureaucratic and tactical distortions discussed earlier (there is not much sign of local authorities responding to central cutbacks by shedding manpower on a large scale, for example, although much was talked of this both by the Labour government of 1974—9 and by the Conservative government elected in 1979 in relation to their respective 'industrial strategies'). Furthermore, even relatively innocent cost-cutting behaviour by local authorities, such as early retirement of surplus teachers, may result in extra costs being loaded on to central government (in that case, through payment of teachers' pensions). Local authorities in the hands of the government's own party may well resist cuts quite strongly; but, as we saw in the last chapter, there is an extra twist to the process because local authorities — with partial control over a large, highly visible and, until recently, rapidly growing, sector of government spending — are organizations that tend, in the normal course of the political cycle, to be captured in large numbers by the political enemies of the party in control of Whitehall, often fairly early in the life of a government.

As we saw in Chapter 5, the uncertain political relationship between Whitehall and the town halls is one of the reasons why quangos are so hard to dispose of. For local authorities, to the normal tactics of bureaucratic survival and resistance to cuts may be added a political motivation to respond to central government initiatives in ways calculated to frustrate the intention of Whitehall and to cause maximum political embarrassment. Even what might otherwise be seen as sensible economies may be interpreted as a political betrayal of the king over the water.

Central government faces a dilemma over its strategies for counter-attack. If it attempts to curb the discretion of local authorities over spending heads and tax-raising powers, it is raising constitutional issues in a way that may risk displeasing the government's friends as well as its enemies. The so-called 'independence of local government' may be said to be threatened, and government may thereby be curbing the ability of its own political forces to frustrate central initiatives at a future time when the 'ins' and the 'outs' at both levels of government have changed places. Alternatively, if government uses informal political pressures to guide local spending rather than formal constitutional measures, the political outcome may be equally difficult. The latter course means that the government's loyal friends suffer disproportionately, being asked to make ever-deeper cuts to pay for the 'profligacy' of local authorities under the government's enemies, who are seen to go unpunished. Short of doing away entirely with over 400 local authorities, the fungibility factor cannot be entirely eradicated. Hence the importance of the tactical interrelations between central government and local authorities as discussed in Chapters 3 and 4.

## The combined effect

The picture that the foregoing discussion conjures up of government in hard times therefore contains a strong element of paradox if not of actual contradiction. It is more than likely that the results of cuts and contraction may be the very opposite of that intended or desired by the 'cutback managers', through institutional processes that display a distinct if perverted rationality. The element of bureaucracy in the delivery of services may fail to take the brunt of contraction and may actually expand, whereas key operations and the most popular targets may be hit hardest — partly because of bureaucratic tactics, partly because of party politics exploiting the fungibility factor at the central—local divide. Public sector jobs tend to be retained at the cost of non-wage items, the hiring of key labour skills, the introduction of possible labour-saving devices and responses to changing patterns of demand, resulting in even lower productivity and ossified or lop-sided resource use — a process that may or may not break down at some point, forcing radical choices to be made. Even then, financial pressures are likely to lead government to dismiss employees at the 'sharp end' of service delivery rather than middle- or top-level bureaucrats. The heightened politicization of the bureaucracy and public service union militancy makes bureaucracy's interest in its own survival more visible to the outside public.

Obviously, the possible knock-on effects of such a development in terms of public and electoral responses to government decline are interesting to contemplate, and it is to the wider aspect of government—public relations that we now turn.

## A WIDER CRISIS OF GOVERNMENT?

What of the wider crisis of government that a prolonged period of hard times may bring? One comparatively optimistic picture of the future is that painted by Richard Rose and Guy Peters in their influential book *Can Government go Bankrupt?* (1978). They demonstrate that there has been a slow-down in economic growth in several Western industrialized countries, accompanied by expanding public policy, a rise in 'take-home pay' (earnings after tax) and growing inflation. From the 1950s to the 1970s there was a pattern of what Rose and Peters call 'treble affluence' (that is, the simultaneous rise of Gross Domestic Product, public spending and take-home pay). But, as Maurice Wright has described in Chapter 1, this pattern began to collapse in the 1970s, most obviously in the UK and Sweden, but also in Italy; and the same is predicted for the more robust economies of France and the German Federal Republic in the 1980s. Increasingly, the annual growth in public policy (measured by rises in public spending, often under a heavy weight of inertia commitments) and take-home pay outstrips the growth (if any) of GDP. To continue to provide for the growth of the former, governments print money to finance higher prices and wage claims and higher public sector deficits.

If we ignore 'steady state' possibilities (that is, take-home pay or government spending staying constant), we can consider four possible combinations, as shown below:

|  | Take-home pay rises | Take-home pay falls |
|---|---|---|
| Cost of public policy rises | 1 | 2 |
| Cost of public policy falls | 3 | 4 |

Rose and Peters, extrapolating from economic trend data, argue that situation 1 (a 'win—win' situation, since government spending and take-home pay both rise) cannot be projected far into the future. Governments will be forced to choose between substantial further rises in government spending and further increases in take-home pay. If they choose situation 2, continuing to raise government spending at the expense of take-home pay, they face the danger of 'political bankruptcy'. Situation 4 is effectively ruled out by Rose and Peters, since they assume that economic growth will continue in the industrialized world. Indeed, they consider that a fall in the historic rate of increase of public spending (not a cut in real terms) will be all that would be required to prevent the growth of public spending from cutting into the value of take-home pay. They therefore predict a mild version of situation 3, but they are not doomwatchers foreseeing the end of the welfare state. Their view is that governments will not need to dismantle the welfare state, but only to slow down the rate of its growth.

This scenario raises two interesting questions about the behaviour of the wider politico-economic system in hard times. One is whether a slowing-down of the rate of growth of public policy (in order to save take-home pay, as in situation 3) can be managed without a head-on smash with historic public expectations of a continuous rise in the benefits to be provided by government. Or is this the classic scenario for a revolution of (disappointed) rising expectations? The second question concerns the exact nature of the political bankruptcy that may result if government makes the wrong political choices in the trade-off between rising government spending and rising take-home pay. We shall discuss these two questions in turn.

## A revolution of rising expectations?

Rose and Peters consider that a slowing down of the rate of public spending is politically feasible because public expectations of continued public spending growth are diminishing or can be scaled down. At the time when their book appeared, the political climate was certainly one of tax revolts rather than of welfare crusades; it was a time of 'strategic retreat' (Wildavsky, 1980) from the ambitious social objectives set for government in the 1960s and 1970s. The assumption of falling expectations is an important one, because it goes against a classic recipe for political upheaval: rising expectations disappointed by a sudden break in improvements. Many writers (such as Stewart, 1980) see the transition from government growth to standstill as a formula for rising conflict. Rose and Peters produce opinion poll data for the UK to support their contention about falling expectations. Too much weight ought not, perhaps, to be attached to any poll results taken at any one point in time (a 1980 MORI poll, for example, indicated that the bulk of respondents would prefer to see public services protected at the cost of higher taxes — meaning, presumably, lower take-home pay in a nil-growth economy). Perhaps more convincing — though absent from Rose and Peters' exposition (Tufte, 1980, pp. 567—8) — would be some kind of correlation between government spending, take-home pay and opinion poll data over time or cross-nationally.

Part of the problem is that the electorate is not an undifferentiated mass, and that one man's 'cost of public policy' is another man's take-home pay. Even leaving aside recipients of transfers and other benefits, a quarter of the labour force is employed in the public sector, which is heavily and increasingly unionized (Rose, 1980a, p. 41, Table 8) and the site of many of the key pay battlegrounds. Indeed, some interpretations of public spending growth (such as Bacon and Eltis, 1976, Self, 1980, or Howard Glennerster's remarks in the last chapter) see it as affording higher wages and better conditions to public employees rather than as dramatically extending the public service or raising standards of service. Will public sector employees and their unions tolerate static or lower levels of real wages over an indefinite period of time, as implied by the government's attempt to break out of the traditional principle of 'comparability' for public sector pay in the 1980/81 wage round? ('Comparability' is the philosophy of keeping public sector wage levels in line with those of the private sector wherever any comparison can be made in types of work.) Will they countenance programme termination and organizational death in some policy areas to pay for advances in others? Will they be willing to trade jobs in the public sector for real wage rises to a larger extent than in the past?

There are in fact two circumstances in which *both* situations 2 *and* 3 might be 'bankruptcy scenarios'. One is the possibility that the electorate at large and/or key power groups in the political system (particularly the more powerful trade unions) will not consistently accept a trade-off between continuing government growth and continuing growth in take-home pay in a situation of low, nil or negative economic growth. Recent evidence, such as it is at the time of writing, and the reactions to spending cuts in Britain since 1974/75, does not clearly confirm the suggestion that expectations from government are steadily diminishing. The other circumstance is that the electorate and/or key power groups might be deeply divided on the issue, with one powerful or numerous section demanding situation 2 and another powerful or numerous section demanding situation 3. As with measures for trade union reform (supported by over 70 per cent of poll respondents in most polls from 1975 to 1980), opinion poll data are not necessarily a reliable guide to political outcomes in such cases.

### Managing the politics of low government growth?

As with economic forecasting, visions of the political future of government in hard times can be 'optimistic' or 'pessimistic'. But, unlike economic forecasting, what counts as 'good' or 'bad' news depends on your political views.

One view — hardly discussed by Rose and Peters — is that the politics of lower government growth might turn into channels far more divisive than the bland politics of the years of 'treble affluence'. Henry Fairlie (1968, p. 245) once remarked that the politics of the 1960s encouraged voters to treat government as a supermarket — a process that he sarcastically dubbed 'The politics of the Gross National Appetite'. But if the goods that everybody expected to find on the supermarket shelves are no longer there in the desired quantities, they may find themselves involved in sharper disputes over the distribution of the goods that *are* there — a familiar experience of shortage situations. Then the argument may shift to the management of the supermarket, or even of the 'supermarket system', bringing the dispute on to a constitutional plane.

Tricky questions relating to the distribution of wealth, income and welfare could be side-stepped in the years of 'treble affluence' from the 1950s to the 1970s. Powerful interest groups could be bought off; income equalization could be achieved through levelling up, so that everybody won, as in Lewis Carroll's caucus race. But growth served as a surrogate for redistribution: even after long periods of Labour government, the relativities of income and wealth in Britain remain undisturbed (Royal Commission on the Distribution of Income and Wealth, 1979; Meade, 1978; Townsend, 1979; Bosanquet and Townsend, 1980).

On this argument, when growth falters (and the illusion of growth through the emollient of inflation), the caucus race of the treble affluence years will be superseded by a more conventional form of competition, in which there have to be losers as well as winners. The management of interest groups may become politically trickier: a government with more to spend year by year will not lack for friends and counsellors, whereas a government with less to spend may find itself in a lonelier position. Hard times provide a good test-bed for theories of corporatism and pressure group government. Similarly, it is possible that a society accustomed to an increasing standard of living year by year, both in terms of take-home pay and of the 'social wage', will become embroiled in disputes over distribution more bitter than have been seen for decades. The prospect opens up of political bankruptcy of a kind somewhat different from that envisaged by Rose and Peters (of which more in the next section), particularly if their assumption of continuing economic growth turns out to be overoptimistic and the spectre of situation 4 appears on the scene for any length of time.

Against this, an opposing view ('optimistic' or 'pessimistic', depending on your preferences) can be built up from several arguments. Rose and Peters' view is that the brakes can successfully be put on public spending by judicious political management. Government spending growth can be reined back by measures such as user charges, a shift from cheque-book government to regulatory government (in which private citizens pay the costs), decriminalizing activities to cut law enforcement costs, and promoting once-for-all, fixed-cost or symbolic activities without a built-in escalator of 'intertia commitments' — such as military displays, the honours system, Queen's Awards to Industry, and so on. Such devices promote the majesty of government at little long-term expense and add to people's self-importance rather than to their material well-being.

Ingenious as such suggestions may be, they seem a little like trying to stop a steamroller with a bicycle brake, and Rose and Peters admit that slowing down the rise in government spending inevitably means changes in the big cash programmes of government. A more substantial argument is that of Peter Self (1980, p. 126), who contends that the brakes on public spending will apply themselves automatically in a period of economic stagnation because much of public spending growth has been a response to economic growth: 'Economic stagnation will reduce the need for further growth in many forms of public expenditure, and . . . if cuts must be made the effects should be more tolerable than under conditions of growing "affluence" . . .'

There is a neat logic in the idea that government growth will automatically self-correct in hard times. But experience at the time of writing suggests the reverse: in late 1980 the British government was facing an extra £2 bn. per year in public spending (mainly in extra unemployment benefits and subsidies to loss-making state industries) as a result of the recession — threatening to more than counterbalance the government's planned cuts in spending between 1980/81 and 1981/82. Moreover, Self's view depends on rather heroic assumptions about rising unemployment causing major reversals in public spending trends by increasing family care of children, the handicapped and elderly, lower crime rates and the like. Large-scale and rapid changes in social behaviour would be required to stem the tide of public spending in areas like health and social security in the face of the continuing explosion in the elderly population. Even in education, where school rolls are falling in aggregate, movement of population may make theoretically possible economies harder to realize than it might seem (schools may have to be built in expanding areas at a rate that it may not be practicable to balance by school closures in declining ones, for example).

There are two further arguments for dismissing the picture of ever-rising expectations as an irresistible force meeting an immovable object of low economic growth (and the consequent need to choose between rises in take-home pay and rises in government spending), with the caucus race becoming transformed into a zero-sum, each-group-for-itself, no-holds-barred political conflict. One is to point to historical precedents. Rose and Peters point out that cuts took place in Britain, the USA and Scandinavia in the 1930s without a collapse of those political systems (though there were less encouraging developments elsewhere and Self — 1980, p. 130 — thinks even the British precedent from the 1930s a misleading one). The other is to argue that economic growth can never keep pace with wants and expectations, so that there will be fierce distributional conflicts at *any* level of economic growth; hard times have nothing to do with it. Indeed, Fred Hirsch (1977), in a celebrated and by now familiar argument, asserted that the distributional struggle is *exacerbated,* not relieved, by material growth. This is because the importance of inherently scarce 'positional goods' (high status, access to empty spaces, and the like) becomes greater as such goods become scarcer. People's wants therefore turn from aspirations that are in principle capable of satisfaction, at least in an expanding economy, to aspirations that in their nature cannot be satisfied for everybody. On the other hand, it could perhaps be argued with equal plausibility that at a time of economic stagnation *more* goods become 'positional goods', so that distributional conflict may intensify when material growth *stops.*

## Government in hard times: heading for political bankruptcy?

The prospect and immediacy of political bankruptcy overtaking government therefore depends on which of these arguments you think most plausible. But what exactly does political bankruptcy mean? As we have seen, Rose and Peters foresee a danger of political bankruptcy if government spending continues to expand at the rate of the (trebly affluent) recent past in an era of lower economic growth and thus threatens the real value of take-home pay (situation 2). By this they mean that people will turn away from demands for government intervention in the economy, perceiving governments to be part of the economic problem rather than a potential solution to it. What they foresee as political bankruptcy is a prospect of growing civic indifference — widespread apathy towards government and a growth in tax evasion and the 'black economy'.

Since governments can come to fates rather worse than mere 'indifference' (as Rose and Peters are well aware — 1978, pp. xiii, 31—5), this is a fairly bloodless picture of political bankruptcy, in line with the anti-doommongering tone of Rose and Peters' assumptions. The regime remains: it is merely isolated from an indifferent citizenry pursuing its own concerns in the black economy. This is a fairly comfortable position for a bankrupt, one might think. Unlike the business parallel, the 'firm' continues to trade, even if fewer people are keenly interested in buying its goods.

There are, however, rather different possible forms of political bankruptcy, as was indicated above. To put it in the most extreme form, governments become bankrupt in a very clear-cut sense when some or all of the following conditions apply. They lose the ability to defend their territories against outside attack or to maintain order within their own territories without foreign military assistance; they cease to be able to pay their own followers except by obtaining money from outsiders on terms that they are unable to dictate; they are unable to prevent foreign currency from becoming the main medium of exchange in their territories. There may be other possible forms of political bankruptcy, but these are unmistakable ones.

Governments can and do go bankrupt in all of these senses. When that happens, a 'bankruptcy receiver' appears. Receivership might mean control by an international credit agency, as with the Council for the Administration of the Ottoman Public Debt in the late nineteenth century (Blaisdell, 1966) — though the International Monetary Fund in the present day tends to stand back from receivership in the sense of direct management. Alternatively, receivership may mean a takeover by another state, as happened in effect to eighteenth-century Scotland, or the supplanting of the bankrupt regime by another with command of more political resources (a more 'corporate' type of state, say, or an 'iron government' of the left or right). Indeed, the notion of 'bankruptcy' without a receiver seems a strange one and Rose and Peters' use of the term 'political bankruptcy' somewhat eccentric (cf. Tufte, 1980, p. 568).

If Rose and Peters' assumptions about continuing economic growth turn out to be overoptimistic and the prospect arises of take-home pay *and* government spending simultaneously *falling* over a period of time (situation 4 — 'treble poverty', as we might call it), bankruptcy might not be confined to a mere 'indifference' to government by the citizenry. The same might happen if Rose and Peters' assumptions about economic growth are correct but it proves to be difficult to damp down expectations of continuing growth in both take-home pay and government-provided benefits, with politics developing into the caucus-race-turned-free-for-all scenario depicted earlier. Greater problems could then threaten. The ability of the regime to keep control and to maintain itself in power might come into question. Bankruptcy is a dramatic and extreme case; but even for more mundane concerns with government's effectiveness, the tactics and behaviour of 'government in hard times' are of rather more than academic interest.

## REFERENCES

Bacon, R. and Eltis, W. (1976) *Britain's Economic Problem: Too Few Producers* London, Macmillan

Blaisdell, D. C. (1966) *European Financial Control in the Ottoman Empire* New York, AMS Press Inc.

Bosanquet, N. and Townsend, P. (eds) (1980) *Labour and Equality* London, Heinemann

Chapman, L. (1978) *Your Disobedient Servant* London, Chatto and Windus

Dahl, R. A. and Lindblom, C. E. (1953) *Politics, Economics and Welfare* New York, Harper and Row

Dunsire, A. (1980) 'Central-local relations in retrenchment: the UK case', paper for EGOS Workshop on Organizational Analyses of the Relationship between State and Local Government, University of Bamberg, September

Fairlie, H. (1968) *The Life of Politics* London, Methuen

Garrett, J. (1980) *Managing the Civil Service* London, Heinemann

Greenwood, R., *et al.* (1980) 'Incremental budgeting and the assumption of growth' in Wright (ed.)

Hall, P. (1980) *Great Planning Disasters* London, Weidenfeld and Nicholson

Hinings, C. R., *et al.* (1980) 'The organizational consequences of financial restraint in local government' in Wright (ed.)

Hirsch, F. (1977) *Social Limits to Growth* London, Routledge

Hirschman, A. O. (1970) *Exit, Voice and Loyalty* Cambridge, Mass., Harvard University Press

Kellner, P. and Crowther-Hunt, Lord (1980) *The Civil Servants* London, MacDonald General Books

Meade, J. (1978) *The Structure and Reform of Direct Taxation* London, Institute of Fiscal Studies

Page, E. (1980) 'Grant consolidation and the development of intergovernmental relations in the USA and the UK', paper for 5th PSA Workgroup on UK Politics, Cardiff, September

Riddell, P. (1980) 'What government wants from oil' *Financial Times* 15 March

Rose, R. and Peters, B. G. (1978) *Can Government go Bankrupt?* New York, Basic Books

Rose, R. (1980a) 'Changes in public employment: a multi-dimensional comparative analysis' *Studies in Public Policy* No. 61, University of Strathclyde Centre for the Study of Public Policy

Rose, R. (1980b) 'Misperceiving public expenditure: feelings about "Cuts"' *Studies in Public Policy* No. 67, University of Strathclyde Centre for the Study of Public Policy

Royal Commission on the Distribution of Income and Wealth (1979) Report No. 7, *Fourth Report on the Standing Reference,* Cmnd. 7595, London, HMSO

Self, P. (1980) 'Public expenditure and welfare' in Wright (ed.)

Stewart, J. D. (1980) 'From growth to standstill' in Wright (ed.)

Townsend, P. (1979) *Poverty in the United Kingdom* Harmondsworth, Penguin Books

Tufte, E. R. (1980) Review of Rose and Peters' *Can Government Go Bankrupt?* in *American Political Science Review* Vol. 74, pp. 567–8

Wildavsky, A. (1980) *The Art and Craft of Policy Analysis* London, Macmillan

Wright, M. (ed.) (1980) *Public Spending Decisions* London, Allen and Unwin

# Index

ACAS 108
advisory bodies 101-3, 109-13
aerospace industry 117, 139, 144
Alcaly, R. E. and Mermel-
    stein, R. 77, 94, 97
All-Volunteer Force 127, 130, 132,
    145
Anderson, Sir J. 35-55 passim,
    104, 118, 121
armed services, manpower 127
Arndt, H. W. 6, 7, 29
Arts Council 105, 119

back door cuts 25
Bacon, R. and Eltis, W. A. 44, 55,
    219, 225
Bancroft, Sir I. 18, 30
bankruptcy of government 192,
    201-2, 218-24 passim
Banks, G. T. 27, 30
Barber boom 9
Barnett, J. 8
base, budgetary, see budgetary
    base
beggar-thy-neighbour responses to
    cuts 191-2, 201, 212
birth rate, see demography
black economy 223
bleeding stumps tactic 17, 139,
    163, 209
Booth, T. A. 27, 30, 180, 195
Boyle, E. 168, 173
British Airways 117
British Council 116
British Leyland 206
British National Oil
    Corporation 20, 108
budgetary base 12-13, 16, 21, 26-7,
    162, 178, 184, 189, 199
bureaucratic behaviour 5, 18, 152,
    164-5
Butler, R. A. 7

Cabinet Office 37, 41, 52, 165
capital spending cuts 5, 12, 23, 78,
    161, 184, 203
cash limits:
    introduction of . 11, 17, 22, 181;
    use for cutbacks 19, 24-5, 50,
    58-9, 61, 75, 89, 186-8, 194, 211
Central Council for Education and
    Training in Social Work 109
central non-departmental bodies,
    see quangos
Centre for Educational
    Disadvantage 161
Centre for Environmental
    Studies 116, 186
Chapman, L. 41, 55, 212, 225
charges for government
    services 63, 83, 85, 94, 184, 211
Charity Commission 119
civil service:
    growth in manpower 100
    growth in number of senior
        staff 40, 54
    index-linked pensions 45
    morale 18, 44, 48
    pay comparability 19, 190, 219
    reduction in manpower 17-18,
        102, 142-3
Civil Service Department 12,
    36-54 passim, 107, 118
    machinery of government
        division 36, 43
    reorganization 43-4, 52
Clegg Commission, see Standing
    Commission on Pay
    Comparability
coefficient of variation 64, 72
Colonial Empire Marketing
    Board 104
comet phenomenon 105
commitments of government, see
    inertia growth

Commonwealth Institute 105
Commonwealth War Graves
    Commission 116
Comptroller and Auditor-
    General 38, 118
corporate planning 21-8 *passim,*
    202
COSLA 62, 76
cosmetic cuts 103, 109-12; *see
    also* token cuts
cost compensation 84-95 *passim*
Council for Educational
    Technology 116
Council for the Encouragement of
    Music and the Arts 105
Crosland, C. A. R. 7, 30
Crown Agents 105
cutback management 5, 192, 216
cuts, definition of xii, 11-13, 62-3,
    126, 130, 137

Danziger, J. N. 82, 87, 98
Decimal Currency Board 105
decrementalism and decremental
    cuts 5, 12, 15, 203, 206, 207
Defence, Ministry of, *see* Ministry
    of Defence
Defence Reviews 132-5
defence spending:
    changes in 126-30
    model of 135-6, 150-1
demography, effect on
    government spending and
    behaviour xi, 19, 93, 145,
    154-72 *passim,* 185, 222
Department of Education and
    Science 157-73, 184-5, 203,
    212, 215
Department of Health and Social
    Security 20, 26-7, 30, 113,
    180, 184-5, 195
Department of Industry 49, 50,
    108
Department of Prices and
    Consumer Protection 19
Department of the
    Environment 28, 42, 50, 93,
    98, 111, 210, 215
Department of Transport 28
Donoughue, B. 201
Downs, A. 165, 172
Dunsire, A. 58, 76, 215, 225

Ecclesiastical Commission 119
Education White Paper 1972 155
educational norms 169

efficiency of government, relating
    to cuts xii, 20, 69, 133, 137,
    141-6 *passim,* 177-93, 208-13
Else, P. K. and Marshall, G. P. 7, 30
equal misery approaches to
    spending cuts 15, 125, 141,
    143, 185, 203, 212-13
expectations from
    government 218-20, 222
Expenditure Steering Group for
    Educational Services 159
Expenditure White Papers 8, 10,
    23-4, 158-9, 162, 173, 176-7,
    184-5, 196

fair shares cuts 143; *see also* equal
    misery
Fairlie, H. 220, 225
fairy gold 12, 15, 120, 137, 163,
    183, 185
financial stringency xi
fiscal pressure 77-96 *passim*
Forestry Commission 119
Fraser, B. 104, 118, 121-2
Fulton, Lord 43, 100
fungibility 213-16

Garrett, J. 204, 225
Geddes' axe 3, 159
Gilmour, Sir I. 46
Glassberger, A. 12, 30, 189, 195

Hayward, J. E. S. *et al.* 27, 30
health authorities 26, 47, 186,
    192-3, 204, 210
Health Service, *see* National
    Health Service
Heath, E. 10, 14, 112, 115
Heclo, H. and Wildavsky, A. 22,
    30, 120-1, 158, 166, 173, 183,
    195
Heseltine, M. 14, 42-3, 55, 111,
    114
Hinings, C. R. *et al.* 21, 30, 178,
    195, 202, 225
hiring freezes 16, 47, 102, 154,
    160, 169, 189, 202, 205, 210-17
    *passim*
Hirsch, F. 222-3, 225
Hirschman, A. O. 211, 225
Hogwood, B. 105
Holland, P. 101, 108, 111, 121;
    and Fallon, M. 101, 121
Housing Corporation 116
housing investment
    programmes 28, 180-1

Imperial Shipping Committee 104
improvement factor in
    education 167
incrementalism 5, 14, 21, 22, 26,
    27, 74, 136, 171, 178, 179, 190,
    194, 199
inertia growth 5, 16, 22, 159, 217,
    221
Institute for Development
    Studies 116
Institute for Health Studies 26
International Monetary Fund 224

job creation programmes 212

Kanter, A. 147, 149
Kellner, P. and Crowther-Hunt,
    Lord 41, 55, 202, 225
Keynesian economics and
    techniques 3, 9, 29
Klein, R. 166, 173
Korean War 126-7, 130-6

Lambeth, Southwark and
    Lewisham Area Health
    Authority 193, 204
Land Authority for Wales 110
Land Commissioners 105
Lasswell, H. 200
last in, first out system of
    retrenchment 101, 160
Layfield, F. 61, 75-6
leisure and recreation services 71
Levine, C. 15, 30, 104-5, 114, 116,
    122, 177, 196
local authority associations 50-1,
    82, 95
local government manpower,
    growth of 16, 32
local government spending:
    block grant system 50, 68, 95-6,
        162, 214
    central government
        guidelines 58-96 *passim,* 180
    cuts in mid-financial year 68-9, 75
    expenditure allowance and
        percentage support 58-61
    growth of spending 56
    propensity to increase
        spending 65-6
Local Government Planning and
    Land Act 1980 51
Lothian region 67-8, 71, 188

McGuire, M. 107-8
macro-economic management 8, 10

Manpower Services
    Commission 118, 119, 180, 207
Medium Term Assessment 8, 10, 23
Ministry of Defence 109, 125-50

National Enterprise Board 20,
    108, 117
National Health Service 26, 100;
    planning system 181
National Heritage Fund 114
National Housebuilders
    Registration Council 115, 117
National Incomes
    Commission 105
National Institute for Economic
    and Social Research 186
National Insurance
    contributions 14
National Plan 10, 168
National Ports Council 112
National Steering Committee
    Against the Cuts 37
National Vegetable Marketing
    Board 105
nationalized industries 9, 12-13,
    19, 45-6, 50-1
NATO 134-5, 139-40, 145-6
natural wastage, *see* hiring freezes
Newsom, J. H. 154, 173
Newton, K. 77, 98
Niskanen, W. 164-5, 173, 186, 196
non-departmental bodies, *see*
    quangos

Office of Management and Budget
    (US) 52
organizational decline 104
Outer Circle Policy Unit 107, 112,
    122
Overseas Development
    Ministry 19
Pay Comparability, Standing
    Commission, *see* Standing
    Commission on Pay
    Comparability
Peacock, A. and Wiseman, J. 91,
    98, 126, 150
Peel, Sir R. xii
Personal Social Services
    Council 109, 113
PESC 8, 13, 22, 23-9 *passim,*
    178-94 *passim,* 204
Physical Training and Recreation
    Councils 105
Pliatzky, Sir L. 43, 55, 101-3,
    106-20, 122, 204

political bankruptcy, *see*
    bankruptcy of government
potential local tax effect 79, 80, 97
Price Commission 19, 106, 112
privatization and
    reprivatization 20, 46, 49-51,
    117, 191
programme budgeting 20
promotion in the public sector,
    effect of cutbacks 171, 190,
    199, 200, 211
PSBR 9, 13, 20, 24
Public Accounts Committee 29
public expenditure:
    growth of 4, 7-8
    reduction of 102
Public Record Office 209
public sector employees 102;
    redundancies 44, 63, 72, 74,
    154-69 *passim,* 189, 205-17
    *passim*

quangos xii, 18, 19, 40, 41, 43, 47,
    55, 100-22, 186, 192, 202, 208,
    215
quantum cuts 12-13, 15, 161, 171,
    200, 206-7, 212
Queen's Awards to Industry 221

rationality in public spending
    cuts 15, 21, 26, 27, 29, 178-95,
    203, 204, 207, 208-13, 216-17
Rayner, Sir D. 41, 42, 43, 44
regional economic planning
    councils 105
regional price control
    machinery 105
relative price effect 137, 174, 175,
    190, 194, 219
reprieve, politics of 206
resource substitution 57, 84, 85-6,
    89, 90, 91, 92, 94, 214
Richardson, J. J. and Jordan,
    A. G. 121, 122
Robbins, Lord 156, 173
Rose, R. 206, 219, 226; and
    Peters, B. G. 213, 217-25
Royal Commission on the
    Distribution of Income and
    Wealth 112, 220, 226

school curricula 156-7
school meals 16, 63, 85, 160, 168
Scottish Development
    Agency 108, 117, 209
Scottish Financial Plans 28

Scottish Office 57, 61-75 *passim,*
    96, 109-10
Self, P. 211, 221-2, 226
sickness benefits 188
SOLACE 95, 96, 98
sore thumb approaches to
    cuts 139, 163, 183, 209
Sports Council 105
Standing Commission on Pay
    Comparability 105, 113, 187,
    190
Stewart, J. 56, 76, 90, 98, 177, 226
strategic coordinator 15, 178, 179,
    181, 182, 188
Strathclyde region 68, 70
Sugar Commission 105
sunset laws 111
Supplementary Benefits
    Commission 113

tax evasion 223
Tithe Commissioners 105
token cuts 15, 120, 121, 144
Tomato and Cucumber Marketing
    Board 105
trade unions 10, 37, 44, 45, 48,
    158, 163, 178, 189, 191, 205,
    206, 210, 217, 219, 220
Transport Policies and
    Programmes 28
Treasury 8-39 *passim,* 46, 52, 53,
    71, 109, 118, 121, 158, 164,
    165, 166, 175, 183, 187, 195
treble affluence 3, 217, 220, 223
tribunals 101-2
TSR-2 133, 137, 144

unacknowledgeable means 120
unemployment, impact on
    government spending xi, 18,
    93, 203, 205, 222; trade-off
    with inflation 9, 29
Upper Clyde Shipbuilders 206
Urban Development
    Corporations 103, 113, 120
urban stress, impact on
    government spending 93

X-efficiency 208

Wildavsky, A. 93, 98, 168, 173,
    180, 196, 204, 218, 226
Wolman, H. 77, 78, 86, 97, 99
Wood, T. 170, 173

zero-based budgeting 22, 177, 182